WOMEN
&
THE NATION'S NARRATIVE

WOMEN
&
THE NATION'S NARRATIVE

Gender and Nationalism in
Twentieth Century Sri Lanka

NELOUFER DE MEL

ROWMAN & LITTLEFIELD PUBLISHERS, INC.
Lanham • Boulder • New York

ROWMAN & LITTLEFIELD PUBLISHERS, INC.

Published in the United States of America
by Rowman & Littlefield Publishers, Inc.
4720 Boston Way, Lanham, Maryland 20706
http://www.rowmanlittlefield.com

Copyright © 2001 by Rowman & Littlefield Publishers, Inc.

ISBN 0-7425-1806-X (alk. paper)
ISBN 0-7425-1807-8 (pbk.: alk. paper)

Printed in India

For my parents
and
Devan

CONTENTS

ACKNOWLEDGEMENTS

This book could not have written without the inspiration and support of many friends and colleagues. I wish to thank foremost, Kumari Jayawardena, for her constant encouragement and generosity of ideas and time, and Ritu Menon of Kali for Women, who kept faith in the project, always provided valuable advice and put me in touch with many who helped me in my research in India.

There were many other friends and colleagues who made valuable suggestions on the chapters and manuscript at its various stages. My thanks to Geeta Patel, Yasmin Tambiah, Kumi Samuel, Sunila Abeysekera, Michael Roberts, Rajeswari Sunder Rajan, Uma Chakravarti, Amrita Basu, Praful Bidwai, Ratna Kapur, Kathryn Hansen, Rimli Bhattachcharya and the late Eqbal Ahmad. I also wish to acknowledge with gratitude the time and information given to me on Anil de Silva by the late Minette de Silva, Mulk Raj Anand, Romila Thapar, Uzra Bhatt, Yvonne Gunawardena, Seneka Bandaranaike and Manel Fonseka. My thanks also to "Juliet" whom I interviewed for my work on the JVP woman combatant, and to Nirmala Nityanandan; to Ranjith Perera for information on Annie Boteju, and Lakshmi de Silva for her translation of John de Silva's verses; to Jean Arasanayagam for keeping me posted on her latest work; to Sumika Perera of the Women's Development Foundation, Kurunegale, and the women of the Uva Welassa Govi Kānthā Sanvidānaya, Buttala.

I am also grateful to the participants at the SSRC "Violence Against Women" conference held in Colombo in 1995, for their comments on chapter 5 on the Sri Lankan woman militant; those present at the lively seminar at Cornell University, Ithaca, in 1998 who listened to my presentation on Anil de Silva and asked eager questions; to my fellow researchers at the Institute for Research on Women at Rutgers University, New Jersey, when I was Visiting Scholar there in the Fall of 1998, and my students at the Department of English, University of Colombo for participating in lively debates on the issues discussed in this book. Very special acknowledgement and thanks are owing to Nadi Jayaweera, Prema Gamage, Ramani Jayasundera and Janaki Abeywardena who helped with interviews, archival work, translation and transcription of tapes for chapter 6 on the Sri Lankan women's movement and the Mothers' Front. Grateful thanks also to the John D. and Catherine T. MacArthur Foundation for a research and writing grant which supported my research for this chapter. Thanks also to the Sri Lanka Social Scientists' Association Gender Research Unit for a grant which enabled me to travel to India and research there.

My thanks too to various libraries and their librarians for their unstinted support: the Sangeet Natak Akademi and the Nehru Memorial Museum & Library in New Delhi; Radhika Sabhawala who opened up the archives of the *Marg* office for me in Bombay; to Father Aloysius Pieris S.J. for access to the Fr. S.G. Perera Memorial Library at the Tulana Research Centre, Kelaniya, Sri Lanka and to Sheila Fernando, also of the Tulana Research Centre.

Very special thanks to my family and friends who supported me in various ways through the writing of this book.

INTRODUCTION

I

THIS BOOK MARKS the production of important "events",[1] temporal moments and selected strands of nationalism in Sri Lanka[2] of the 20th century, particularly within dominant Sinhala Buddhist and militant Tamil nationalisms. Its main focus however lies in the way gender has been, and continues to be, a central trope within them. Through a discussion of how women from diverse professional, class, caste, religious, ideological, ethnic and linguistic backgrounds have engaged with nationalism, the book attempts to foreground the relationship between gender and nationalism and how feminism engages with the ideology of the nation. If tenets of bourgeois respectability, ethnic exclusivity, patriotism, self-sacrifice, etc., are cornerstones of the collective imaginary of the nation, it shows how women have both participated in this project and contested it, forwarding other, alternative ways of imagining the nation. At the same time it marks the fact that nationalism and patriarchy are never static institutions; they shift, at times adopt, a certain feminist stance and adapt to exigency. The engagements of the women foregrounded in this book show how women can, and have been, appropriated by such a protean nationalism. But they also show when and how women act on their own behalf, in their own right, and negotiate patriarchy, capitalism and political opportunity, as well as contradictions within nationalism itself, to their advantage. The book is engaged, then, in signalling that gender is crucial to an understanding of nationalism and vice versa. It also marks the fact that feminism, when it occurs, is not an autonomous practice but deeply bound to the signifying network of the national contexts which produce it.[3] As such, feminism too, like nationalism, is rich in paradoxes and ambiguities.

Women have been incorporated into nationalist projects in diverse and often contradictory ways. Nationalism, particularly in the Third World's post-colonial terrain, has been commensurate with the rise of feminism, women's movements and the construction of the "modern" woman through social and legal reforms encompassing education, marriage and inheritance laws, and religious/cultural customs. Equal rights for women has been a part of this campaign, from obtaining the vote to entry into public service. Nationalism has also subordinated women, at times through these very social and legal reforms, to keep them at the boundaries of the nation by controlling their sexuality, mobility, the trope of motherhood, rights of citizenship and a variety of personal laws that became codified with the advent of the modern nation state.[4] Indeed these very boundaries of the nation have needed, for their organisation, the subordination of women even as they are posited in nationalist projects as central in the grounding of the nation. Thus even when women have been the sites of liberal reform, it has "always contained a degree of instrumentalism, a sense that transforming women's place in society and the state represented an opportunity that was only partially about women themselves".[5] Despite repeatedly affirming the centrality of women to nationalist projects—whether as signifying sites of modernisation or for their allegorical value as mothers of the nation—women have in this respect been primarily a discursive terrain on which significant socio-cultural tenets of the nation are produced. Women are constructed as the nation's subjects—not only as citizens, but also as members of ethnic, class and caste groups—differently to men.[6]

Four discursive arenas provide useful insights into the way nationalism is shaped and gendered; their significance as shifting sites of control and struggle in the story of nationalism and gender in Sri Lanka will be seen throughout this book. First, nationalism produces normative ideas about sexuality and gender with which it closely intersects and on which it rests.[7] Its discourse also constructs a division of gender which renders the male as the author and subject of the nation,[8] while the female stands for the nation itself, in need of male protection, the reproducer and nurturer of future generations and transmitter of cultural values. As reproducer she carries the responsibility of avoiding miscegenation to ensure ethnic, class, caste or racial "purity". Her sexuality has to be policed and regulated to this end in the service of the nation. In another context, when European nationalism from the 17th century onwards began to fuel the imperial conquest of territories in the Americas, Africa and Asia, it was projected, in its colonialist discourse, as aggressively masculine in its penetration of feminised colonial territories.[9] Wars have, through the years, been fought in defence of the nation by "sons of the soil". Modern technologies of aggression take place, yet again, within a framework of a penetrative male discourse. The very names of the most recently developed missiles on the Indian subcontinent—Trishul (trident of the god Shiva) on the Indian side, and Hatf (the lance of the Prophet Mohammed) on the Pakistani side, simultaneously invoke male prowess and resonate as symbols of Hindu and Islamic iconography. Following the Indian nuclear tests of May 1998 Bal Thackeray, the leader of the Shiv Sena which expounds a right-wing Hindutva ideology proudly proclaimed, "We are not eunuchs anymore"; and when Nawaz Sharif, Pakistan's Prime Minister, delayed responding to India's nuclear challenge with tests of his own, he was the recipient of glass bangles by a section of the public intent on shaming him for his lack of male virility and courage—hence the "gift" of women's ornaments. Evident here is the notion that male virility and aggression are the traits that protect a feminised nation. Politicians and a military unable to fulfil these roles fail the nation. Conversely, women who break the mould of a feminised subjectivity and refuse the obligatory roles of chaste and dutiful wives and daughters become the target of attack. Such emasculation and female transgression blur gender distinctions and produce a confusion seen as compromising the potency of the nation.[10] This in turn evokes an anxiety that permeates political rhetoric as well as popular culture, with very specific consequences for both men and women.

During the formation of the modern nation state, when the concept of a fraternity of national subjects took hold of 18th century Europe after the French Revolution, women were conspicuously left out of this fellowship. They were excluded from its civil law through a dispossession of their inheritance in favour of their brothers, and through the legal regulation of their sexual, biological and reproductive roles.[11] Muslim and Hindu personal laws continue, in South Asia, to deprive women of inheritance and equality in marriage.

In India, under the Hindu Succession Act of 1956, only patrilineal forms of inheritance are legitimate. Accordingly, a Hindu woman cannot inherit a share of ancestral property at birth as her brothers do. It is only to her father's self-acquired wealth that she can lay claim equally with her brothers.[12] In Sri Lanka, under the *Thesavalamai*, the laws governing Tamils of Malabar origin who live in Jaffna, in the north of Sri Lanka, women cannot dispose of their property without written male consent. Under the Muslim Intestate Successions Ordinance of 1931 which recognised the right of Muslims to inherit according to their sect, women within the Shafie sect (the majority Muslim sect in Sri Lanka) can only inherit half the equivalent of the male, although there is some protection for her in that her property cannot be willed away. Again under Muslim personal law in Sri Lanka, it is only the male guardian's consent that is required for a woman's marriage. Under the Hudood Ordinance, operative in Pakistan, one man's evidence in a court of law is considered the equivalent of two women's. In this way women have been constructed as partial citizens of the nation-state. Moreover, that women's regulation is seen to take place in the private spheres of the domestic and familial, rather than the public domain of the state has hitherto encouraged the erasure of women and gender from discourses on the state and nation.[13] It has been the task of feminist scholarship of the late1980s and 1990s to dismantle this idea of a polarised, dichotomous public/private binary. Partha Chatterjee, in a path-breaking essay for the time, noted that in mid to late 19th century India, the Bhadralok nationalist elite invested heavily in a private domain epitomising indigenous/spiritual values because the public sphere, associated with the material, was contaminated by the presence of the coloniser. While in public the male Bengali elite had lost its power, it could still determine events and discourses in the private domain. Women were central signifiers of this private domain.[14] It has since been the task of feminist scholars to show that Chatterjee's understanding of the Bhadralok's "resolution" of the women's question as a subaltern move is predicated on an erasure of women's agency,[15] that in fact, "this division between outer and inner, with its homologies no longer corresponds to the lived reality",[16] and that women have redefined their limits and (re)crossed their boundaries to make the private/public not water-tight, but porous.

The second arena is the nexus between nationalism and modernity. The growth of feminism and women's movements in the 20th century is distinctly related to the modernising impulse of the nation-state. What agentive moments and acts women have been able to achieve have taken place under circumstances that pushed towards a new modernity. Kumari Jayawardena has shown that in the 20th century it was at the historical junctures of anti-imperial struggles that women participated most keenly in nationalist projects.[17] As the colonised elite at the vanguard of anti-imperialist struggles were keen to modernise their societies to claim parity with their colonial masters, women's emancipation became an essential and integral part of this process. Modernity would better equip native society to jettison its colonial bondage, and creating a "New Woman" became part of this campaign. Thus the terminology of the "New Woman" which had become fashionable in 19th century Europe was adopted in the colonies with zeal. From the publication of a book on women's emancipation entitled *The New Woman* by Kassim Amin in 1901, to the association in 1919 of Egyptian women under the Société de la Femme Nouvelle, the new agenda for women spread to East Asia. Japan saw the establishment of the Association of New Women also in 1919, and in 1919 and 1920 respectively, magazines entitled *The New Woman* were published in China and Korea.

Jayawardena cautions that what actually defined this "New Woman" varied from region to region according to historical specificities and cultural traditions.[18] Nevertheless, in colonial situations the idea of women's emancipation allowed women a degree of freedom they had not enjoyed before either in pre-colonial or early colonial society. Obtaining access to colonial

education, albeit with different emphases than what was on offer for men, they went on to professional careers, becoming doctors of western medicine and leading educationists. When women
were part of militant struggles as in Palestine, China and Vietnam they secured a degree of mobility and public presence they
had not enjoyed before in their traditional societies. In Palestine,
from 1917 onwards, urban women openly demonstrated against
the Balfour Declaration, travelling to villages, holding demonstrations at both Muslim and Christian holy sites thereby subtly
subverting the highly segregated gender roles within traditional
Arab society.[19] In India, the slogan of swadeshi and the ensuing
boycott of British goods, made even the handicraft sector, often
associated with women, a site of political significance.[20] Women
took to the streets for social service—helping in health care, slum
education, cottage industry. In Sri Lanka, women took an active
role in organising against British imperialism through the Suriya
Mal movement. Launching their campaign in 1933 on Armistice
Day, or Poppy Day on which poppies were sold to raise funds for
British soldiers, they named their campaign after a common local flower, *suriyamal,* instead of the poppy associated with the
western war effort. The proceeds of their sales went towards
educating an undercaste girl.[21] These women creatively subverted
an imperial symbol for radical ends. In Sri Lanka today, there
are women militants who, as frontline combatants in nationalist/
revolutionary groups, are active participants in nationalism. The
women cadres of the Liberation Tigers of Tamil Eelam (LTTE)
undergo as rigorous a military training as their male colleagues,
are confident users of weaponry and other military technology
at their disposal, and are part of elite fighting squads such as the
Sea Tigers and Black Tigers, the latter being the death squad
from which LTTE suicide bombers await their call-up. Suicide/
sacrifice is already gendered, in that women have traditionally
been called upon to make sacrifices for the family as wife and
mother, as well as for the community as mothers who sacrifice
warrior sons during war. But the LTTE women have redefined
this role to collapse the distinction between private and public by
making their sacrifices highly visible and manifest.

Modernity, however, is a complex set of co-ordinates. These

women can also embody the hallmarks of what Rajeswari Sunder Rajan terms a *sufficient* modernity that spells out the cost of such emancipation. This is when, in recognition of the needs of national development, human rights and civil liberties, women are no longer denied a role in "the time-space of the modern". But, as Sunder Rajan points out,

> When women become conspicuously visible in the spaces of modernity (such as the street and the work-place, places of mixing of the sexes), they are treated as having chosen the "risk" of harassment voluntarily—and treated accordingly. In other cases, more subtle ideological pressures are enacted to contain women's "modernity", to incorporate them within its class-caste frame. . . . In influential anti-Enlightenment critiques, when gender and modernity are read together it is only to indict "modernity" for producing *anomie*, aggression and reactive orthodoxy in men, "feelings" which are then (inevitably) directed as violence against women. This comprehensive indictment not only leaves no room for ascribing other reasons for violence against women—of which there are myriad, complexly interrelated—it also refuses to recognise the benefits of modernity, not least for women.[22]

Modernity also incorporates a reinvention of tradition to fit its needs. This is where a containment of women's modernisation can be most profoundly enacted. Within a context of anti-colonial nationalism, modernity was often read as *already* a part of indigenous tradition. In Sri Lanka, within Sinhala nationalism, images of the ideal Arya Sinhala woman, appreciation of the Sinhala language and Buddhist culture were part and parcel of the nation's emerging modernity and, as will be shown with special reference to the nationalist Sinhala theatre (Chapter 2), women were made its embodiment. Western culture, according to this strand of nationalism, brought with it a disguised modernity, a false consciousness with the hidden agenda of wiping out the indigenous. Within such a nationalism women were encouraged to modernise, but with only a sufficient, selected modernity as would benefit the emerging nation. At the same time, there were women for whom the ability to make their own choices and construct their own subjectivity, even if this meant an acceptance of some traditions, were important rights. As Deniz Kandiyoti noted, women did in this way make "an irreversible entry into political discourse and the question of their rights became a privileged site for debates concerning questions of modernisation vs. cultural conservatism and integrity".[23]

This struggle between notions of *sufficient* modernity and women's agency was addressed by women. A forceful and humourous rendering of it can be found in a satirical dialogue entitled, "Her Wedding Morning" by Ina Trimmer, a Sri Lankan woman of Burgher descent.[24] The dialogue is between a mother and daughter on the morning of the latter's wedding, and represents the viewpoints of two different generations of Sri Lankan women. The mother, Ango Nona, is a fifty year old woman who speaks "broken English", a target of satire in the dialogue which locates her within a Sinhala-speaking lower-middle class milieu. Seeking upward social mobility for her daughter she has worked hard to provide the latter with an English education. But she is, at the same time, beset by anxiety at her daughter's achievements. The daughter's independent outlook and self-confidence produce ambivalence in the mother, who no longer feels in control or needed in the society her daughter will now be part of. This produces a nagging and irrational response in her. She accuses her daughter Leela of bad habits, of smoking, of repudiating tradition by wearing bobbed hair and dressing immodestly—"Like dolls dressed up, finger-nails painted, toe-nails painted, how to know what else. Lace jacket showing the body," she fumes. Leela meanwhile is a self-assured young woman who drives a car, is glad of her mobility and looks forward to the future with ease and confidence. She asks, in educated Lankan standard English:

But we are not a bad lot, Mother, in spite of all these things. Are we now? We can look after ourselves which you all couldn't. Whenever you went out a servant accompanied you just as if you were a child, while we are at home anywhere. We don't want servants to walk behind us; we are not afraid of anything. You must admit girls of the present day are a jolly capable lot.

A key argument between mother and daughter centres around the wedding dress. The mother wants Leela to wear a white muslin jacket and pink silk skirt in keeping with an older fashion adopted by Sinhala women in the mid 19th century. Leela prefers a georgette sari, eliciting her mother's scorn. She chides, "Go, go, go. Dress, will you, like a 'thewditchee' (a flighty woman) with lace jacket and the white saree like a 'paynayray'(sieve). Annay for me, very ugly.'¹ Leela argues that the skirt is part of English attire. "We are Sinhalese," she says "must dress like Sinhalese, not imitate the Western nations." In this transitionary period of Sri Lankan society, as values of behaviour and dress change, it is the daughter's right to *choice* of dress that is compelling. Leela complies with the nationalist sentiment of the times but makes clear that for her, its dictates on dress are part and parcel of the modernity she represents. A strict separation between the discourses of westernised modernity vs. indigenous tradition does not apply: they overlap. Her own agency is at work here and this is when Sri Lankan women are best able to creatively use traditional symbols for new meanings, finding ways "to put new experiences in the old package".²⁵

Third, nationalism gives play to contesting individual and collective identities. How does the contest affect men and women who are subjects of the nation? During anti-colonial struggles, discourses of nationalism strategically forward a homogenous, cohesive collective identity that is oppositional to the imperial power and culture. Indigenous languages, religions, customs and traditions become foregrounded in this move and women, as embodiments of community, are made to carry their "best" values. At the same time, a colonised culture is one which is multi-layered, deeply influenced too by the coloniser's culture. Through education and emulation western values, habits, modes of thought and dress become part and parcel of the indigenous. Indigenous middle class elites cross borders, depart for the metropolis, receive education and professional training there and return, committed to a cosmopolitan identity rather than an exclusively nationalist one which, in its bid for political hegemony, seeks to erase heterogeneity.

If this kind of nationalism in its fetish for group purity, territorial exclusivity and spatial boundary, is opposed to the very concept of cosmopolitanism that makes those boundaries porous and carries "the imperative to register the moral and cultural existence of non-citizens and to force that existence on a reluctant and well-defended national consciousness",²⁶ what is the backlash suffered by women who embark on such a project? Is the backlash gendered? Are the consequences any different depending on whether they are domiciled abroad or situated within the territorial borders of the nation? Moreover, how do they defend themselves against the charge of elitism when cosmopolitanism is seen as a cultural position that, in a colonial context, is born of privilege and complicity with the coloniser, and in today's world, serves the needs of global capitalism? Does cosmopolitanism always mean a detachment from the nation? The forging of a Sinhala consciousness through theatre, and the life and work of Anil de Silva and Jean Arasanayagam as women forced to negotiate between cosmopolitanism and nationalism even as they argue for a national imaginary which *is* cosmopolitan, are case studies that shed light on these questions.

Finally, there is the relationship between nationalism and women's movements. If cosmopolitanism has so far been viewed as essentially a cultural construct, does it also have potential as a political position and platform from which the nation can be imagined differently? What is the role of women's movements in the construction of such an imagination? It is the case that, at the dawn of the 21st century, women's movements have established more global links than ever before. In working for women's rights as universal human rights, intervening in cross-border conflicts, lobbying the UN and other international agencies for a range of goals from eliminating violence and discrimination against women through the CEDAW treaty to insisting on gender justice in programmes implemented by the UN and the World Bank, defining gender-related war crimes and pushing for the ratification of the International Criminal Court, women's movements have built on an internationalism that can be read as the political arm of cosmopolitanism. What then, of national women's movements? Have they been able to adhere to this internationalist model of forwarding a concept of universal human rights through a *lateral* cosmopolitanism that seeks to install *within* the nation's territory, a culture which allows for pluralism, the inclusion of the "impure", a democracy free of caste and ethnic coercions?[27]

Such a lateral cosmopolitanism would build on and institutionalise the work already being done by many small Sri Lankan groups, for instance, that have forged coalitions at an intra-national and regional level, on a wide range of issues from labour security, human rights and women's rights, to protection of the environment and inter-faith dialogue. These efforts, however, remain small and individualised, dependent on the commitment of their leadership to the issues of coalition-building. The work of two women's groups, the Women's Development Foundation which grew out of the Progressive Women's Front of Kurunegala and the Uva Welassa Govi Kānthā Sanvidānaya (Uva Welassa Women Farmers' Organisation) of Buttala are presented in Chapter 6, as two small organisations involved in forging a notion of lateral cosmopolitanism that complements a "transversal" politics[28] which allows for the differences in membership and identity of each group to be maintained even as they come together to form coalitions on selected issues. The work of these two women's groups with plantation Tamil labour, women of the north and east, disadvantaged farmer communities of the south-east and the Mothers' Front, show that they have the ability to (re)cross the issues from women's rights to human rights and forge inter-ethnic links which deliberately challenge the strictures of nationalism, in order to re-imagine the nation in a far more pluralistic way. What prompts these organisations to engage in such work in the first place? What are the factors which make them successful? Can the politics of lateral cosmopolitanism within the nation also allow a cultural cosmopolitanism that accommodates deep and meaningful cultural exchange between different communities and classes without seeking to homogenise and/or to appropriate their difference? The answers to these questions can provide useful insights to the Sri Lankan women's movement of today, and how it carries forward the struggle towards pluralism and women's rights as human rights into the 21st century.

Feminist scholars have drawn attention to the fact that measuring the success of women's movements needs different yardsticks because their composition and strategies are not necessarily orthodox. A women's movement comprises a range of women's organisations and networks encompassing women's wings of political parties, NGO coalitions, trade unions, academics and professional women's networks. They stand, at times in coalition, at times alone, for a diverse array of goals and strategies. They incorporate both middle class and working class groups. Some of them choose to work with the state while others do not. Their goals have not only been those of raising awareness, equal opportunities and gender justice, but also of employment generation, health, education, legal aid, community and slum development, consumer protection for women and cultural production. Thus, yardsticks such as membership numbers or the success of orthodox "tactics of disorder" such as public protests and demonstrations are not always the best gauge by which women's movements can be judged.[29] Many women's organisations opt for working privately, away from public view. They do not keep written records of their meetings, and in certain cultures depend more on informal networks and kinship groups rather than organised party or association membership.[30] However, standards of judging women's movements have to necessarily take into account whether they have been able to shape an alternative social consciousness or not. This is where the role of women's movements within a broader social movement such as nationalism comes into focus. Quite often it is the case that even if a particular goal of the women's movement has been achieved, it has been unable to transcend and change the larger collective consciousness that goes beyond ethnic/racial nationalism for instance, to accommodate equality and justice for all the citizens of a nation. The discussions that follow on the women militants of the Janathā Vimukthi Peramuna (JVP) and LTTE and the Mothers' Front address these issues from the context of their Sri Lankan specificities.

II

A society in transition, particularly at moments of struggle over colonial rule or political and cultural representation in the post-independence nation-state, is inevitably in a state of emergency. Its revolutionary language, hegemonic anticipations, shifting constructions of ethnic, class, caste and cultural economies, the state's counter-moves including the declaration of Martial Law or Emergency rule to quell dissent, make it a site of contestation in which the state of emergency is not the exception but the rule.[31] Such an interregnum in which normalcy is suspended has a particular bearing on women. On the one hand it frees them from traditional restraint, allows them public participation in socio-political movements, provides a space for unorthodox protest and enables physical mobility and public comradeship with men, disallowed under "normal" conditions. On the other hand, state repression, war and anarchy have meant a closer supervision and protection of women, particularly when their bodies become the symbolic site of communal, class and caste enmity. They are raped, tortured and mutilated in the name of honour and shame. They become the booties of war, forced into sexual labour, pregnancy and chattelhood at the hands of the enemy.[32]

This book marks several such moments of emergency in the process of constructing the nation, to see how Sri Lankan society has been shaped by them and how selected women have engaged with the political and socio-cultural paradigms that are drawn and re-drawn within their framework. Chapter 2 marks how renowned Sinhala nationalist playwright John de Silva used the Tower Hall stage to make a template of ethno-Sinhala Buddhist identity, and how the convention of female impersonation and the entrance of professional actresses like Annie Boteju were put to use in its service. Such a mapping cannot take place without reference to the Buddhist revival of the mid to late 19th century, the rise of a local bourgeoisie and the colonial government's response to its anti-British sentiments. Chapter 3 takes into account the nationalist gaze on journalist, art historian and biographer, Marcia Anil de Silva, whose life (1909–1996) spanned almost the entire century. As the daughter of prominent political parents active in Ceylon's labour union and lobby for universal franchise, Anil's response to that gaze cannot be located in the nation's narrative unless set against the fierce backlash by an upper caste, upper class Sinhala lobby which, anticipating hegemony at independence, opposed the rise of the labour movement in Sri Lanka. Chapter 4 discusses author Jean Arasanayagam's quest for an identity that would integrate her into contemporary Sri Lanka. The identities she subscribes to as a woman of Dutch

Burgher descent married to a Tamil, privileged in her class and command of the English language, yet currently dispossessed of legitimacy within the nation because these very identities simultaneously stamp her liminality, must be read in reference to S.W.R. D. Bandaranaike's "Sinhala Only" call of 1956. This set the seal for post-independence communal conflict and marginalised both Tamil and Burgher communities from Sri Lanka's mainstream political arena. Chapter 5 looks at the issues surrounding women's agency through choices made by young women combatants of the Janathā Vimukthi Peramuna and the LTTE; they are located within the context of the unfulfilled promises of 1956, an imagined socialist revolution that failed, and the rise of militant Tamil nationalism with its demand for a separate Tamil state as the only solution to Sri Lankan Tamil self-determination. Pertinent to all of the above are the gains and losses of the women's movement of Sri Lanka which either opened up or foreclosed political, economic and social possibilities for these women. Chapter 6 sets out the work of the Sri Lankan women's movement in the 1980s and 1990s as it responded to the ethnic war and JVP uprising of the late '80s. The Mothers' Front was formed in direct protest at state repression and the "disappearance" of southern youth during the late 1980s. Its campaign, described even today as a "golden moment" of the contemporary Sri Lankan women's movement, has been one of the most successful women's struggles in recent times.[33] Focusing on the women of the Mothers' Front ten years after it was formed, this chapter explores the conditions that have enabled some to forge empowering possibilities for themselves, allowing a progressive feminist politics within national politics, while others are co-opted into patriarchal political hierarchies.

The events of emergency have been both a response to, and justification for, the authoritarian stamp of respective governments. In 1915, following the Sinhala-Muslim riots which the colonial government read as a culmination of anti-British sentiment by the Sinhalese, martial law was declared. Large numbers of the Sinhala Buddhist intelligentsia were imprisoned and sentenced to death by a military tribunal. Henry Pedris was one of the more prominent Sinhalese to be executed in this manner. Public venues such as the Tower Hall, Sri Lanka's national theatre, were closed in an attempt to stall the spread of anti-British sentiment. The government's handling of the riots was so precipitate that eventually, when the Colonial Office in London reviewed its actions, Governor Sir Robert Chalmers was recalled and those imprisoned released on payment of a fine. In the second decade of the 20th century which saw labour unrest and the rise of militant trade unionism, the general strike of 1923 and the port, taxi and tramway strikes of 1927–29, British capitalists owning businesses called for stringent trade union legislation, the confiscation of trade union funds and the speedy crackdown on trade unionists and key political figures behind the unrest. The colonial government came under intense pressure to implement the Trade Union and Trade Disputes Act of 1927, designed to suppress labour union activity. It was unable to implement any of these only because of the electoral win, back in Britain, of the British Labour Party which refused to support the Act.[34]

After Independence in 1948 the reduction of the rice subsidy by the United National Party (UNP) government led to a series of protests in July 1953 spearheaded by the left parties—the Lanka Sama Samaja Party (LSSP), Communist Party (CP), Viplavakari Lanka Sama Samaja Party (VLSSP), United Front and Federal Party. These protests, which included hunger strikes, culminated in a huge rally on Galle Face Green on 23rd July. Thereafter, the agitation gathered momentum towards the call for an island-wide *hartāl*, or stoppage of work, on 12th August 1953. This was particularly successful in the western province and Colombo south. There was violence and turmoil when ten people were killed in clashes with the police and a state of Emergency and curfew declared. D.S. Senanayake, the first Prime Minister of independent Sri Lanka resigned over these events in October that year.[35] The Sri Lanka Freedom Party's (SLFP) "Sinhala Only" policy of 1956, which made Sinhala the language of education and administration and caused the first post-independence communal violence between the Sinhala and Tamil communities, resulted in the declaration of Emergency from May–June 1958 and the proscription of the Federal Party and Jātika Vimukti Peramuṇa, each representing the two extremes of the language issue.[36] Following the assassination of S.W.R.D. Bandaranaike, leader of the SLFP, in September 1959 by a Buddhist monk who felt that Bandaranaike had conceded too much to the Tamils on the language issue, his wife Sirimavo Bandaranaike assumed leadership and became the world's first woman prime minister. Her government did not enjoy a prolonged period of stability either. In February1961 the Federal Party organised a satyagraha or campaign of non-violent civil disobedience in the northern and eastern provinces over the language issue, which met with a harsh response from the government. The Federal Party was proscribed and its leaders and MPs detained. The following year, an attempted military coup in January1962 jolted the government yet again, and by 1964, an Emergency was declared to counter a wave of labour strikes in protest against economic mismanagement, and minority dissatisfaction. These now threatened the unity of the government itself, causing defections from its ranks to the opposition, resulting in a precariously low majority.[37]

The next three decades saw even more prolonged periods of Emergency. The 1971 insurrection by the Janathā Vimukthi Peramuna resulted in a brutal crackdown by the SLFP government on youth (mostly university students) suspected of being in the movement, and elections due in 1975 were postponed until 1977. A state of Emergency gave the government the necessary power to both pursue its crackdown and prolong its term of office. Immediately after the 1977 elections an Emergency was declared by the new UNP government following political party clashes, which soon turned into Sinhala-Tamil communal violence. The years 1987–89 witnessed what is now popularly known as "the reign of terror" when the security forces, on orders from the UNP government, caused thousands of predominantly male youth to "disappear" in the south of the country during the second phase of the JVP uprising, that was itself brutal in its use of violence. The rise of militant Tamil nationalism from the 1970s onwards culminating in the demand for a separate Tamil state, the government's response to this in the form of the Prevention of Terrorism Act of 1979 and—following the July 1983 LTTE ambush of 13 Sinhala soldiers and the communal violence that ensued—the full-blown separatist war that currently engulfs the nation has meant that the state of Emergency is more and less a fixture. It is suspended only occasionally for purposes of elections or lifted as a gesture of goodwill on the part of new governments, as happened from August 1994 to April 1995 when the People's Alliance led by Chandrika Bandaranaike Kumaratunge came to power. With the military successes of the LTTE in April–May 2000 in the taking of Elephant Pass which controls land access to the Jaffna peninsula, Emergency regulations were beefed up by the PA government. Specific sections of the Public Security Ordinance, originally enacted in 1947, a year before independence, were promulgated. The country was placed on a war footing, demonstrations and protest marches banned and news and information on the war heavily censored. Sri Lanka's colonial and post-colonial journey has not been amenable to aspirations of democratic political participation and cultural plurality. The failure of its post-colonial political elite and successive governments to implement far-reaching political and social reform that addresses inequalities of political representation, education and employment, even as its society is often cited as "an example of democratic institutions backed by high standards of social development", has made Sri Lanka's post-coloniality abundant in paradox.[38]

States of emergency are also "always a state of *emergence*".[39] This is when a re-visioning of society and its economies takes place, changing the direction in which the nation journeys. Each phase, although not watertight, constantly re-visits previous experiences and lays the ground for those who follow; it has had its thinkers, writers, artists and leaders who have attempted to re-align the nation's history, deconstruct imperial myths and fashion its own modernity. The authoritarian state itself has played its part. Amongst those imprisoned by the British colonial government in 1915 was John de Silva, whose plays from 1902 onwards —*Sinhala Parābhava Nātakaya* (A Satire on the Modern Sinhalese) and *Sirisangabo Charitaya* (The Character of Sirisangabo) in 1903—were anti-British in sentiment. The charges against him were that he held weekly public meetings to which Muslims were not permitted entry.[40] It is reported that de Silva sang the popular lyrics from his plays in jail,[41] reiterating their Sinhala Buddhist ideology as he did so. His plays presented the grand and noble Buddhist heritage of the Sinhalese by way of contrast to the British and the western, and argued eloquently for the resurgence of the Sinhala language. The conflation of Sinhala and Buddhist ethno-religious identities thus became a given. Nationalists and participants in the Buddhist revival of the late 19th century reformulated the Mahavamsa version of history, a chronicle written in the 6th century A.D., which presented Sri Lanka as a place blessed by the Buddha and Buddhism, and the Sinhala people as those chosen to uphold its tenets.[42] Reiterating the links between a rightful/legitimate state, Buddhism and the Sinhalese, John de Silva's plays and songs sung in jail were eloquent protests against the illegitimacy of the British colonial government and Christianity. They also excluded non-Sinhala minorities even if they had resided in Sri Lanka for hundreds of years.

More than fifty years later, women combatants of the JVP and LTTE would emerge from a crisis of unemployment and political marginalisation, to attempt a radical transformation of their society and re-draw the state. JVP woman combatant, Juliet, who was involved in the April 1971 insurrection in which her brother Sarath Wijesinghe died, fled government reprisals to re-group in the jungles of Wilpattu, gathering around her a new community of like-minded individuals aspiring to a new, regenerative socialist revolution. It is said that Dhanu, the suicide bomber who killed Indian Prime Minister Rajiv Gandhi in 1991, was selected by LTTE leader Prabakharan for the mission so that she could avenge her rape by the Indian Peace Keeping Forces. These acts of victimhood transformed into agentive moments, mark their protagonists as those who have broken rank, dispensed with or reinvented tradition and re-drawn their roles in society. This task is made easier because, as noted before, in the interregnum between the state as they know it and the anticipated state they struggle for, normalcy is suspended and prevailing rules do not apply. This state of emergency encourages transgression. Thus young women from Sinhala Buddhist or Hindu Tamil communities, who would otherwise conform to traditional cultural and social values, here take up arms, live and die with male comrades, eschew early marriage and motherhood. The mothers, wives and sisters of the "disappeared" take to the streets under the umbrella of the Mothers' Front and adopt unorthodox strategies such as public cursing and shaming, invoking the wrath of the goddess Kali on the government in revenge for the loss of their loved ones and providers. Although such invocations are within indigenous custom, here the Mothers' Front adopts them publicly rather than as the private supplication these rituals usually take. Patriarchy still puts in place strictures that will pull these women back into the domestic sphere once the struggles are over, but most women never quite go back to square one. It is in this gap between the point from which they started and the point to which they return that the transformation of women's lives and its processes are signified. It is also in this gap that women's movements can mark their achievements and assess how far they could have pushed to re-imagine the nation and when, and where, they failed to do so.

Other women, like actress Annie Boteju and journalist-art historian Marcia Anil de Silva, made use of the cross-currents of their time to assert their own vision of modernity. Capitalising on the transition in early 20th century Sinhala theatre from folk to urban, stylised to naturalistic, ritualistic to secular, offeratory to commercial and so, traditional to modern, Annie Boteju entered the stage in 1917 to huge public acclaim. She not only set the seal of respectability for actresses—where before they had been stigmatised as "loose women" and/or debarred from the stage altogether—she also played her part in making the theatre enter into contractual obligations with its performers, a significant milestone in its journey towards becoming urban, commercial and modern. Anil de Silva's crossing of territorial borders as she left Sri Lanka, the land of her birth, to make her homes in Bombay, Paris and London in the 1940s and '50s took advantage of the possibility of domicile within the "Commonwealth" (and Paris through marriage), before emigration and visas became sites of regulation/exclusion by various states. Her journeys also drew on an *internationale* that gave her Communist Party sympathies a home in Bombay and Paris, and a cosmopolitan outlook that had been shaped in Sri Lanka even as it came under siege by a right-wing nationalism's exclusionary logic. Jean Arasanayagam emerged as a fresh poetic voice in the 1960s whose work, reflecting the feminist creed that the personal is political, continues to engage with the nation's battlegrounds to this day, ceaselessly questioning the destruction caused by the ethnic war, its culture of militarism and in praise of plurality as a *structural reality* of the nation.

The struggles by these women have been long and arduous, and achievement has not come without a price. Their moments of creative re-visioning can be marked too by a liminality which forecloses complete equality for them within the nation. Even when a star like Annie Boteju played a central role in reinforcing early 20th century Sinhala Buddhist nationalism through the theatre, she remained outside its privileges of capital accumulation and equity reserved for the male. She died a pauper. Anil de Silva lived her life in exile, driven out of Sri Lanka by a powerful caste and political lobby that targeted her as much as her father. Jean Arasanayagam's quest for a nation which values her heterogeneity remains elusive, and the question will be asked as to whether women of the JVP, LTTE and Mothers' Front have been able to attain independence by themselves without support from their respective male leadership, political party or member of parliament.

Within South Asia, the representation of women in legislature and government remains abysmal. Its preponderance of women heads of state as presidents or prime ministers reflects the region as feudal and dynastic rather than blessed with an enlightened political constituency that returns feminist and politically progressive women as its leaders. Most South Asian women live on the outer rings of political power. Although women comprise 51 per cent of the population in Sri Lanka, and Adeline Molamure served as a senator as early as 1931, the current representation of women in parliament stands at a mere 4 per cent, down from the 4.8 per cent of the 1994 parliament. In India, although there is a high level of representation of women in the *panchayats*, the campaign by women's groups for 33 per cent reservations in parliament has not yet been fruitful. In Pakistan, before the October 1999 military take-over by General Pervez Musharraf, there were only eight women in the Nawaz Sharif government (two in the Senate and six in the National Assembly, two of whom were cabinet ministers). After the military take-over only one woman serves in a national security council of seven. In Nepal, where women form 50.1 per cent of the population, there are only 12 women in the house of representatives (the lower house) comprising 205 members, and nine women out of a total of 60 in the national assembly or upper house. In Bangladesh, although 10 per cent of parliamentary seats and 25 per cent of local government bodies have been reserved for women, they are mostly filled through nominations by male colleagues.[43] Women have by and large, been outside the male-dominated political arena and masculinist discourse of the nation.

The cricket field stands as an apt metaphor of this exclusion. Cricket has acquired iconic status in South Asia as *the* national sport of Sri Lanka, India, Pakistan and Bangladesh. Governments and the private sector invest heavily in it, and the game and its players receive state and religious patronage.[44] Fans commit suicide when their team is defeated and abuse their cricketers when they fail expectations. Such is a cricketer's national standing, on whose performance vast amounts of money ride and a public weary of its nation as a failed utopia enter into a shared national pride, that his privileges are extraordinary. In Sri Lanka cricketers purchase prime land well below market value in a boon gifted by the government. They enjoy duty free permits for luxury vehicles with no limit on engine capacities—regulations politicians and professionals must conform to. These entitlements mark cricketers as favoured subjects of the nation. As it is constituted today, cricket is a sport which debars women from the field (and therefore its perks) at the highest club, national and international levels. Sponsorship for women's cricket is well below the levels available for the men's game, and no woman sits on cricket's governing boards. The privilege of being flag-bearers for their respective nations and when successful, the accolades that come with it, are reserved exclusively for eleven men. The national sport in South Asia is the preserve of men.[45]

Women have, therefore, been amongst the harshest critics of the dominant nationalisms that hold up a community and/or the nation-state, for they have had to engage with the fact of their difference within the nation: their difference from men as citizens, as well as members of ethnic, religious, class and caste groups whose affiliation they have to symbolically bear. In the Sri Lanka of today, where ethno-nationalism has produced one of the harshest ethnic wars in South Asia in which thousands of lives have been lost, property destroyed, welfare, education and health programmes neglected and a culture of violence taken root, it becomes imperative to examine women's interventions as they have contested ethno-nationalism and the autocratic, patriarchal nation-state.

III

A significant feature of post-enlightenment modernity values the rights of the individual. The era of divine privilege is over, and equal opportunities for all has been the rallying cry of modern social movements. From the call for universal suffrage that would give women the vote, to women's education, reservations in public institutions and legislative bodies for minorities and women, social movements in the 20th century have spearheaded the concept of civil, social and political rights. In the colonial world these demands have often gone hand in hand with demands for independence, and in the post-colonial state, that of significant democratic power-sharing. Women have been at the forefront of some of these movements.

For Annie Boteju, Anil de Silva, Jean Arasanayagam and the women combatants of the JVP and LTTE, the choices they made in life, whether about careers, marriage, dress, language or political expression, could not have taken place without the previous efforts of other women in varied fields. Anti-British nationalism, and cultural decolonisation as one of its crucial planks, encouraged several women to reappraise their motherland and contest the British state. Just as Annie Boteju took part in the anti-colonial nationalist project through her roles and performances in the Sinhala theatre, other women from different linguistic and class backgrounds answered the call of nationalism through writing poems, short stories and, finally, novels.[46] While the Sinhala literary tradition boasted a lineage of women's writing that began with the Sigiri graffiti composed between the 7th and 10th centuries,[47] and the verse in the late 18th and early

19th centuries of Gajaman Nona,[48] writing by Sri Lankan women in English had to wait until women's education in English took hold in Sri Lanka in the 1820s.[49] The earliest Engligh writing by Sri Lankan women dates back to 1884. This was when two sisters, Jessie Alice Goonetileke and S. Jane Goonetileke published short stories in the first volume of *The Orientalist* in June 1884. The women's stories, entitled "The Tiger and the Blood Sucker" by Alice Goonetileke and "The Story of Twenty Five Idiots" and "The Woman and the Twenty Five Robbers" by Jane Goonetileke drew from indigenous folk stories and figures, both human and animal. However, just as Sri Lankan men who began to write in English during the 19th century (Sir James Alwis' *Leisure Hours*, a collection of literary papers and original verse published in 1863 is one such early work) were influenced by the British literature they had studied in schools, novels available in libraries, and literary pieces published in the local English newspapers and journals for their edification, so too did the women follow the pattern and attitudes of British writers. The result was that, even though a nascent nationalism amongst Sri Lankan women writers encouraged them to draw on their own folklore and surroundings, much of this work was imitative and derivative in thought, images and language. Their delineation of native characters and comic situations took its cue from European travellers who had commented on similar subjects. Yasmine Gooneratne notes how the editor of the influential *Ceylon Magazine*, John Capper, himself inspired by Dickens in his portrayal of character, influenced a number of Sri Lankan writers in the way they foregrounded native characters as comic, cunning, indolent, fastidious and/or adopting a bedraggled grandeur.[50] The poems of Sri Lankan writers were paeans to the native landscape, imitative of a romantic tradition which had come down to them not only through their education and literary periodicals, but also a body of writing by British expatriates who wrote of the England they had left behind with great nostalgia.[51] Take for instance the poem "Our Motherland" (1918) by Nancy Wijekoon.[52] Nancy Wijekoon was a schoolteacher who had joined the Young Lanka League which, inaugurated in 1915, was the earliest radical nationalist organisation in Sri Lanka. She published poetry recognised as seditious by the British. It is reported that H. L. Dowbiggin, Inspector General of Police, ordered surveillance of her during the 1915 disturbances.[53] "Our Motherland", while closely following the cadences of a Christian hymn and drawing on imagery from British romantic poetry in its evocation of the Lankan landscape, cast 1915 as a heroic stand for freedom, and is unambiguous in its upholding of Sinhala nationalism. Despite its derivativeness in form and imagery, the poem's references to an ancient lion race and the Sinhala people as heroes, warriors and martyrs who have pledged themselves to freeing the motherland, are also unmistakably local and topical:

> Our Mother-Land
> Smiling plains and stately mountains,
> Star-crowned heights and gem-decked vales,
> Golden fields and verdant meadows
> Palmy groves and flower-strewn dales.
>
> Lanka, mother-land of heroes,
> Lanka, famed in legends old,
> Ever theme of song and story,
> Mother, help us to be bold.
>
> Help us fight thy cause with ardour
> Fill us with the love of thee,
> Let us revel in thy glory,
> Sound thy praise o'er land and sea.
>
> May we hearken to the story
> Of thy fame in ages past,
> And with courage born of union
> Make thy fame forever last.
>
> "Sons of Lanka," proud our title,
> Nor for thrones of wealth untold
> Shall we barter this our birthright,
> More to us than countless gold.
>
> Lion-fierce and strong and deathless,
> In our veins there runs the blood
> Of the brave and dauntless heroes,
> Now at rest beneath the sod.
>
> By that blood, oh Mother Lanka,

Swear we to be true to Thee.
Use our hearts and lives, oh Mother
In the fight for Liberty!

The campaigns of the early Sri Lankan women's movements played equally important and complementary roles to that of cultural nationalism in significantly changing socio-political conditions for Sri Lankan women. Annie Boteju who reigned as star actress of the Sinhala stage in the 1920s and 1930s, and Anil de Silva who began her career as a journalist in the late 1920s and campaigned for her father's political platform for the Ceylon National Congress in the 1930s, belonged to a period in which the women's movement in Sri Lanka was decidedly successful in its campaigns despite being in its formative years. The early part of the 20th century was a time when expansion in women's education and the consequent entry of women into professions had encouraged a political consciousness among them. As early as 1904 under the leadership of Mary Rutnam, a medical doctor of Canadian origin married to a Sri Lankan Tamil, the Girl's Friendly Society and the Ceylon Women's Union were formed. While the former provided a meeting point for women to discuss issues of interest, the latter was oriented towards women's health care, nursing, education and the discussion of women's rights. At its annual general meeting in 1909, an item on the agenda was a "Dialogue on Women's Rights" by five young Burgher women, inspired perhaps by the suffragist campaigns in Europe and North America and reported in the local press.[54] Later, in 1925, it was a women's organisation known as the Mallikā Kulangana Samitiya which first moved a resolution at the sessions of the Ceylon National Congress for women's right to the vote. This campaign for women's franchise was taken on more systematically by the Women's Franchise Union (WFU), inaugurated in 1927, which had Mary Rutnam and Agnes Nell, Anil de Silva's mother, as founder members. At its public meeting on 7th December 1927, Lady Dias Bandaranaike, mother of S.W.R.D. Bandaranaike (Prime Minister of Sri Lanka from 1956–59), presided. The WFU made representations to the Donoughmore Commission appointed to look into constitutional reform in Sri Lanka, and succeeded in its aims when, in 1931, Sri Lanka became the first British colony to enjoy universal franchise unlinked to property and educational qualifications.

Tamil women, too, had been at the forefront of yet another organisation inspired by Mary Rutnam. This was the Tamil Women's Union which began in 1909. Later, Tamil women like Nalamma Murugesan and Maheswari Segarajasingham participated as delegates in the first session of the Ceylon National Congress in 1919.[55] The Muslim Young Women's Association was inaugurated later in 1937.[56] While some women's groups focused more on social service, inspired by the efforts of Indian women who were called into social service in the interest of swaraj, others like those which culminated in the All Ceylon Women's Conference in 1934 and of which Mary Rutnam was President, took on the state. It passed resolutions calling for the maintenance of high standards in the medical and nursing professions, restriction of ribaldry and jocularity (sexist comment) in the law courts, separate and suitable accommodation for women in remand, removal of gender discrimination in entry into the civil and public services, inclusion of Mahilā Samiti[57] methods of adult education to women of Sri Lanka, and the extension of the Technical College to include extra-mural classes for girls.[58] The conference also called for free education for girls, more young women to enter the university and greater participation of women in politics. In 1936–37, a Women's Charter was drawn up by the National Women's Trade Union League which called for full political and civil rights for women, education and work opportunities, security of livelihood, social and labour legislation to ensure minimum wage, better working conditions, and leisure time during night work.[59] Not all of these demands met with immediate success but these women's groups had placed women's civil and political rights in the public domain early on in the 20th century. The significance of their contribution in making women's rights a public discourse cannot be underestimated in both the course of politics as well as the trajectory of the women's movement in Sri Lanka.

Work needs to be done on whether there were direct links between the women active around these issues, and those like Annie Boteju who came from a Sinhala speaking world but was as involved in defining the terms of a future, modern post-colonial nation through a different discourse. Sinhala publications of the time which drew from the local English press, and journals like that of the Ceylon Reform Society could have been vehicles for cross-fertilisation, providing information and arguments on women's education, franchise, political participation and the intervention of various women's groups on these issues. Moreover, the appearance of women on the public stage, speaking at political meetings, school assemblies and women's gatherings to demand suffrage, entry into public service, better education and healthcare, etc., would have inspired and led the way for other women, and perhaps even actresses like Annie, to take on stage/ public roles for themselves. Whether there were direct links or not, it is a fact that the first half of the 20th century was a time of increased activity and debate in the field of women's civil rights, which in turn could not have failed to have a bearing on those like Annie Boteju for whom public spaces opened up and a profession became a possibility.

The 1930s in particular saw significant political activity on the part of women, this time under the leadership of the traditional left. From the Suriyamal campaign to trade union agitation, women of the left organised against imperial/capitalist exploitation. Selina Perera (1909-86) and Vivienne Goonewardena (1916-96) were two exemplary women activists who caught the public imagination. Combining struggles for socialism, feminism, anti-imperialism and anti-fascism, they militantly challenged the status quo in the 1930s, showing that larger social movements could complement an engagement with women's issues and a cosmopolitan politics. Selina Perera was in the limelight in Sri Lanka only during her time in LSSP politics within the country. Having graduated from the University of London where she offered Pali and Sanskrit as subjects, she returned to Sri Lanka in 1935. Taking part in the Suriyamal campaign, she became one of the founder women members of the LSSP in December 1935[60] and was its treasurer.[61] She took part in its campaign for elections to the state council in 1936 and during World War II when the male leaders of the LSSP were arrested by the British colonial government for their leadership of the plantation strikes and

anti-imperial stance. Selina Perera assumed a public role, address-
ing public meetings and appearing on the picket lines. She gained
a reputation for militancy, and directly challenged the police when
harassed and threatened by them. In 1942 when she was proclaimed a wanted offender by the British administration, she
left Sri Lanka in disguise and joined the approximately twenty
LSSPers who had already escaped prison or evaded arrest and
gone into hiding in Bombay.[62] When some of them were arrested
there and deported back to Sri Lanka in July 1943, she, Vivienne
Goonewardena and Colvin R. de Silva escaped to Calcutta, finding refuge in the Bolshevik Leninist Party of India (BLPI) headquarters there. However, with the break-up of the BLPI and Indian pre-Partition politics, Selina became increasingly disillusioned
with the political climate of the time, although she remained active in political agitations of the left in Calcutta. She adopted the
name Sheela Perera, taught English for a livelihood and led an
austere life until her death in 1986. She visited Sri Lanka only
once during her prolonged stay in India.[63]

Vivienne Goonewardena, inspired by revolutionary women of
the international socialist movement like Rosa Luxemberg,
Alexandra Kollontai and Clara Zetkin, as well as her own family
members who were deeply involved in the anti-imperial struggle,
and Selina Perera who was a school friend, joined the LSSP soon
after its inauguration. Unlike Selina she spent most of her political life in Sri Lanka, in the public eye, agitating on a range of
issues from the demand for independence to labour rights, the
reduction in prices of household goods and milk-food and the
establishment of creches that would allow mothers to work.[64]
The latter were issues of direct concern to women. Like Selina,
Vivienne also went into hiding in India following the crackdown
on the LSSP by the British. But while Selina remained in Calcutta,
Vivienne returned to Sri Lanka in 1946 and went on to be the
foremost woman leader of the LSSP. She campaigned in the 1947
elections, becoming a municipal councillor in 1950. She served
as a member of parliament from 1956-60, 1964-5 and 1970-7.
Like Selina, Vivienne gained a reputation for militancy. She had
legendary brushes with the police, a quick wit and a fierce
tongue.[65]

During their lifetime, both Selina and Vivienne had shown that it was possible for women to occupy public roles and stand up to the heckling, shaming and derision they encountered as women in politics, and still retain the respect of the public and the labouring classes they worked for. They also showed the way to a cosmopolitan politics that was not focused solely on matters within the nation, but also those beyond its borders. While Selina involved herself in socialist politics in Calcutta, Vivienne was vocal in her protests against US aggression in Vietnam, Cuba, Mozambique, and Zionist aggression in Palestine. She protested the nuclear arms race and the installation of US bases in Diego Garcia. She asked that the Sri Lankan government disallow the Pakistani airforce use of Sri Lankan airports as a fuelling point in its strikes against Bangladesh during its 1971 war of independence. "Her social outlook" therefore, "and her concept of emancipation. . . were not limited to one sector but encompassed all forms of exploitative relations and discriminations."[66] Patriarchy was one of them.[67]

One of the most vocal and intriguing organisations that grew out of the left movement was the Eksath Kāntha Peramuna (EKP or United Women's Front), the first women-only political organisation of its kind in Sri Lanka, which brought middle and working class women onto a common platform. It was formed in 1947, a year before independence, and its membership consisted entirely of women who were members of the left-wing Lānka Sama Samāja Party (LSSP). Some of its leading members like Doreen Wickremasinghe, Vivienne Goonewardena and Sita Wickramasuriya were married to left-wing politicians. Others like Edith Gymroi Ludowyk, the Hungarian-born wife of Lyn Ludowyk, Professor of English at the University of Ceylon, Irangani Meedeniya, Cora Abraham, Shirani Jayawardena, Parameswari Kandiah and Jeanne Pinto were activists of the left, some from their student days.

The EKP came into prominence on March 8, 1948 when it held a public rally to celebrate International Women's Day. Its activities and interventions received wide publicity, particularly in the *Times of Ceylon* as its editor, D.B. Dhanapala, was a personal friend of some EKP members. Its ideological battle was reflected in its rejoinders to the Central Board of Women's Institutes which was formed in October 1930 and, following the Bengal Mahilā Samiti, had taken on the name Lanka Mahilā Samiti (LMS). The EKP had an ambivalent attitude towards the LMS. While it praised the organisation for its work in the rural sector through home gardening projects and animal husbandry, it condemned the LMS's limitations in working within a system of capitalism, for making "no suggestion that any attempt should be made to change the basic economy of the village, or the system responsible for it, but a desire that within the set pattern of life now existing, whatever could be done to help the villagers to make the best of their poor circumstances would be done". The EKP on the other hand saw its "duty (as being) not merely to help people make the best of a bad world, but to understand why it is bad and to help them realise, through experience in fighting for their rights, that they can change it".[68]

The EKP was particularly suspicious of the Lanka Mahila Samiti's close involvement with the post-independence UNP government, as the LMS relied heavily on government infrastructure to carry out its projects. It also attacked the middle-class composition of the executive of the LMS, noting the pitfalls of their patronage of them and their accepting a different standard of living for the poor. It wasn't as if the EKP was against the middleclass per se—it could not afford to be, given its own composition. In what comes across as almost a recruitment drive directed at LMS workers it acknowledged that

Just as it needed women of the middle class to give a start to the work of the Mahila Samiti, so does our movement need a middle class lead. We appeal therefore to such women who have already shown by their work for the Mahila Samiti that they have a social conscience to consider our stand. If they are in agreement with it, we ask them to have courage and join us too.

Mindful of its constituency on the left, the EKP also took up the struggle for workers' rights. At its March 8 rally held at the Town Hall, women workers from the Tamil, Muslim and Sinhala communities, like Lailamma, Zahara Umma and Ponsihamy addressed the gathering, and either proposed or seconded resolutions calling for the immediate reinstatement of workers who had lost their jobs due to trade union action; better housing facilities; and an immediate decrease in the cost of living. This address was reported in the *Lankādeepa* of the Sinhala press.

The EKP's Edith Ludowyk was one of the first feminist voices in Sri Lanka to initiate an argument that the women's movement would take up as a defining concept later on. This was that women's liberation meant an acceptance of women's difference rather than arguing for sameness with men. She wrote in 1948:

> If socialists fight for women's rights, it does not mean that they want to prove that men and women are alike. Men and women are not alike and it is well that this is so. There are many things which men and women can do equally well; men can do some things better than women and women can do others better than men. Nothing is more foolish than futile comparisons.

Equal opportunity on the basis of difference, then, was the EKP's platform. One issue it keenly fought was the inclusion of women into the public service for which women's groups had been agitating since the 1930s. Its strategies were multi-pronged. Consultations were first held with Senator Cissy Cooray and the Finance Minister on the entry of women into the Ceylon Civil Service. The EKP also took the Department of Education to task for specifying that only males need apply for the General Clerical Services examination. Its petition went up to the Public Services Commission which declared that it was government policy to employ only males in the public service. The EKP then had LSSP MP Pieter Keuneman raise the issue in parliament. When the Finance Minister replied that the matter was under consideration, the EKP realised that the government was employing a delaying tactic. It then sought to form a joint front with other organisations to agitate for its demands. Helen Gunasekera, secretary of the EKP, wrote a letter to the *Ceylon Daily News* (July 3, 1948) announcing support for its cause from the General Clerical Services Union, the Registered Trained Nurses Association, the Association of Chartered Accountants, the Agricultural Officer's Association, the Association of Government Apothecaries, the United Lanka Congress Party and the LSSP. Letters of support from the Young Men's Buddhist Association (YMBA) and Sri Nissanka, President of the North Western Province's Peasants' and Workers' Front were also listed.

Earlier, Helen Gunasekera, in an article entitled "How the World Treats its Women" (*Ceylon Daily News* June 19, 1948) had persuasively stated the EKP's case on the issue of women's entry into the public service. Comparing the Ceylon government's stand with those of other countries, she provided a chart featuring 45 countries, listing the global position of women under the headings, (*a*) Less chance of promotion; (*b*) Women employed only in lower grades; (*c*) Equal pay; (*d*) Lower pay than men; (*e*) The marriage bar; (*f*) No marriage bar; (*g*) Full pay maternity leave. Showing that many countries had opened their doors to women in their respective public services, Helen Gunasekera declared, "The demand for employment of women in all branches of the public services is not a revolutionary one. But in this case, as in many other matters, Ceylon is backward." She drew particular attention to the Indian case stating that, "In India, where the status of women is supposed to be more strongly influenced by tradition than in Ceylon, the Government of India Act in 1935 gave Indian women more rights of employment in the Public Services than we enjoy in Ceylon in 1948".

It would take another 15 years before the campaign that the EKP mounted to allow women entry into the public service would bear fruit. In 1963 the first admissions of women to the administrative service as well as to the accountants and shroffs services were made, but on a quota basis. In 1975, in response to UN International Women's Year, a 25 per cent increase in the intake of women into the administrative service was made, but it was not until 1980 that quotas were abolished altogether.[69]

IV

What did the women's movement offer post-independence Sri Lankan women? Women of Jean Arasanayagam's generation, who came into the public sphere in the late 1950s and early 1960s as teachers, lawyers, doctors, nurses and clerical officers, reaped the benefits of widespread women's education. Free education from primary to tertiary levels had been introduced in 1945. This made education far more egalitarian, boosted its general level in the country as well as numbers seeking employment. Literacy rates for women became the highest in South Asia. In 1963 it was 67.3 per cent, steadily increasing to 87.9 per cent by 1994.[70] Similarly, life expectancy rates steadily improved for Sri Lankan women who now enjoy one of the highest life expectancy levels in the Third World. From a 41.6 average in 1946, women's life expectancy rose to 74.2 in the projections for 1991/96.[71] Maternal mortality dropped from 16.5 per cent in 1945 to 0.2 per cent in 1995.[72] These gains were the result of sound public policy initiated by both the colonial and post-independence governments. However, while these were achievements to be proud of, there were other significant trends of the post-independence era that would have a debilitating impact on the country's youth in general, and women in particular. This was where the post-independence Sri Lankan women's movement faced its greatest challenges.

The Youth Commission, which sat in 1989 to analyse the causes of youth unrest in the country, issued its report in 1990. It looked back over two decades of youth dissatisfaction and identified some of its main causes. The politicisation of the public services, impacting on recruitment, transfers, promotions and dismissals disavowed merit for political affiliation, leaving youth with no political patronage severely disadvantaged.[73] A gradual politicisation since independence of village and provincial institutions eroded hitherto dynamic social organisatons in which youth of both sexes played an active role. Despite class and caste differences, community clubs and *praja mandalas* brought youth together in a constructive pursuit of vocational training, community work and sport. The politicisation of these clubs as well as village councils and co-operatives further marginalised those who did not belong to the favoured party.[74] The education system, geared to passing the G.C.E. A level examination and gaining university entrance, failed many youth whose aspirations remained unfulfilled. University entrance became increasingly competitive. Conversely, with little or no vocational training, these youth could not find sustainable employment. Highly educated women were particularly disadvantaged. The following table on unemployment according to educational qualifications makes this clear:[75]

	1971		1981		1985/86	
	M	F	M	F	M	F
	%		%		%	
Passed G.C.E. A level	0.7	1.0	01.7	3.3	04.9	12.8
Passed Degree or above	0.3	0.6	01.0	0.4	04.0	0.8

Even those women who did get into the public sector were under-represented. In the Sri Lanka Administrative Service (SLAS) they comprised just 22 per cent in 1993; in scientific services only 20. 1 per cent in 1995, and in planning services 29. 7 per cent of the total employed.[76]

Responding to the needs of young women under these circumstances was a daunting challenge for the women's movement. Many women's organisations that had achieved so much before independence and had kept a discussion of women's rights alive in the public domain, were unable to sustain their efforts; in the 1960s and '70s they failed to mobilise a mass movement around these issues. Women's wings of left parties were stifled and the left leadership was singularly short-sighted in its attitude towards youth in general. This was another cause that led to youth frustration and drove them to militant politics. Ranjith Amarasinghe writes of the LSSP:

Youth leagues were one of the main sources of recruitment for the party at lower levels. Although membership of a youth league did not ensure party membership, it was essential that a potential party member should have experience either at a Samasamaja youth league or at a trade union affiliated party. The youth league was the first contact with the party for a majority of the recruits. The top positions of the Youth League Congress were, as a rule, filled with people drawn from among the leading cadres of the party hierarchy and, therefore, the youth league's role as an avenue for upward mobility within the party was limited.[77]

Apart from foreclosing possibilities for youth to rise within the party structure, the left parties had made no serious attempt until 1963 to translate key Marxist texts into Sinhala and Tamil for the large number of non-English reading party cadre, or produce any substantial new theoretical writing on national conditions.[78] This vacuum was filled in its own way by the JVP which, when it began functioning in 1965, initiated its cadres through five key "lessons" which critiqued the colonial plantation economy, the left's failure to enlist a socialist state and India's occupying role throughout Sri Lankan history.[79] Moreover, with the LSSP entering into coalition politics with the SLFP in 1960 it rejected, as a matter of policy, any revolutionary/extra-parliamentary means of installing a socialist state in Sri Lanka.[80] Unable to find a suitable ideological home within the mainstream left, educated disaffected southern youth who wished to transform their lives and re-draw the state and society had, by the mid-1960s, nowhere else to. go but to a militant group like the JVP. This paralleled events in the north. Disgruntled with the elite power-brokering of parties like the Tamil United Liberation Front and the Federal Party, several Tamil groups formed by the late 1970s such as People's Liberation Organisation of Tamil Eelam (PLOTE), Tamil Eelam Liberation Organisation (TELO), Eelam Revolutionary Organisation of Students (EROS) and the LTTE attracted large numbers of youth to armed struggle. Both the JVP and Tamil militant groups took on distinctively nationalist overtones particularly in the 1980s, that preached ethnic exclusivity and separatism, and launched violent campaigns to attain their goals.

The demise of the EKP itself and its legacy is an interesting case study of both the potential and pitfalls confronting the Sri Lankan women's movement, as much as it is a commentary on the left. The EKP, even while it functioned, was not taken seriously by male members of the left-wing parties.[81] As long as their women were seen to be doing good work, the EKP was humoured and allowed to function. It was not mobilised on a larger scale for the agendas of the left, nor did it seek a more defining role for itself within the left. This constituted a lost opportunity for the left in general. According to Ranjith Amarasinghe, it was not until 1953 and the success of the *hartāl* that the left united in a common cause, although this had been advocated for some time by the LSSP.[82] The EKP, however, had realised this goal earlier, in 1947, in offering a common platform for women of the LSSP and CP. Once the left parties coalesced and strengthened their position in a common front however, their women's wings suffered commensurate downgrading. In Amarasinghe's study of Trotskyism in Sri Lanka, women's contribution to the movement is barely noted. Nowhere is the EKP mentioned. The Samasamāja Kāntha Peramuṇa or LSSP Women's Front merits one brief paragraph: this brevity is proof that, within mainstream political analysis of the left as well as its party leadership, women were denied the possibility of having made a significant contribution to party policy and decision making; today, most of them are, in fact, denied the opportunity to do so.

The Kāntha Samithis or Women's Committees within today's left-wing parties are the legacy of the EKP.[83] These organisations are dominated by party ideology which has little feminist content, and reflects the shift that has taken place within the traditional left itself. For example, the Kāntha Samithis of the constituents of the current People's Alliance government of Chandrika Kumaratunga, are inexplicably quiet on the government's policies of privatisation and the expansion of the export processing zones in which many women are employed. These issues have been taken up by various NGOs rather than mainstream political parties. Kāntha Samithis have been singularly unable to influence general party policy and their members are marginalised into playing a role within the Kāntha Samithi rather than being active in the party bureaucracy or think-tank. They retire to their party headquarters as soon as they are summoned to concentrate on something else, merely supplying numbers for party rallies. When SLFP MPs Mangala Samaraweera and Mahinda Rajapakse decided to form the Mothers' Front in July 1990 as a voice of protest against the abduction and killing of SLFP and JVP party activists and youth, it was from the Kāntha Samithis of the various SLFP branches that women were initially recruited. Some of them had suffered the abduction of their husbands, brothers and sons. Chapter 6, which reappraises the Mothers' Front retrospectively, looks at what has happened to some of these women and how their lives have changed or not in the ten years after its formation. While the widespread disappearances of the 1987–89 era are not prevalent today, arbitrary detention of Tamil males suspected of LTTE involvement continues nevertheless. The

disbanding, on LTTE orders, of the Jaffna Mothers' Front which
had taken up cases of detention and disappearance in 1984, and
the failure of the southern Mothers' Front to forge significant
links with women of the north and east to erect a common, pan-
island platform against violence, has meant that, today, these
arrests go virtually unnoticed by some of the same women's
organisations that came together under the umbrella of the Mothers' Front, active in the issue of disappearances a decade ago.

The absence of these Kāntha Samithis in their party newspapers tells its own story. The LSSP newspaper, *Samasamāja* does
not even contain a separate page on their work and concerns.
The same was true of the Communist Party newspapers, *Aththa*
(The Truth) and *The Forward*. The JVP of the 1980s, on the
other hand, devoted quite a bit of space to its women's wing in
its party newspaper, *Niyamuwa*. But, as discussed in greater de-
tail in Chapter 4, like the Kāntha Samithis, the JVP women's
wing was unable to make significant inroads into party policy or
its hierarchy. Its own committee consisted of the entire JVP male
politbureau as ex officio members, and it was often subjected to
an instrumental use by this leadership. As for the LTTE, women
were inducted as cadre only after it could no longer recruit large
numbers of Tamil male youth, following the Indo-Lanka agreement of 1987 and the crackdown on the LTTE by the Indian
Peace Keeping Forces (IPKF). Much international publicity has
been given by the LTTE to its women's wing, known as the Birds
of Freedom. But this is not unconnected with international funding available for women's empowerment and political participation. A closer look at the role of women within the LTTE, however, leads to questions about the nature of their empowerment.
The structure and ideology of the LTTE leave little room for the
freedom of women to determine their own destiny. As with the
JVP, the women of the LTTE occupy no positions in the
organisational hierarchy, and are therefore outside the decision-
making process. As Radhika Coomaraswamy states:

They are not initiators of ideas, they are only implementers of policy made
by someone else, by men. This authoritarian model of decision-making
does not really empower women as political and social beings. They become cogs in the wheel of someone else's designs and plans. They are not

the creators, the visionaries, the entrepreneurs, of any political or social project. They are only following orders, or enacting someone else's strategy. They are the consumers, not the producers of the grand political project.[84]

The transformation, through such recruitment, of Tamil women as celebratory not of life, but of death and martyrdom in the name of the emerging nation, and the militarisation of society that they sanction by their actions cannot be liberatory for them or their societies, whatever the short-term gains. That their search for autonomy, even when it repudiates allegiance to individualism and traditional family ties in exchange for other identities representing abnegation, sacrifice, martyrdom, renunciation and discipline, are nevertheless ideological terrains that are themselves gendered. Are these women fully aware of this gendering? What have been their gains and losses? And what are the problems they pose for feminism when their agentive moments have, necessarily, to be considered with the question of their accountability in the destructive and authoritarian regimes they participate in?

V

After seventeen years of bitter ethnic war, there are many Sri Lankan women who are currently redefining their lives not through party affiliation or the compulsions of the women's movement, but as a result of the exigency born of conflict. These are women in the war zones. Much has happened in their lives that has transformed their traditional roles as wives, mothers and daughters of the community. They have been displaced following the destruction of their homes and villages and have found themselves in refugee camps; they have been widowed and become heads of their households, responsible for their children and elders; they have been compelled to seek jobs outside the home. In the absence of their menfolk they have had to assume public roles in dealing with the armed forces, state bureaucracy, medical authorities and humanitarian aid agencies. They have had to file applications for various emoluments and petitions for legal redress. Those living in conflict and "border" areas have had to regularly negotiate check-points and military personnel. All of this has meant that deep structural changes are taking place in the families and communities that live in these areas, and that through fragmentation and reconstitution, a significant revolution is taking place in the lives of these women.[85]

Social scientists have noted that women in refugee camps no longer conform to the traditional roles demanded of them. They move between gender and caste lines quite freely, boys and girls of different castes play with each other and young widows refuse to erase their *pottus*, the mark of married Tamil women.[86] Young women who have integrated into the local economy by finding jobs outside the refugee camps express reluctance at returning to their original homes. Displacement for them constitutes a place of ambivalence. While it is a constant reminder of loss and trauma, it has also provided them a space of "regeneration and hope for a future unfettered by the past".[87]

At present, however, these women lack a generalised cultural discourse, outside of the refugee camps and the interregnum in which normative behaviour is adapted or suspended, that will sustain these transformations. Young widows in camps who are anxious about returning home, fear precisely this: a return to the status quo once the period of transition has ended. Nor are the camps themselves entirely free of patriarchal strictures. There are continuities of pre-conflict administrative hierarchies as well as gender control within them, which form the bases of the refugee's *naturalisation* of their camp as home. Camp committees often comprise members of administrative councils which prevailed in the refugees' home areas, and women whose husbands are with them complain that they are under constant surveillance by their men. In this way the refugee men reassert their authority within the camp as well as rehearse their familial, patriarchal roles in both a nostalgia and reconstitution of their lost homes.[88] So deep is the cultural discourse that demarcates gender through "roles", that even those women whose lives have been positively transformed by displacement express their anxiety at returning with great ambivalence and guilt.

Moreover, when interregnum becomes prolonged, normative traditional codes tend to become even more entrenched within the camp. In a study of 75,000 displaced Muslims of the northern province, forcibly evicted following ethnic cleansing by the LTTE and in camps in the Puttalam district since 1990, it was found that customary practices regulating women were heightened.[89] Faizun Zackeriya and Zulfika Ismail found that during 1992–97, there was an increase in school drop-outs amongst Muslim girls living in these settlements, and consequent early marriage; 70 per cent of the sample had attained only a primary level of education and 60 per cent of them had ended up in early marriage. In 1971 in the Mullativu district, the average age of marriage for girls was 16.6 years; in Mannar 19.1; in 1997 these figures were the same. The causes for this are fairly self-evident. Insecurity of displacement made parents marry off their daughters early so that they would have the added protection of their husbands. Economic deprivation is another factor which parents attempt to alleviate through marriage; 67 per cent of the marriages under study took place during 1991 and 1997, when the government introduced a Rs. 25,000 employment benefit for newly-married couples. Many marriage brokers had, in fact, skimmed off this sum as their commission, but this was also a time when customary practice regulated young Muslim women even more harshly than before, a response to the increased contact between girls and boys during camp life and women seeking outside employment. As the researchers noted, Muslim culture and codes became the lynchpin of a continued communal identity throughout displacement. Mosques were built, Quranic classes held and Islamic pre-schools organised in every camp. Women's wings of the religious groups of each camp were formed to teach the "true Islamic way of life". In this way women were selected as repositories of community values, and for many of them this became the dominant identity they bore in the camps.

Apart from the trauma of displacement, the camps have also been sites of increased domestic violence. Women who entered into early marriage are amongst the most vulnerable in this regard. Women have had to bear the brunt of high male unemployment, and a high rate of separation and divorce, mostly without maintenance benefits. Incidents of rape and molestation have been recorded and women have been prey to local men of the area. These violations have gone unreported. Parents keep silent because, being displaced, they are dependent on the goodwill of the "host" community. Suicides, previously not reported in their villages of origin have also occurred amongst this displaced Muslim population.

Researchers point out that significant transformations also have occurred. Muslim women from these camps seek employment in the Middle-East, a practice previously unheard of. The seclusion of Muslim women is breaking down due to the exigency of camp life, affording increased physical mobility and contact with others outside their immediate family. Women have gained increased economic independence and girls and boys interact much more freely than they were allowed to in their villages of origin. However, NGOs and humanitarian aid agencies working in these areas tend to reinforce the dependency syndrome of Muslim women rather than encourage a sustainable transformation of their lives. This is because they do not effectively address issues of class, gender and social mobilisation that have an impact on the women and their roles within camp society. This "lack of social recognition and a culturally appropriate idiom to articulate, legitimate and support women's transformed roles and empowerment in the midst of conflict, trauma, and social disruption"[90] is one of the main challenges that lies ahead, then, for the women's movement in Sri Lanka, if it is to build on what is empowering for women in the transformations currently taking place.

VI

The story of Sri Lankan nationalisms cannot be written without reference to India. Both countries have, in the modern period, shared a British colonial heritage but before that, from ancient times, India has been the source of inspiration and influence for countless migrations, the advent of Buddhism, traders, intellectuals and artists to Sri Lanka. Sri Lankan folk theatre is replete with Indian characters from Bengal, Andhra, Malabar, the kingdom of the Cholas and Kalinga,[91] and the story of modern Sinhala theatre cannot be told without appraising the influences of the Bengali and Parsi theatre of India on it. From Indian musicians, performers and stage designers who worked closely in the Sinhala theatre in the early decades of the 20th century, to cameramen and editors in the Sinhala cinema in the 1940s and 1950s, to Shantiniketan as alma mater for Sri Lankan painters, actors and musicians, there was a dynamic borrowing and cross-fertilisation between the two countries. Sri Lankan nationalist leaders like Anagarika Dharmapala were deeply influenced by Indian nationalists and, inspired by the Theosophical Society, engaged in Buddhist education and reform in India. When Anagarika Dharmapala was banned by the British government from returning to Sri Lanka after the 1915 Sinhala-Muslim clash, it was in India that he sought refuge. There were close ties too between the political leadership of both countries. Sri Lankan nationalist politicians travelled regularly to India to attend Congress sessions, and the post-independence first families of India and Sri Lanka, the Nehrus and the Bandaranaikes, formed close friendships. Jawaharlal Nehru was chief guest at the Buddha Jayanthi celebrations held in Sri Lanka in May 1957 to celebrate 2,500 years of Buddhism and in turn, S.W.R.D. Bandaranaike was a distinguished guest at India's celebration of the event. Public holidays were declared in India and Sri Lanka, respectively, when S.W.R.D. Bandaranaike was assassinated in 1959, and Nehru died in 1964.[92] And when the JVP launched its insurgency in April 1971 Indira Gandhi was quick to help the beleaguered government of Sirimavo Bandaranaike.

Most importantly for the theme of this book, the Indian women's movement played a central role in inspiring and complementing the efforts of various Sri Lankan women on issues of women's rights and development. The Lanka Mahilā Samiti closely followed the Indian Mahilā Samitis' example of community development work, focusing on self-employment, health and welfare of women. The visits to Sri Lanka in the 1920s and '30s of Indian women like Sarojini Naidu, Kamaladevi Chattopadhyaya and Vijayalakshmi Pandit inspired the local political elite to take up the cause of women's franchise and education, and issues of the undercaste (see chapter 3, and Sarojini Naidu's influence on George E. de Silva). Both male and female reformists in Sri Lanka took inspiration from Indian women reformists on these issues. The editors of *Young Ceylon* used the magazine's women's page to constantly keep their readership aware of the strides being made by women in the colonies as well as Britain, Europe, the Middle East and Far East, but they paid special attention to the meetings and discussions of the Indian women's movement. *Young Ceylon* regularly announced the meetings of the All India Women's Conference and carried excerpts of addresses by their Presidents; this coincided with the editor's own goals for improvement in women's education, entry into public service, the professions and the legislature, and improved working conditions for women. The *Young Ceylon* of June 1934 (vol. 3 no. 2) reported on the National Council of Women in India's fourth triennial conference and quoted from the Maharani of Baroda's address to this conference on the necessity of spearheading girls' education; it published excerpts from addresses by Sarojini Naidu and Malinibai Sukhtankar to women's conferences in Madras and Berar respectively, calling for women to unite in working for social reform, and for increased self-reliance even if their goals were different depending on regional needs (vol. 4 no. 6, October 1935); it carried an excerpt from Kamaladevi Chattopadhyaya's address to the South Canara District Women's Conference on the importance of women entering politics (vol. 7 no. 6, October 1938); it highlighted the programmes of the Indian Women's University (vol. 4 no. 2 June 1934) and wrote on the formation of the Indian Women's Fellowship of Service, inaugurated in Bombay and dedicated to "creating a standard of disciplined service which shall be worthy of the high ideals and deep devotion of Indian womanhood"(vol. 5 no. 1, May 1936); it announced the list of women elected to the Indian legislature in 1937 (vol. 5 no. 11, March 1937) and reported on Mrs. Nilima Devi's address on "Indian Women and the New Constitution" which criticised the valuing of a woman's domestic role at the expense of her equal rights as a citizen (vol. 5, no. 12, April 1937). These Indian women who forwarded an agenda for reform and equal opportunities were thereby lauded in a move calculated to mobilise Sri Lankan women to enter the public sphere and serve the needs of the nation and their gender.

India is present, therefore, in each chapter of this book in a manner that also signifies shifts that have taken place in its relationship with Sri Lanka. For many Sinhalese in a deeply divided Sri Lankan nation-state, India has progressed through the 20th century from acknowledged "Mother India", fount of cultural inspiration, leader and fellow traveller in the anti-British, anti-colonial struggle, to post-independence adversary as giant neighbour and South Asia's dominant power. Despite the close ties that endured even after independence, the symbiotic relationship of Sri Lanka to India began to change after each nation-state carved out its terms of sovereignty and engaged in social engineering to fit its needs.

The issue of citizenship for estate workers of Indian origin residing in Sri Lanka became a contentious one. The first independent UNP government of Sri Lanka sought negotiations with India on repatriating Indian Tamils who had been brought by the British to labour on the tea estates. India, however, stalled on the issue, seeing it as a domestic problem for Sri Lanka. Political aloofness between the two states ensued.[93] Visas and travel certificates, not necessary before Indian and Sri Lankan Independence, now became a requirement. It was not until 1964 and the Sirimavo-Shastri pact that serious negotiations on the issue of citizenship for estate workers of Indian origin took place. Under the agreement Sri Lanka would grant citizenship to 375, 000 estate labour while 525,000 would be repatriated to India.[94] Subsequent negotiations increased this quota on both sides, but it has taken over three decades to settle the issue, with all estate labour of Indian origin presently in Sri Lanka finally enjoying long overdue rights of citizenship. Added to the issue of citizenship were other irritants: the question of fishing in each other's territorial waters, smuggling, the Kachcha Thivu dispute and the attempt by India in 1957 to ban the broadcasts of Radio Ceylon to India, popular with listeners and advertisers at the time. The Indian government proclaimed the broadcasts as culturally corrupting, improper and in contravention of the Commonwealth Broadcasting Convention.[95] All of these were to take a toll on Indo-Sri Lankan relations.

As India began to implement a foreign policy that established its dominance in South Asia, and its Prime Minister Indira Gandhi gave sanctuary and training in the 1970s to Tamil militants who would eventually launch their bid for a separate Tamil state in Sri Lanka, tensions between the two states mounted. The JVP discourse of the 1980s portrayed India as a bully and India began to feature in nationalistic rhetoric as a threat to Sri Lankan sovereignty and the Sinhala identity. The nadir of tension between India and Sri Lanka was reached when, following the Indo-Lanka agreement of 1987, the Indian Peace Keeping Forces arrived in Jaffna as part of the deal brokered by Rajiv Gandhi. Gandhi lost his life for that deal when he was assassinated by a female LTTE suicide bomber in 1991. But India continues to assert a powerful presence in Sri Lanka although, following the withdrawal of the IPKF in 1989, it has not played an overt role in the Sri Lankan separatist war. Most recently, however, the controversial Indo-Lanka trade agreement and India's refusal in May 2000 to give military assistance to Sri Lankan troops marooned and surrounded by the LTTE in Jaffna, have renewed the sense of unease many Sri Lankan Sinhalese feel about India.[96]

It is perhaps proof of India's dominance in the region that, while Sri Lanka's history cannot be narrated without the Indian factor, India can afford to marginalise or even completely ignore comparable Sri Lankan influences on India. Anil de Silva was a founder member of two important institutions in the arts in India in the 1940s—the journal *Marg*, and the Indian People's Theatre Association whose very idea was hers. She was also actively involved with the ideas and goals of the Progressive Writers' Association. It was she who first introduced the art of George Keyt to India by organising his first exhibitions in Bombay and featuring his art in *Marg*. She lived in Bombay from 1941–49, was a close associate of members of the Communist Party of India, and an admirer and archivist of Indian art. Together with Mulk Raj Anand she spearheaded, through *Marg*, the appraisal of Indian art as a pan-Asian heritage. Yet, few in India today know about Anil de Silva or her place in the arts, politics and life of Bombay of the 1940s, although she does figure in a few works of scholarship and writing by Indians authors—notably in Sudhi Pradhan's edition of the documents of the Marxist Cultural Movement in India,[97] Raj Thapar's memoir *All These Years*,[98] Zohra Segal's autobiography, *Stages*[99] and in the introduction by Susie Tharu and K. Lalitha to their anthology, *Women Writing in India.*[100] Tharu and Lalitha mention that Anil was the secretary-general of IPTA and then go on to give a short description of her as "one of the principal ideologues and organizers of the movement in its initial stages".[101] Nowhere do they mention that Anil was from Sri Lanka.

Anil, on the other hand, was able to adopt Bombay as her home with ease. The city's cosmopolitan composition helped, but so did the very close connections her parents had with Indian political figures. Her father, George E. de Silva, was a leading nationalist and political figure in the 1920s, whose career culminated as President of the Ceylon National Congress in 1930 and Minister of Health in 1942. He knew the personalities of the Indian freedom struggle well and was host, amongst others, to Mahatma Gandhi and Nehru (including his wife Kamala and their daughter Indira), Kamaladevi Chattopadhyaya and Sarojini Naidu when they visited his home in Kandy. In turn, he attended every annual session of the Indian National Congress. For Anil therefore, Bombay, at the height of World War II and India's independence struggle held a familiar political and cultural fascination. Besides, so close were the leaders of Sri Lanka's left-wing parties to their Indian counterparts prior to independence, that when the leaders of the LSSP and CP went underground following the colonial government's crackdown on their parties, it was to India that they fled. Anil's flat in Bombay was raided by the Indian police on the orders of the British colonial government when it was hunting the fugitives.

It has been largely the feminist movements in both countries that have attempted to continue vital civil society links between Sri Lanka and India even at the height of their respective governments' conflictual relationship. Through personal contact, conferences, workshops and publications women's groups of both countries have learnt of each other's issues and concerns, strategies and challenges. Representatives from the women's movement of India and Pakistan came to Sri Lanka following Rajini Thiranagama's murder by the LTTE in 1989, to show solidarity and participate in protest/peace marches organised by Sri Lankan women. Such solidarity has *politically* best epitomised the cosmopolitanism that Anil de Silva and Jean Arasanayagam foreground culturally.

It may be reasonably argued that such a show of transnational solidarity is possible because women's organisations have, in the interests of universal standards of human rights, countered their respective states and attempted to build an alternative culture to nationalism. This has not been easy. In the post-colonial world where local feminists are constantly charged with adopting an alien, western rhetoric of feminism, the debate between nationalism and internationalism comes to the fore, at times eroding the strength of local women's movements. Ratna Kapur notes that women's organisations in India have had to counter these charges by locating themselves firmly within nationalism, resulting in a watering down of the penal, legislative and customary law reforms that they have been pressing for.[102] However, as already noted, the women's movement is diverse and defies homogenisation. Its issues can vary as do its strategies. It has the ability to (re)cross issues in a manner which mirrors the cosmopolitan. In South Asia, many women's groups have gone against the grain of dominant nationalism and the drive of their nation-states. Women in India have protested against anti-Muslim communalism and nuclearisation; in Pakistan they have protested against militarisation and military rule; in Bangladesh they have joined forces against curbing of freedom of speech and Islamic fundamentalism; in Sri Lanka they have been at the forefront of the peace movement, calling for a negotiated settlement to the ethnic conflict. These responses have squarely confronted dominant and politically powerful ideologies either sponsored by the state or aligned to religious groups.

Bruce Robbins writes,

Support for feminism, human rights and the environment comes in both national and international scales or emphases, but ways exist in which such support could be channelled into struggles that recognize some, though not all, of what each party wants, and which could thus avoid a debilitating choice between them. This is a goal for the political imagination in the new millennium."[103]

In a South Asia intimately connected through geography and

history, there are many cross-border issues that are pertinent to its women's movements. The 1947 partition of India and Pakistan and the on-going dispute in Kashmir, considered the "unfinished business" of partition, has drawn feminists to study its effects on women and call for de-militarisation of the region and normalisation of Indo-Pakistan ties.[104] Women's groups from Bangladesh, Nepal and India have been involved in lobbying for a treaty on the trafficking in women across their borders. Women in Sri Lanka joined in negotiating the language of this treaty through the South Asian Association of Regional Co-operation (SAARC) Peoples' Forum. Moreover, borders between issues themselves have been successfully crossed and re-crossed by some women's groups in what approximates to a "lateral cosmopolitanism" within the nation. In Sri Lanka, a burgeoning NGO sector as well as an autonomous women's movement organisationally unlinked to political parties enabled women's groups to work on issues which were of strategic feminist interest in the early 1980s. By the end of that decade, however, with the JVP insurrection and "disappearances" in the south, and the separatist war in the north and east, the burning issue was that of human rights. Many of these women's groups took on human rights work before returning to working on women's issues in the latter half of the 1990s at a policy level. (See chapter 6.) This mobility between issues is where women's groups have shown most independence, in an empowering feminist politics that encompasses human rights and challenges what is most pernicious in nationalist ideology. All of these have repercussions on, and concern, the national. How women's groups take this into cognisance, yet avoid the exclusivities of nationalism even as they draw strength from nationalism's sense of community, justice and self-determination in building a lateral cosmopolitanism within the nation and a South Asian internationalism, is the challenge for the future.

Notes

[1] I take my frame of reference from Rogers Brubaker who calls for theorizing nation as event, as something that suddenly crystallizes rather than gradually develops; "as a contingent, conjuncturally fluctuating and precarious frame of vision and basis for individual

and collective action, rather than a relatively stable product of deep developmental trends in economy, polity or culture." in *Nationalism Reframed: Nationhood and the National Question in the New Europe.* Cambridge: Cambridge University Press, 1996, p. 17. However, as Brubaker himself goes on to define the nation and nationhood as a category of practice that has institutionalised cultural and political forms, the centrality to them of nationalist ideology that is incremental and has accumulated as an "archive" in the Foucauldian sense, cannot be dismissed.

2 Sri Lanka was known as Ceylon before 1972. However, I refer to the country as Sri Lanka throughout except when the word Ceylon appears in quotations or in the names of registered companies and political organisations.

3 Deniz Kandiyoti, p. 13. "Identity and Its Discontents: Women and the Nation," in *Dossier 20*, December 1997.

4 See Nivedita Menon, "Women and Citizenship," in Partha Chatterjee (ed.), *Wages of Freedom: Fifty Years of the Indian Nation-State.* New Delhi: Oxford University Press, 1998, pp. 244–5. Many Acts drafted and codified by Congress leaders after Indian Independence put an end to the diversity of Hindu personal law as practised in different regions. Some of these Acts actually destroyed already existing, more liberal provisions for women. Thus, the Hindu Succession Act of 1956 which made only patrilineal inheritance legitimate, deprived women from matrilineal communities in Kerala and Karnataka of their birthright to parental and ancestral property.

5 Elizabeth Wood, *The Baba and the Comrade: Gender and Politics in Revolutionary Russia.* Bloomington: Indiana University Press, 1997, p. 13. This is also borne out in Partha Chatterjee's study of the Indian nationalists' resolution to the women's question in *The Nation and Its Fragments: Colonial and Postcolonial Histories.* New Jersey: Princeton University Press, 1993.

6 Nira Yuval-Davis argues therefore for a concept of "citizenship as a multi-tier construct, which applies to people's membership in a variety of collectivities—local, ethnic, national and transnational". Thus the issue of women's citizenship should be considered "not only by contrast to that of men, but also in relation to women's affiliation to dominant or subordinate groups, their ethnicity, origin and urban or rural residence." *Gender and Nation.* London and New Delhi: Sage, 1997, p. 68.

7 Begona Aretxaga, "What the Border Hides: Partition and Gender Politics of Irish Nationalism," in *Social Analysis 42*, no. 1, March 1998, p. 23; George L. Mosse, *Nationalism and Sexuality: Middle Class Morality and Sexual Norms in Modern Europe.* Madison: University of Wisconsin Press, 1985; Lois A. West, Introduction in

Feminist Nationalism. New York &London: Routledge, 1997; Elleke Boehmer, "Motherlands, Mothers and Nationalist Sons: Representations of Nationalism and Women in African Literature," in Anna Rutherford (ed.), *From Commonwealth to Post-Colonial*. Sydney: Dangaroo Press, 1992.

[8] Elleke Boehmer, op. cit., p. 233.

[9] See Sara Mills, *Discourses of Difference: An Analysis of Women's Travel Writing and Colonialism*. London: Routledge, 1991.

[10] Begona Aretxaga, op. cit., p. 24

[11] Carole Pateman, *The Disorder of Women: Democracy, Feminism and Political Theory*. Stanford: Stanford University Press, 1989, chapter 2.

[12] Nivedita Menon, op cit., p. 245.

[13] Nira Yuval-Davis, *Gender and Nation*, p. 13.

[14] Partha Chatterjee, "The Nationalist Resolution to the Women's Question," in Kumkum Sangari and Sudesh Vaid (eds.) *Recasting Women: Essays in Colonial History*. New Delhi: Kali for Women, 1989, pp. 233–253.

[15] Himani Bannerji, "Projects of Hegemony: Towards a Critique of Subaltern Studies' 'Resolution of the Women's Question'," *Economic and Political Weekly* 35, no. 11, March 11–17 2000, pp. 902–20.

[16] Joan Kelly, quoted in Jasodhara Bagchi, Introduction to *Indian Women: Myth and Reality*. Hyderabad: Sangam books, 1995. p. 7.

[17] Kumari Jayawardena, *Feminism and Nationalism in the Third World*. London: Zed Books, 1986.

[18] Leila Ahmed contends that Kasim Amin's ideas "actively reproduced colonial thinking about women's status in Muslim society", quoted in Nadje Al-Ali, *Secularism, Gender and the State in the Middle East: The Egyptian Women's Movement*. Cambridge: Cambridge University Press, 2000, p. 57.

[19] See Sherna Berger Gluck, "Shifting Sands: The Feminist-Nationalist Connection in the Palestinian Movement," in *Feminist Nationalism*, op. cit., p. 101–129.

[20] Jayawardena, op. cit., p. 22.

[21] Ibid., p. 134.

[22] Rajeswari Sunder Rajan, Introduction in *Signposts: Gender Issues in Post-Independence India*. New Delhi: Kali for Women, 1999, pp. 7–8.

[23] Kandiyoti, op. cit., p. 127.

[24] Ina Trimmer, "Her Wedding Morning," *The Times of Ceylon Christmas Number*, 1941.

[25] Zohreh T. Sullivan, "Eluding the Feminist, Overthrowing the Modern? Transformation in Twentieth Century Iran," in Lila Abu-Lughod (ed.), *Remaking Women: Feminism and Modernity in the Middle East*. New

Jersey: Princeton University Press, p. 236. Sullivan describes how the chador, or veil, was used by Iranian women as both a symbol of modernity and protest. In 1936 the Shah of Iran forbade the chador as part of his programme for the emancipation of Iranian women. By 1979, Iranian women of all castes and classes were voluntarily wearing the chador as a symbol of protest against the Shah's regime. It became an emancipatory symbol rooted in Islamic culture that marked their protest against the Shah's repressive, corrupt and pro-American regime. These same women would be surprised however when, with the advent of Ayatullah Khomeni, the wearing of the chador was made compulsory for women who ventured into public spaces. Thus the chador figured again when 30,000 Iranian women took to the streets on March 8, 1979 to protest against compulsory veiling. What was pertinent to Iranian women was not that the chador signified oppression/tradition, but that their autonomous choice as to whether to veil themselves had been denied them.

26 Bruce Robbins, *Feeling Global: Internationalism in Distress.* New York & London: New York University Press, 1999, p. 7.

27 Ibid, p. 76.

28 Nira Yuval Davis, *Gender and Nation*, pp. 125–133.

29 Mary Katzenstein, quoted in Amrita Basu (ed.), Introduction, *The Challenge of Local Feminisms: Women's Movements in Global Perspective.* New Delhi: Kali for Women, 1999, p. 14.

30 Dahabo Farah Hassan, Amina H. Adan and Amina Mohamoud Warsame, "Somalia: Poetry as Resistance against Colonialism and Patriarchy," in Saskia Wieringa (ed.), *Subversive Women: Women's Movements in Africa, Asia, Latin America and the Caribbean.* New Delhi: Kali for Women, 1997, p. 167.

31 I borrow here from Homi Bhabha, "Remembering Fanon", Introduction to Frantz Fanon's *Black Skin White Masks.* London & Sydney: Pluto Press, 1986. p. xi.

32 The 20th century has seen some of the most horrendous atrocities committed on women during war. In Europe, the recent pogroms and wars in Bosnia-Herzegovina and Kosovo in the 1980s and 1990s and on the Indian subcontinent, the 1947 violence against women at Partition are examples of these.

33 Sunila Abeysekera, keynote address, Indian Association of Women's Studies Conference, Jaipur, December 1995; Malathi de Alwis, "Motherhood as a Space of Protest: Women's Political Participation in Contemporary Sri Lanka," in Patricia Jeffery and Amrita Basu (eds.), *Appropriating Gender: Women's Activism and Politicized Religion in South Asia.* New York & London: Routledge, 1998, pp. 185–202; Rohini Hensman, "The Role of Women in the Resistance to Political

Authoritarianism in Latin America and South Asia," in Haleh Afshar (ed.) *Women and Politics in the Third World.* London & New York: Routledge, 1996, pp. 54–55.

[34] Visakha Kumari Jayawardena, *The Rise of the Labor Movement in Ceylon.* Colombo: Sanjiva Prakashana, n.d. First published Duke University Press, 1972. chapter 11.

[35] See E. F. C. Ludowyk, *The Story of Ceylon.* London: Faber & Faber, 1962, p. 289 and Y. Ranjith Amarasinghe, *Revolutionary Idealism and Parliamentary Politics: A Study of Trotskyism in Sri Lanka.* Colombo: Social Scientists' Association, 1998, pp. 99–104.

[36] Tarzie Vittachi, *Emergency '58: The Story of the Ceylon Race Riots.* London: Andre Deutsch, 1958, p. 55.

[37] Y. Ranjith Amarasinghe, *Revolutionary Idealism and Parliamentary Politics*, op. cit., p. 157.

[38] Jayadeva Uyangoda, "A State of Desire? Some Reflections on the Unreformability of Sri Lanka's Post-colonial Polity," University of Colombo, forthcoming.

[39] Homi Bhabha, op. cit., p. xi.

[40] D. V. Hapuarachchi, *The History of Sinhala Drama 1860–1911.* Colombo: Lake House, 1981. p. 230.

[41] Wilfred Gunasekera, "Life and Times of Dramatist John de Silva with Special Reference to His Hitherto Unknown Poetic Acumen," presentation at the Royal Asiatic Society, Sri Lanka, 26 January 1998.

[42] Michael Roberts, "Sinhala-ness and Sinhala Nationalism," work in progress for the Marga project on Ethnic Reconciliation, November 1999. See also Gananath Obeysekera, "The Vicissitudes of the Sinhala-Buddhist Identity through Time and Change," in Michael Roberts (ed.), *Sri Lanka. Collective Identities Revisited Vol. 1.* Colombo: Marga, 1997, chapter 12. Obeysekera's argument is that "being Buddhist is inseparable from being Sinhalese" and that until the advent of the European coloniser in the 16th century, "being a Sinhalese implied being a Buddhist". p. 355. The identities constructed by the nationalist elite from the mid 19th century also drew their terms of reference from other, earlier important collectivities within the Sinhala polity such as caste, notions of patriotism and relationship to the king etc.

[43] Roushan Jahan, "Men in Seclusion, Women in Public: Rokeya's Dream and Women's Struggles in Bangladesh," in Amrita Basu (ed.), *The Challenge of Local Feminisms: Women's Movements in Global Perspective*, p. 90.

[44] President Chandrika Kumaratunga spent time with the captain of the Sri Lankan cricket team, conveying her good wishes before the team's departure in September 1999 for the Sharjah tournament, and almost all the Buddhist players in the Sri Lankan cricket team wear "*pirith*

noolas", thread blessed by a Buddhist priest, on their wrist. Captain Sanath Jayasuriya wears several of them.

45 "Cat's Eye," the feminist column published in *The Island* newspaper has intervened consistently on the gendered nature of cricket.

46 The first novel to be published by a Sri Lankan woman was in 1914. It was entitled *The Broken Heart* and written by Mangala Nayagam Thambiah of Tamil ethnic origin. (Selvy Tiruchandran, work in progress for a project on Women's Writing in Sri Lanka.) Another Tamil woman author who wrote novels in the 1920s was S. Sellammal. (Kumari Jayawardena, *Feminism and Nationalism in the Third World*, p. 129.)

47 The Sigiri graffiti are verses written in Old Sinhala, the bulk of them by pilgrims to Sigiriya, the rock fortress of King Kasyappa, built in the 5th century. Incised on a plaster wall, known as the mirror wall, these verses comment on the "golden" women of the Sigiri frescoes. See Richard Murphy, *The Mirror Wall*. Newcastle-upon-Tyne, Bloodaxe Books, 1989. One poem written by a woman ridicules the love poems written by male pilgrims in admiration of the Sigiri women in the frescoes:
"We being women sing on behalf of this lady,
You fools! You come to Sihagiri and recite these verses hammered out with four-fold effort.
Not one of you brings wine and molasses remembering we are women."
Quoted in Ranjini Obeysekere, *Sri Lankan Theatre in a Time of Terror: Political Satire in a Permitted Space*. Colombo: Charles Subasinghe & Sons, 1999, p. 22.

48 Gajaman Nona, (1758–1814) is associated with the literary renaissance known as the "Matara period". Her poems included supplications to Sir John D'Oyly, the Government Agent of Matara, a major town in the south of the island.

49 The first girl's boarding school was set up in Uduvil, Jaffna, in 1824 by Methodist missionaries Harriet and Rev. Myron Winslow. See Kumari Jayawardena, *The White Woman's Other Burden: Western Women and South Asia During British Rule*. London: Routledge, 1995, pp. 34–37. In 1857, Bishop's Gate School, later known as Bishop's College and one of the earliest girl's schools in the English medium, was inaugurated in Colombo.

50 Yasmine Gooneratne, *English Literature in Ceylon 1815–1878*. Dehiwela: Tisara Prakasakayo, 1968, pp. 157–60.

51 Ibid., Chapter 11.

52 Nancy Wijekoon, "Our Motherland," *Young Lanka*, vol. 1 no. 1, July 1918.

[53] Kumari Jayawardena, *Feminism and Nationalism*, op. cit., p. 127.

[54] Kumari Jayawardena, *Dr Mary Rutnam: A Canadian Pioneer for Women's Rights in Sri Lanka*. Colombo: Social Scientists' Association, 1993, pp. 16–18.

[55] Kumari Jayawardena, *Feminism and Nationalism*, op. cit., p. 128.

[56] *Young Ceylon*, Vol. 6 no. 1 May 1937, p. 35.

[57] Mahilā Samitis were Women's Committees involved in social work in India.

[58] *Young Ceylon*, Vol. 3 no. 4, August 1934, p. 148.

[59] *Young Ceylon*, Vol. 5 no. 9, January 1937, p. 336.

[60] Hector Abhayavardhana, "Selina Perera—The Forgotten Socialist Militant," *Pravada* 4, nos. 10 & 11, 1997. p. 19.

[61] Pulsara Liyanage, *Vivi: A Biography of Vivienne Goonewardena*. Colombo: Women's Education Research Centre, 1998, p. 17.

[62] Hector Abhayavardhana, op. cit., p. 19.

[63] Ibid., pp. 21–2.

[64] Pulsara Liyanage, op. cit., chapter 8.

[65] Kumari Jayawardena, "Vivienne Goonewardena: 'La Passionara' of Sri Lanka," *Pravada* 4, nos. 10 & 11, 1997, pp. 16–18.

[66] Pulsara Liyanage, op. cit., p. 78.

[67] Vivienne Goonewardena encountered patriarchy early in life within her own home, when her conservative father denied her permission to enter university even though she had won an exhibition to read for an English Honours degree. He was persuaded to allow Vivienne to go to university only after the strenuous arguments of his friends. Later he ostracised her when she married Leslie Goonewardena who belonged to a different caste.

[68] *The Times of Ceylon*, 30 January 1948.

[69] *Women and Men in Sri Lanka*. Colombo: Dept. of Census and Statistics, 1995.

[70] *Statistical Profile of Sri Lanka*. Colombo: Dept. of Census and Statistics, 1998, p. 14. The figure for 1994 does not include the northern and eastern provinces.

[71] Ibid., p. 9.

[72] Ibid., p. 33.

[73] *Report of the Presidential Commission on Youth*. Colombo: Government Publications Bureau, 1990, p. 2.

[74] Ibid., pp. 16–17.

[75] Ibid., p. 109.

[76] *Changing Role of Women in Sri Lanka*. Colombo: Dept. of Census and Statistics, 1997, p. 132.

[77] Ranjith Amarasinghe, op. cit., pp. 184–5.

[78] Ibid., p. 187.

[79] Jani de Silva, "Praxis, Language and Silences: The July 1987 Uprising of the JVP in Sri Lanka," in Michael Roberts (ed.), *Sri Lanka. Collective Identities Revisited Vol 2.* Colombo: Marga, 1998. p. 192.

[80] Ranjith Amarasinghe, op. cit., p. 136.

[81] Sita Wickramasuriya, personal communication, 1997.

[82] Ranjith Amarasighe, op. cit., pp. 104–5.

[83] See Neloufer de Mel and Ramani Muttettuwegama, "Sisters in Arms: The Eksath Kantha Peramuna," *Pravada* vol. 4, nos. 10 & 11, 1997. pp. 22–26. My thanks to Ramani Muttettuwegama for her insights on this section.

[84] Radhika Coomaraswamy, "Women of the LTTE," *Frontline*, 10 January, 1997, p. 62.

[85] For an excellent analysis of this phenomenon see the Cat's Eye column "Engendering Peace: Women's Empowerment and Political Violence", *The Island*, 14 April 1999, p. 19.

[86] Dharini Rajasingham-Senanayake, "After Victimhood: Cultural Transformation and Women's Empowerment in War and Displacement," paper presented at the conference on "A Comparative Study of the Issues Faced by Women as a Result of Armed Conflict: Sri Lanka and the Post-Yugoslav States", Hendela, Sri Lanka, December 1998.

[87] Ibid. Rajasingham-Senanayake also makes the point that human rights discourses and humanitarian aid agencies working towards returning refugees to their original homes need to be more sensitised to the needs of the women themselves, and problematise the assumption of return as a fundamental premise.

[88] Malathi de Alwis, "The 'Purity' of Displacement and the Re-territorialization of Longing," paper presented at the conference on "A Comparative Study of the Issues Faced by Women as a Result of Armed Conflict: Sri Lanka and the Post-Yugoslav States, Hendela, Sri Lanka, December 1998.

[89] Faizun Zackariya and Zulfika Ismail, "Early Marriage and Perpetuation of the Cycle of Violence in a Displaced Situation", in *Confronting Complexities: Gender Perceptions and Values.* Colombo: CENWOR, 1998, pp. 25–51.

[90] Cat's Eye, *The Island.* 14. 4. 1999.

[91] Ranjini Obeyesekere, *Sri Lankan Theatre in a Time of Terror: Political Satire in a Permitted Space.* Colombo: Charles Subasinghe & Sons, 1999, p. 30.

[92] S. U. Kodikara, *Indo-Ceylon Relations Since Independence.* Colombo: Ceylon Institute of World Affairs, 1965, p. 50.

[93] Ibid, pp. 37–8.

[94] Sunil Bastian, "Plantation Labour in a Changing Context," in Charles

Abeysekera and Newton Gunasinghe (eds.), *Facets of Ethnicity in Sri Lanka*. Colombo: Social Scientists' Association, 1987, p. 183. See also Amita Shastri, "Estate Tamils, the Ceylon Citizenship Act of 1948 and Sri Lanka Politics," in *Contemporary South Asia* 8 no. 1, March 1999, pp. 65–86.

[95] S. U. Kodikara, op. cit., p. 63.

[96] The LTTE's military success in April–May 2000 in retaking some of the lost territory of Jaffna in 1995 gave rise to an ironic situation in which the harshest critics of the 1987 Indo-Lanka accord now looked to India for military assistance. Rev. Sobitha Thero, a spokesman for this lobby, justified this about-turn on the grounds that the difference between 1987 and 2000 lay in the fact that this time, India was being invited to help out in the conflict rather than subjecting Sri Lanka to its dominance and will.

[97] Sudhi Pradhan, *The Marxist Cultural Movement in India*, Vol. 1: *Chronicles and Documents, 1936–1947*, Calcutta: Mrs. Shanti Pradhan, 1979.

[98] Raj Thapar, *All These Years: A Memoir*. New Delhi: Seminar, 1991.

[99] Joan L. Erdman with Zora Segal, *Stages: The Art and Adventures of Zohra Segal*. New Delhi: Kali for Women, 1997.

[100] Susie Tharu & K. Lalitha (eds.) *Women Writing in India Vol. 2*. London: Pandora, 1993.

[101] Ibid., p. 79.

[102] Ratna Kapur, "Nationalism and Feminism," talk at the International Centre for Ethnic Studies, Colombo, 29 April 1999.

[103] Bruce Robbins, *Feeling Global*, op. cit., p. 173.

[104] See Ritu Menon and Kamla Bhasin, *Borders & Boundaries: Women in India's Partition*. New Delhi: Kali for Women, 1998; Rita Manchanda, "Kashmir's Worse-off Half," in *Himal* 12, no. 5, May 1999, pp. 30–3. A large number of women also belong to the Pak-India Forum for Peace and Democracy which engages in Track 2 diplomacy, lobbying for normalising ties between the two states.

Annie Boteju

1

SETTING THE STAGE, GENDERING THE NATION
John de Silva's Nationalist Theatre and the Entrance of Annie Boteju

THE LINKS BETWEEN the growth of modern Sinhala theatre and early 20th century nationalism in Sri Lanka highlight issues that are central to understanding the processes of nationalism, the importance of gender within them, and drama as a medium of popular culture. This chapter foregrounds the beginnings of modern Sinhala theatre, deeply influenced by British colonial theatre, Bengali nationalist theatre and the touring Parsi theatre from Bombay. It marks the significant transition in Sinhala theatre from traditional to modern as it changed from being rural, ritualistic, stylised and offeratory to becoming urban, secular, naturalisitc and commercial. It specifically locates the nationalist theatre of John de Silva (1857–1922), a founding father of modern Sinhala theatre, within this trajectory. This was a period of significant change for women, reflected in female portrayals on stage. This chapter examines both the ideological and performative nature of these portrayals; how the ideal Arya Sinhala woman was constructed in John de Silva's plays to justify a hegemonic status for the Sinhala race, language and its Buddhist culture; and the theatre convention of female impersonation and its performative language, through which such representations of the female and the feminised were conveyed. It also marks the moment of transition from female impersonation to the phenomenon of the star actress as we know it today, by examining the conditions under which, in 1917, Annie Boteju entered the Tower Hall stage as the first professional Sinhala actress. Boteju's life and career, her incorporation into nationalism, her agentive role within it and her contribution to the modernising of Sinhala theatre are foregrounded as significant junctures in the gendering of the nation.

The print media play a crucial role in forging a sense of community and a common, collective consciousness through newspapers, broadsheets and books (particularly in the vernacular), for citizens who may not know each other but enter into, and reinforce, shared assumptions, world-views and cultural practices.[1] The role of theatre in forging such an imagined community, similarly, cannot be underestimated. It is a medium in which hundreds of people participate at the same time. Mime, song, dance and dialogue in theatre allow even those who cannot read, and to whom print is not available, access to the collective imagining. This ensures that theatre remains a powerful vehicle for disseminating ideology and socio-political comment. It is this didactic use, together with the participatoriness of theatre and its ability to reach out to all classes depending on the language employed and situations dramatised, that Sinhala playwrights like John de Silva and Charles Dias exploited in the early 20th century. They developed the young Nūrti tradition (an amalgam of indigenous folk theatre known as the Nādagam and forms of the Parsi theatre) which had begun in Sri Lanka in the later decades of the 19th century to a full-fledged national, and nationalist, theatre by the early 1920s. Their goal was to forge a Sinhala consciousness amongst the audience which would be central in the anti-colonial/British drive that gathered momentum by the late 19th century.

In this project Sinhala women, as embodiments of the community, took on particular roles. The plays of John de Silva are sites on which these roles are prescribed and enacted as example. From Sita in the *Rāmāyanaya* to the queen in *Daskon Nātakaya* (1888), Sirisangabo's queen in *Sirisangabo Charitaya* (1903) and Ehelepola Kumarihamy in *Sri Vickrama Rajasinghe* (1906), queens and aristocratic ladies drawn from historical legends and Buddhist Jataka stories perform the roles of dutiful wives, good mothers and chaste partners. The aristocracy, by its very nature, was inaccessible, distant and therefore to be "aspired" to. The constructions of aristocratic feminised identity were therefore formulated to fit a patriarchal framework metonymic of a larger

nationalist discourse and design. They would inculcate respect
for the indigenous culture, show up the foreign ones as debased
and inspire the audience, through the personal sacrifice, decorum and selflessness enacted on stage, to be courageous participants in the nationalist struggle for independence.

How were these constructions given legitimacy within the
medium of theatre? What power did they have? And how did
they reflect what Sri Lankan women were themselves aspiring
to? Counterpoised to the chaste and dutiful woman as embodiment of the nation are those who have come under the influence
of western colonial rule and culture. They are pilloried in the
nationalist theatre as in John de Silva's *Sinhala Parābhava
Nātakaya* (A Satire on the Modern Sinhalese) performed in 1902.
This was the time when Buddhist girls' education had expanded
in response to Christian missionary education on the island and
middle class families were keen to have their daughters benefit
from the new educational opportunities. Nationalist patriarchs
saw in this move an inevitable change in the role of women in
society. To them aspirations to an English education and foreign
examinations detracted from indigenous values and encouraged
neglect of a woman's domestic duties. Their response, essentially
one of anxiety to such change, was to 'fix' their ideal of womanhood by denouncing women's education except within the terms
of a *sufficient* modernity. Women were disallowed the
cosmopolitanness permitted to men, and their duty to nurture
future generations in Sinhala culture, language and the Buddhist
religion was reiterated with greater vigour.

That this ideal woman was played by a man on stage com-
pounds the significance and complexity of such female representation and subjectivity. The institution of female impersonation
widely prevalent in the theatre of the Indian subcontinent held
sway in Sri Lanka until the second decade of the 20th century.
What did it mean to have the desirable, and therefore respectable, feminised traits of a woman, as constructed by nationalists
during this period, visually and gesturally signed on stage by male
bodies and projected by male voices? How did these articulations dictate the way women dressed, spoke, moved and behaved
on and off-stage? Was female impersonation primarily a discourse

for and about men rather than women? Did it merely signify rather than give voice and agency to women on stage? Did female impersonation then become a translation of conservative feminised identity rather than a radical critique or transgression of it?[2] Moreover, how did the institution of female impersonation respond to the challenge posed to its professional monopoly by actresses who wanted to enter the stage? The most renowned female impersonators were once the star attractions of popular theatre. What were the reasons that led to their eventual decline? Conversely, how difficult was it for actresses to break through the tradition of female impersonation?

The stage entry of Annie Boteju was not an easy one. Women actors had to struggle to enter the profession and contend with long cultural traditions that denied them access to theatre as a performing art, and stigmatised those who did as loose women. Often they had to face the rivalry of female impersonators struggling for their own livelihoods. When women were allowed onto the Sinhala stage in commonplace theatre practice from the second decade of the 20th century on, their incorporation was made under certain circumstances. What were the possible stage entrances and exits for an actress? What ethnic communities and/or class did they come from? What were their material circumstances? How were feminised ideals and respectability reflected by them? In examining these factors it is possible to see how the position of women both on and off-stage (their role on-stage prescribed normative off-stage behaviour) was gendered to suit the patriarchal needs of the nation. But they also point to how women negotiated these paradigms and made use of the new circumstances shaping the Sinhala theatre, to transcend some of patriarchy's more repressive features.

Transition to Modernity: Theatre as Hybridity

As with the nationalist theatre of Bengal which began in earnest in the early 19th century, its Sri Lankan equivalent (which emerged from the 1880s onwards) was a response to the need for a new national identity that took on a particularly hybrid form.[3] In Bengal the urge was to revive a Sanskrit tradition in western theatrical forms. Following the lead of institutions which furthered British orientalist scholarship, like the Asiatic Society of Bengal (established in 1784) and the Royal Asiatic Society (founded in England in 1823), the Bengali intelligentsia involved with theatre had become "serious and proud scholars of Indian antiquity".[4] The Sanskrit theatre tradition offered them a rich trove of stories, myths and legends from the *Mahābhārata*, the *Rāmāyana* and the *Purānas* which it had dramatised in elaborate canonised form, reinvesting the indigenous with cultural value. It boasted the *Natyāsastra*, a theoretical treatise on Sanskrit dramaturgy by Bharata (written circa 1st or 2nd century), legendary plays such as Kalidasa's *Śakuntalā,* and playwrights like Bhasa, Sudraka and Bhavabhuti. The theatre tradition flourished in the Hindu royal courts, declining only with the advent of the Moghul Empire, and gave the Indian nationalists an unbroken tradition of over two thousand years of elite literary dramatic form to draw on for nationalist purpose. In Bengal, from 1831 to 1867, 82 original Bengali plays had been published, most of which were either direct translations of Sanskrit drama, or drew heavily from them for plot and style.[5]

In Sri Lanka however no such elite literary tradition of theatre had survived. Theravada Buddhism had had a detrimental impact on the development of elite theatre. In its doctrinal form it emphasised individual meditation over collective, participatory ritual, shunned adornment of the body, spectacle and the seeking of pleasure. It had therefore been antithetical to the arts of dance and theatre. E.R.Sarachchandra noted of this doctrine, "With its ideal of individual salvation, it tended more towards solitary contemplation and the attainment of insight (*vidassana*) than towards congregational practices or participation in community life."[6] A few instances of Buddhist dramatic ritual were in existence such as the *Bana,* or sermon, in question-answer format and the *Dorakada Āsna,* a ritual enacted seven days after taking *pirit,* a ceremony in which priests recite stanzas with advice on righteous living.[7] But unlike India where dance-drama and participatory ritual were features of entertainment and religious devotion in royal courts and Hindu temples, in Sri Lanka they were, by and large, shunned.

This was not to say that performative traditions were totally absent in Sinhala courts. The *Ratnāvalia* was adapted by Gurulugomi (12th/13th century AC) from Sri Harshadeva's drama. The plays of Kalidasa and poetic drama based on the Jataka stories were performed at the courts of Sinhala kings.[8] In the Polonnaruva period King Parakramabahu I (1153–1186 AC) was a patron of the arts and his queen, Rupavati, was a dancer.[9] Sinhala kings often followed their South Indian counterparts, and so Hindu performative traditions entered their courts and Hindu ritual practices became part of Buddhist ritual. As Ranjini Obeysekere notes,

> Throughout the history of Buddhism in Sri Lanka, one is aware of the tension between the highly individualized form of the religion as it was expected to be practiced by monks or individuals seeking salvation, and the continuous and ongoing pressure for it to be transformed into a practical religion of this-worldly support for the laity in their day-to-day activities.[10]

However, it was not the laity who recorded literary activity but the monks who were the "scribes and guardians of the textual tradition". As Theravada Buddhism permitted them an engagement only in arts such as painting, sculpture or writing (solitary, individual activity), and barred them from the arts of dancing, singing or playing musical instruments, the monks kept no record of secular theatrical activity which incorporated the latter elements. The Sinhala literary texts that were preserved came from within the monastic Buddhist tradition. Theatre, being outside this tradition, did not become part of the archive.[11]

What did survive in Sri Lanka were folk theatre traditions such as the mimed *Sokari* and the dance-drama of *Kōlam*.[12] The form known as Nādagam, or folk opera, took root in the early 19th century, influenced by Tamil dance-drama and musical styles such as *vadamōdi*.[13] There was also the genre of *Pāsku* or the Easter Passion Play, a legacy of Portuguese colonialism,[14] which had taken root in the Catholic areas of Jaffna in the north and spread south to the western coastal belt above Colombo where a significant number of Catholics live. But it was with the Nūrti, which emerged from the 1880s onwards, that a new urban form of Sinhala theatre developed and became a powerful vehicle for nationalist ideology.

In Calcutta as well as Bombay, western drama and dramatic style had found its way into Bengali, Gujarati and Marathi theatre by the mid 19th century. A combination of factors—from a British education which anglicised the native, to school English drama societies, touring British theatre troupes and the production of European plays by expatriates living in India—made western theatre visible on the Indian subcontinent. Given colonial cultural paradigms, English plays were valued as cultural products and thought worthy of imitation. They attracted the officials of the Raj, its military and educationists. The Bengali nationalist elite began their theatrical activities mainly as a response to colonial English theatre in Calcutta. They forged a particularly hybrid theatre form as they drew on traditional Sanskrit sources and adapted them to the proscenium stage, translating Sanskrit plays into English or English drama, particularly Shakespeare, into Bengali.[15] European theatre terms began to inflect Sanskrit ones, at times obscuring the distinctions between the Indian and European cultural contexts and their performance styles.[16] Elsewhere, in Bombay, all of the productions of the Parsi theatre until about 1875 were in English and Gujarati, with plots based on the Persian *Shah Nama* and Shakespearean plays.[17]

In Sri Lanka, too, there was an English-educated middle class that held English drama, particularly Shakespeare, in high esteem and adapted his plays to local forms. Long before the tours of the Parsi theatre to Sri Lanka which began in 1882, Shakespeare was performed. The first Shakespeare play to be performed as nādagam was *Cymberline* (September 1859) followed by *The Two Gentlemen of Verona* produced by Proteus Valentine in 1868; *Portia Nādagama* based on *The Merchant of Venice* (June 1881) and *Romeo and Juliet* as a nādagam produced by D.B. Wanigasuriya in 1874.[18] John de Silva adapted five Shakespearean plays,[19] and in his preface to *Othello* (produced in 1909) stated that they would enrich the native language, and that Shakespeare belonged not only to Englishmen but to all communities and races.[20]

Such an appropriation of Shakespeare is evidence that the nationalist intelligentsia was unafraid to draw from colonial tradition, and endeavoured to usher their societies into a "universal" (elided with European) heritage by exposing them to the "best" in European literature and the arts. Absent at this stage of nationalist discourse is the denunciation of all western imports that later characterised some of its strands. Playwrights like de Silva were consciously eclectic in their borrowings from the West, and their adaptations of the existing nādagam into a hybrid nūrti form—of which he and playwrights like Charles Don Bastian were pioneers—epitomised this trend.

The influence on nūrti of the touring Parsi theatre from Bombay (itself eclectic, drawing on traditional forms of Indian theatre including oral story-telling traditions and pageants as well as Shakespeare and Victorian melodrama) was immense.[21] The Parsi theatre[22] which performed in Colombo was a huge commercial success. Never before had such sophistication been seen on stage. Scenes with elaborately painted backdrops, décor, fancy costumes, enchanting tales of magical happenings (dramatisations from the *Arabian Nights* were particularly popular) provided spectacular theatre fare. The success of this theatre made local dramatists sit up and take note, recognising too its commercial potential. Two years after the first touring Parsi troupe, C. Don Bastian founded The Sinhala Nūrti Society and with it, the adaptation of new (largely western) stage technologies and forms such as the proscenium arch, naturalistic scene design, props, costuming and acting styles to elements of nādagam. Heterogeneity marked the new genre of nūrti and the beginnings of modern Sinhala theatre.

Nūrti, albeit not homogenised, contributed to the direction that the modernisation of Sinhala theatre took. First, playwrights like Don Bastian and John de Silva drew their plots from nādagam stories much as the Bengalis had turned to Sanskrit drama or the popular form of *Yātra* (even though the latter was looked down upon by the intelligentsia).[23] The need was to revive a sense of history and cultural continuity and tap into the benefits of using stories and legends that had popular folk value. One historical tale that was popularly performed as nādagam was that of Ehelepola, a Kandyan chieftain who betrayed the last King of Kandy to the British. De Silva made this story the core of his play, *Sri Vikrama Rajasinha: Our Last King.* It was successfully produced in 1906 and gained wide circulation when printed as a booklet, selling an estimated 16,000 copies by 1925.[24] Second, the playwrights introduced the drawing of a front curtain, scenes and acts as in the western theatre to both nādagam and nūrti, incorporating definite time-frames and a firmer linear development of plot. The use of more sophisticated stage technologies and tricks also required a distancing of the action from the audience for which the proscenium and curtains became indispensable. Third, popular tunes following those of the Parsi musicals were introduced instead of the ragas sung in nādagam. Vishvanath Lowji, a composer from Bombay, collaborated with John de Silva for many years, producing some of his plays' most popular tunes. These songs were then recorded and were commercially very popular; they played an important role in popularising de Silva's theatre and disseminating its nationalist ideology both in urban areas and the provinces. Fourth, costuming became more elaborate as did the backdrops and stage décor.

Capital was needed for all of the above. This period saw the emergence of a native professional and entrepreneurial bourgeoisie, and it was largely this class that made capital available for the nūrti plays. John de Silva's diary[25] jots 358 names and addresses of those who donated funds for his plays. Their professions, ranging from Mudaliyārs[26] to advocates and proctors, jewellers, shopkeepers, timber and plumbago merchants, arrack renters, newspaper editors and school inspectors, represent a wide cross-section of society—while their addresses reflect the spread of nationalist feeling throughout the southern and north- western provinces. Benefactors ranged from the local aristocracy— Sir Solomon Dias Bandaranaike, Sir S.C. Obeysekera and Sir Paul Pieris of the Bandaranaike clan of Horagolla; Mudaliyars Harry Obeysekera of Kurunegala, Harry Jayawardena of Tangalle and J. Wickremaratne of Matara; the Diyawadana Nilame P.B. Nugawela of Kandy; advocates A.E. de Silva of Colombo 7 and Frances Mollamure of Kegalle; proctors I.B.L. Moonamalle of Kurunegala, Harry Ellawala of Ratnapura and Harry de Mel and L.B. Jacolyn of Avissawella; plumbago merchants Amadoris Mendis and Hendrick de Mel of Borella; those in the medical profession like Dr. Emmanuel, Dr Roberts of St.James's Colpetty and Dr. Brito Babapulle of Grandpass, and government school inspector S. Welawan of Galle. Some benefactors were Christian, others Buddhist, indicating that at this time (1904) the emerging sense of cultural nationalism was able to unify across caste, religious and professional divides.

Noteworthy, however, is that while John de Silva did have sponsors from the Colombo Chetty (Charles Chitty of Borella), Muslim (Cassim Ismail and Abdul Cadar, advocate), and even Parsi (Mr. Nilgiriya of Fort) communities, there are no Tamil sponsors noted in his diary, largely because his language left out the Tamil spectator. Moreover, as time went by this theatre began to address specifically Sinhalese audiences, sowing the seeds of an ethno-nationalism that made the Tamil, Muslim, Malayali and Burgher minority communities the Others within the emerging nation. The names of the drama societies John de Silva founded epitomise this trend and show the trajectory of a Sinhala hegemony at work. From The Ceylon Oriental Dramatic Company of 1885, a name that pegged its identity in relation to the west and the occident, the societies were named the Sinhala Arya Subodha Natya Sabha (1902), and the Vijaya Ranga Sabha (1913) which later became the Sri Lanka Drama Society. What we have here is an increasing emphasis on ethno-cultural identity and the historical legacy of the Sinhalese—Vijaya for instance being the legendary founder of the Sinhala race.

For much of the time this nationalist theatre made Sinhala consciousness synonymous with Buddhist identity. When the Tower Hall was inaugurated as Sri Lanka's national theatre on 6 December 1911, it was opened by Anagarika Dharmapala who declared, "May this theatre hall be of great assistance to the furtherance of the cause of the Religion and the Nation", religion being exclusively Buddhism, marked on the occasion by a *pirit* ceremony officiated by monks from the Vidyodaya and Vidyalankara *pirivenās* or monasteries.[27] John de Silva's plays would begin with an offering to the triple gem. As already noted in the Introduction, the Mahavamsa version of history that these nationalists reproduced upheld the Sinhalese as a chosen people because of their Buddhist faith, and Sri Lanka as a blessed place because of the presence of Buddhism. De Silva's plays drew their plots from Buddhist Jataka stories. Temperance (as an attribute of Buddhist values) had become a significant feature of the anti-British nationalist campaign by the late 19th century.[28] From plays like *Sinhala Parābhava Nātakaya* (1902) to *Surā Sondayā* (1917) John de Silva repeatedly upheld this value, reinforcing a metonymic link between abstinence and the nation/religion itself, presenting the consumption of alcohol as a betrayal of Buddhist and, therefore, national values.

However, that de Silva's list of sponsors included Christians meant that the plays held a wide appeal for Sinhala nationalists. They accommodated and elicited nationalistic pride in the Sinhala language, royal lineage, traditions, customs and artistic achievements that many Sinhalese, irrespective of class, caste and religious background, felt was their common heritage. Thus de Silva's plays, as vehicles for nationalist expression were able to unify the Sinhalese. Their support and capital, vital to the development of nūrti itself, was crucial to the revival of ancient Sinhala history, mythology and Buddhist Jataka stories. L.D.A. Ratnayake, reviewing John de Silva's *Sri Sangabo,* noted the "magnificence and beauty of the ancient, sacred city of Anuradhapura, the Ruwanvelisaya, . . .Vahalkada, ponds, bridges, roads, etc.", not to mention the realism of the Attanagalla forest, implying elaborately painted dropped scenes.[29] The pageantry and sheer spectacle of the coronation of the last King of Kandy in *Sri Vikrama Rajasinghe,* with the staging of *leekeli* and *kalagedi* dancing (dances with sticks and water-pots), various drummers and the King himself in jewelled costume would have produced spectacular theatrical effect. This in turn would enable the "theatrical realizations of the ideas of nationhood" which gave the imagined, grand, national self-fashioning, a palpable, "near-empiricist proof of the discourse".[30]

The heterogeneity of the nūrti form also had valence with the cultural orientation of its playwrights. Born in 1857 to a Sinhala-speaking middle class family, John de Silva entered a milieu that was conscious of the need to westernise even as it remained the rooted in its Sinhala Buddhist traditions. His early education was at a Christian missionary school and then at the Royal Academy, and his first jobs were as a teacher of English at St. Joseph's and

Wesley College, boy's schools run by Catholic and Methodist missionaries respectively. He then proceeded to Law College, becoming an advocate of the District Court in 1890. The professional opportunities laid out by the British for middle class Sri Lankan men was what John de Silva took advantage of. Amongst his friends were prominent Burgher and Englishmen within the legal profession.[32] His first publication was in English, *A Compendium of Ceylon History* (1882) which he edited with the help of the Cultural Affairs department for the benefit of British expatriates in Sri Lanka.[33] That he mastered the English language and reinforced, through his adaptations of Shakespeare, its elite cultural foundations even as he wrote outstanding plays and lyrics in Sinhala to revive a Sinhala heritage were potent signifiers of his cosmopolitan bi-culturalism.

Enacting Gender: Women in the Sinhala Theatre

Significant and yet entirely in keeping with nationalist patriarchy is the fact that this cosmopolitanism was neither reflected nor encouraged in the portrayals of the ideal Sinhala woman in de Silva's plays. Why was this so? As noted earlier, the woman within nationalism has a symbolic function and is made to carry the community's ideal values. In nationalist discourse, which asserts the superiority and legitimacy of one race, community and religion over others, the practice of hybridity is often elided in a powerful homogenising move. If woman is a site on which such identity is constructed, she cannot be seen as heterogeneous and fluid in nationalistic moments. The need of the hour is for her to be fixed, or telescoped to the past as a bearer of tradition and a proud history, envisioning through that casting back, an authoritative future modernity.

Thus when Sri Lankan women began to demand an English education for themselves, the reaction of nationalists like de Silva, (himself a beneficiary of such an education) was to lampoon the pursuit.[34] In *Sinhala Parābhava Nātakaya,* Satire on the Modern Sinhalese (1920), it is westernisation that has debased the Sinhala community; it is entirely fitting that the women characters most lampooned in the play are those that aspire to a new sense of

modernity through westernisation.[35] A song in the play railed
against such women in the following terms:

Now, the Singili lady, rice and curry she cannot eat,
But she's got accustomed to drinking claret and whisky neat.

She has flung out the skirt and jacket and wears a bonnet now,
Foolish habits in this land flourish, thrive and grow.

The science of the saucepan into a corner they throw,
They take to the quill pen instead and long epistles flow.

More and more the ladies grow so languid and so slack,
From the weight of French and Latin that's loaded on each back.

The work of mortar and pestle is now no longer done,
Gradually the lovely arms and legs have slender grown.

There is much lawn tennis and cricket in our land and the Singili
dame,
Has got in plenty of practice and learned to play such games.[36]

Here is the patriarchal nationalist's anxiety about the changes
a western education will bring to Sri Lankan women. It even
justifies harsh domestic labour—pounding flour in a mortar and
the drudgery of cooking—as more becoming for women than
acquiring skills in new languages and sports. This anxiety became progressively strident as the demand for English education
increased, particularly amongst the Sinhala Buddhist constituency. The need to counteract the influence of Christian missionary schools on girls encouraged the creation of Buddhist girls'
schools by the late 19th century. Between 1880 and 1890, 40
Buddhist schools for both girls and boys were started under the
aegis of the Buddhist Theosophical Society. In 1889 the Women's
Education Society began four schools for girls, but they functioned in the vernacular, and the daughters of middle-class and
affluent Sinhala Buddhist families continued to attend Christian
missionary schools for their training and education. Very soon,
therefore, the most prestigious of the Buddhist girls' schools were
the English medium ones, created in response to the demand for
English education. Sanghamitta Girls' School, founded by the
Women's Education Society in 1889 and later, Buddhist Girls'
College (which became Visakha Vidyala, the leading Buddhist girls'

school in Colombo) founded by the philanthropist, Selestina Dias in 1917, were such English medium schools. Buddhist Girls' College, in particular, was modelled on British schools. Buddhism was not in the curriculum and conversation in Sinhala was punished with the imposition of a fine. Its emphasis was more as a finishing school for girls, and to this end its subjects and activities included English, piano playing, drawing and tennis.[37]

The westernisation of Sinhala women either threatened nationalist patriarchs or, at best, drew an ambivalent response from social reformers seeking to modernise Sri Lankan society. *The Ceylon National Review* published by the Ceylon Social Reform Society, edited by Ananda Coomaraswamy and W.A. de Silva, carried an article by F.L. Woodward on women's education in its first issue. Woodward noted:

In the East. . . there are signs of an awakening activity in the women's sphere. The more enlightened peoples are beginning to see that their policy of the seclusion of womenfolk, so long kept up, has many drawbacks. The men are becoming more cosmopolitan in thought, language and ways: the women however, are being left behind like ship-wrecked sailors on a desert isle, who see their luckier comrades rescued by a passing ship.[38]

Yet, even as the author acknowledged the need for Sri Lankan women to modernise through education, he expressed anxiety about the consequences:

There is, here in Ceylon, a tendency to put a value on the Cambridge Certificate. In fact, I am told that a girl possessing such has a better chance of making a wealthy and successful marriage. But how many girls can keep house, make a good curry, and delight the heart of their help-mate by their womanly ways and domestic skill?

The real need, then, was to modernise Sri Lankan women only to the extent that they would be suitable partners for the English-educated Sri Lankan male. Essential were middle class social graces, the ability to be a good mother and housewife, capable of looking after her husband's belongings and property through good book-keeping, etc.[39] Beyond that there was no need, even for those advocating the cause of reform, to educate and empower women in their own right. While it was the preserve of men to reflect the transition of Sri Lankan society from colonial to postcolonial, eastern to western, homogenous to heterogeneous, traditional to modern, its women were denied fluidity, with no real ability to cross these boundaries. They were the constant and fixed signifiers of the "best" in their native traditions. Repeatedly John de Silva's tragic heroines and legendary queens enacted this restrictive and prescriptive role on the Tower Hall stage. Ehelepola Kumarihamy in *Sri Vikrama Rajasinghe: Our Last King* stood for all of the above. She is first presented singing a lullaby, underscoring her symbolic role as mother of her children and the nation, in which she extols the necessity of developing the ancient arts and skills of the Sinhalese through knowledge of the Sinhala language. She is also the dutiful wife who declares that it is not the habit of a well-bred/upper caste (*kulanganāwa*) Sinhala woman to question a husband who has just returned home, asking where he has been and why he is so late.[40] (The husband, of course, has been plotting with the British against the King of Kandy.) He is the male who, with access to the public sphere, has laid himself open to contamination by the foreign coloniser. So necessary is this "duplicity-as-foreign-induced" to de Silva's nationalist project that the weaknesses and feudalism of the King himself are erased, except in the last scenes which, albeit within the laws of the time, depict the outrageous punishment he metes out to Ehelepola's wife and family. The Ehelepola sons are beheaded and the Kumarihamy is forced to pound her infant to death in a mortar before being drowned with her daughter in the Kandy lake. In his Preface to the play de Silva wrote that his motive was to present the good qualities of the last King to the younger generation of Sinhalese, thereby rectifying the portrait of him by the British as tyrannical and barbaric.[41] To this end the King is made into a sovereign generally worthy of loyalty. To this end, too, de Silva takes pains to present Sri Vikrama Rajasinghe as a Nayakkar king who nevertheless upheld the tenets of Buddhism. Meanwhile, in direct contrast to her husband, Ehelepola Kumarihamy, contained in her domestic sphere, suffers no contamination—she remains "pure" and firmly rooted in her indigenous culture and values until the very end.

The irony of the fixity of this ideal woman is heightened when we consider that the vehicle for this paradigm was the particularly hybrid and eclectic nūrti form which drew from many traditions. The irony is compounded by the fact that, until 1917, de

Silva's women characters, following theatre traditions elsewhere on the Indian subcontinent and in the local nādagam and *pāsku* play, were portrayed by men. In Sanskrit theatre women, drawn from the ranks of devadasis or dancing girls, had taken part in theatre. In the *Natyāsastra* a code of both female and male impersonation is referred to. It states that, "A woman also may assume, if she likes, a man's role in actual practice" (xxxv:31–32) and advocates that "the roles of gods and delicate persons should always be performed by women". (xxxv:38)[42] In the performance tradition of *Bhārat-Nātyam*, female dancers enacted the narrative sung by male vocalists. The earliest reference to female performers in Bengal comes around 1200 A.C. when women took part in the works of the poet Jayadeva in the court of Laxman Sen. The poet's own wife, Padmavati, was a dancer who dancèd the narrative in *Rama-Saraswati* while the poet sang his verses.[43]

The Brahminical codes of Kautilya and Manu had shunted most women, as well as the undercaste, out of the public gaze. Kautilya in the *Arthasāstra* (300 B.C.) declared "singing and dancing occupations of the Sudras" only, and Manu prohibited students from studying the arts of dance, music and song.[44] Medieval Indian drama devised a code in which the male and female essences were combined in a single performance—portrayed by a male actor or dancer. The social stigma attached to women of "honour" being seen in public forbade the respectable South Asian woman from taking part in plays.[45] In modern times, when women did appear on stage (in Calcutta in 1873,[46] in Colombo in 1886)[47] they were quite often prostitutes or dancing girls, already stigmatised for their professions. This immediately made them more vulnerable to a host of exploitative situations.

The story of Binodini Dasi (1863–1941), one of the earliest and most successful actresses of the Bengali theatre bears this out. Binodini came from a background of abject poverty and prostitution. A girl actress, she joined the Great National Theatre of Calcutta at a monthly salary of ten rupees, plus food. Raises in salary were by five rupees and even then, regular wages had to be fought for. At one time, exhausted after a long run of performances, Binodini was granted 15 days leave (she had asked

for a month) from the Great National Theatre to recuperate.
Her manager refused to pay her for the duration of her leave,
derisively mocking, "What salary?.... You've not done any work."
When she demanded a regular contract, that too was dismissed
and Binodini chided for being "difficult".[48] Binodini then made
up her mind to quit the Great National Theatre and perform at a
new theatre but even here, her vulnerability as a woman and her
humble origins played their part in preventing her from gaining
the recognition she felt she deserved. She was promised that this
new theatre would bear her name but her male colleagues registered the theatre as "The Star". Binodini was deeply disappointed
but, realising that she was completely "in their hands", decided
there was no option but to go along with them.[49] Hers was a life
and career in which, as she herself described, the practice was
"to move from the protection of one man to that of another".[50]
That protection often entailed sexual favours, about which the
actresses hardly had a choice. This lent the theatre an aura of
disrepute and the actress was both pursued and shunned for her
sexuality. Elite and middle-class women of "respectable" families were either forbidden or were themselves reluctant to participate in this theatre even as spectators.

In Sri Lanka women did not act in nādagam. The stock roles
of Sokari Amma, the goddess Pattini, Suniya the she-devil, Lenchi
and queens Ridhdhi and Manikpala were portrayed by men;[51]
nor were women allowed to help in these productions.[52] However, there is evidence that a few of them participated as spectators. It is recorded that in March 1870 young women were in the
audience for a performance of *Ehelepola Nādagama,* and in its
production as a puppet show in Dickoya in 1876.[53] Later, when
the *nādagama* was performed at the house of Charles de Soysa in
1870 in honour of the Duke of Edinburgh's visit, the audience
comprised both men and women from diverse Sinhalese, Tamil,
Muslim and Burgher communities.[54] In August 1884 a woman
named Mary Matilda wrote in *Sarasavi Sandarasa,* a Sinhala journal, that she watched nūrti twice together with her husband, and
was pleased that the plays were fit fare for respectable men and
women.[55] There is also reference to working class women forming part of nūrti audiences.[56] Although they were lampooned in

the Sinhala press as *thuppahi* (debased/hybrid) and disrespectable because of their class, their attendance nevertheless shows that the plays had popular appeal and attracted people of all classes. They were therefore powerful vehicles of popular culture in the service of the nationalist cause.

The *pāsku* or Easter Passion play, a legacy of 16th century Portuguese rule in Sri Lanka, also debarred women from its stage.[57] It was not until 1939 that there was an attempt to introduce women to the *pāsku,* and the controversy that followed indicates the extent of patriarchal authority over and interest in the normative roles for women. In the *pāsku,* whose episodes were introduced and linked by a male narrator, the main characters of Christ, the Virgin Mary, Mary Magdalene, John the Baptist, etc. were initially represented by statues carried by people rather than by live actors. Women figured, if at all, only as a chorus when, as in the passion play performed at Duwa, they wept and sang passion hymns when Christ, carrying the cross, met Mary Magdalene, the Virgin Mary and St. John.[58]

It was only in 1923 that live actors played the main roles for the first time in a passion play. Lawrence Perera of Boralessa adapted the Oberammergau passion play and, influenced by nūrti, produced *The Shridhara Boralessa Passion Play* that was theatrical and leaned towards realism in style. He had a cast of over a hundred with actors drawn from the village, comprising masons, carters and sawyers representing its varied professions.[59] But here too, women's roles were enacted by men. As time went by and responding to its popular acclaim—the play became an annual event with special trains carrying people to see it—Lawrence Perera decided to make it an even more credible piece of theatre. Towards this he announced, and included, four amateur actresses from the village in the cast in 1939. He drew inspiration from the Oberammergau and Nancy passion plays, as well as those performed in India which by this time had begun to use actresses. Perera already used women in the chorus for his Duwa passion play, but when he sought to use actresses for the main female roles he came into direct conflict with the Catholic Church. The Archbishop of Colombo banned the scheduled 1939 performance claiming that "the introduction of women would tend to detract from the spirit of piety and devotion with which a Passion Play should be staged";[60] Lawrence Perera was excommunicated from the church for his pains.

It was not that urban audiences were unused to seeing women on the stage. In June 1884 when a performance of *Uncle Tom's Cabin* by a foreign theatre company was held, there were 15 women and 12 men in the cast.[61] Moreover, touring American and European circuses had performances by female dancers and acrobats. As these circuses were advertised as family entertainment, Sri Lankan women accompanying their children, husbands and relatives comprised part of the audience. Women were also present at all-night *bali thovil* ceremonies as participants/audience in the ritual, and their presence at performances of nādagam and nūrti has already been noted. In fact, a call in the Sinhala newspaper *Lakrivikirana* of March 17, 1887 for making nādagam more respectable, opined that it should be safe both in moral intent and in the physical space of the theatre for women to watch. The demands included that nādagam performances begin early and end by 11.p.m. at night, that tents be erected and tickets sold to keep out the rabble and so avoid fights.[62] In seeking public safety and ensuring that nādagam be accessible to the Sri Lankan middle class, the *Lakrivikirana* was in effect calling for the theatre to be made respectable. The number of women in the audience would be the index of the success or failure of such an endeavour.

The Catholic Church, however had a singularly heterosexual male audience in mind when it reacted to Lawrence Perera's introduction of actresses in the Passion play despite the presence of women in it. Fear of male arousal by female performers which would disrupt male devotional engagement with the subject of the play was at the core of its dictate. That there were women willing to act in plays is proved by this episode. But they were denied access to the stage, this time by the Patriarchs of the Church. It was too dangerous for women to represent themselves on stage.

But did female impersonation really distance the male audience from the erotic pleasures available within stage representation and performance? In both western and eastern theatre traditions, the convention of female impersonation evolved from young boys playing female roles. Parsi theatre companies recruited boys at about age nine to play these roles and they usually remained with the company for several years.[63] In the Elizabethan theatre too young boys played female roles and Shakespeare, in particular, made exemplary and complex use of this convention to play on class, gender and sexual signifiers through cross-dressing.[64] In Shakespeare's plots this is shown as an economic or situational necessity. In *Twelfth Night* Viola disguises herself as the page-boy Cesario to overcome the misfortunes of shipwreck, and in *Merchant of Venice*, Portia and Nerissa disguise themselves as male advocates to gain entry into court on behalf of Bassanio, against Shylock. While the cross-dressing is on, subversion of gender stereotypes is possible and homo-erotic desire is made available. At the end of the plays however, once cross-dressing has fulfilled its desired goals, the gender status quo returns. Where young boys—playing women—dressed as men had licence to transgress and de-stabilise Elizabethan gender, class and sexual norms; where men could fall in love with transvestite boys and women, could appear "manly" and engage in male pursuits, the "resolutions" of Shakespeare's plays are within patriarchal convention, which returns the women characters to the domestic sphere as dutiful wives and respectable ladies in the service of (male) heterosexual desire.

In the tradition of female impersonation on the Indian sub-continent on the other hand, there is no overt attempt made at plot level (other than in comedy about mistaken identity) to play on the sexual anxieties that cross-dressing elicits. The female impersonator plays a woman throughout—what is adopted is a "realistic" performative style in representation. We need to bear in mind however that the very language of late 19th and early 20th century theatre reviews only allowed for a discourse of realism; in all available accounts of male actors playing female roles it is the authenticity of their performances as female personae, and the credibility of their impersonation that is commented upon. D. Andrew Perera, a.k.a. Andarai Appu, played many of the female leads in John de Silva's plays and on the Tower Hall stage.[65] It is noted that when he played Juliet in the 1912 production of

Romeo and Juliet at Tower Hall, Lady Benson, an actress with the Shakespeare Drama Company (who had herself played Juliet on the London stage and was on a visit to Sri Lanka) was beguiled into believing that the role was played by an actress! Enthralled at how a man could perform so credibly, she had gifted Perera a gold ring when backstage, he took off his wig to prove that he really was a man.[66] The applauding of such impersonation shows the extent to which realism in performance was valued. It was not without its own sexual ambiguities however, deeply tied to the pleasures of viewing theatrical performance. Marjorie Garber notes that,

One of the cultural functions of the transvestite is precisely to mark. . . displacement, substitution, or slippage from class to gender, gender to class; or, equally plausibly, from gender to race or religion. The transvestite is both a signifier and that which signifies the *undecidability* of signification. It points towards itself—or, rather, towards the place where it is not.[67]

In the convention of female impersonation, it is precisely on this ambiguous site, in the undecidability of male/female, that the spectacle of pleasure lay, as a largely male audience participated in the female impersonator's disguise of "authentic" female. Many renowned female impersonators like Bal Gandharva of the Marathi theatre and Jaishankar Sundari, were star attractions of the day precisely because of their ability to portray female roles in a singing voice in-between male and female, *undecidable*, continually slipping gender to excite erotic and audio-visual pleasure for the theatre spectator.[68] If, as in the Parsi theatre, characters were good or bad and resolution therefore always at hand,[69] then the ambiguity of female impersonation went against the grain of such definite closures.

This theatre, then, even—and perhaps particularly—without the actress, was always a site of subliminal erotic pleasure. Enhancing this pleasure for the largely male audience was also the way "the image of woman circulates in the representational economies of dominant culture". For if there is, by and large, an absence of woman on the stage as a speaking subject *herself* then, as Kate Davy suggests, female impersonation "marks a kind of cultural neologism in the form of an image that resists definition" (the undecidability of Marjorie Garber) and at the same time "generates an excess of meanings. . . Female impersonation provides, in short, a seemingly endless source of fascination because, unlike male impersonation, the man who appropriates his 'opposite' is not simultaneously effaced by it."[70] Thus for Davy, "while it certainly says something about women" female impersonation "is primarily about men, addressed to men, and for men".[71]

Details of female impersonation on the Sinhala stage are scant even in the Sinhala and English press of the day. The performances are praised if they adhere to realism but otherwise there is hardly any mention of performative gesture, gait, details of costuming, etc. What we can say about female impersonation in Sri Lanka at the turn of the 19th and early 20th centuries has to be pieced together. The legacy of female portrayals as it has come down to us in contemporary theatre—the camp gestures, the satirical poses, the feminised gait—provide clues. Other valuable sources are the auto/biographies available of Indian female impersonators and recent scholarship on Indian theatre. Given the enormous influence of the travelling Parsi theatre as well as Bengali theatre on Sri Lankan playwrights, actors and musicians of the time, similarities in performance styles and costuming between Indian theatre and the Sri Lankan nūrti can be reasonably assumed; differences should be borne in mind however, to record how the theatre continually adapts and transforms itself to new localities, situations and exigencies.

In biographies of Bal Gandharva (1888–1967), Dnyaneshwar and Mohan Nadkarni respectively describe the performative tools and techniques with which the actor imitated women.[72] A typical female performance would have Gandharva wearing long hair (in his heyday up to the waist), with flowers in it, pottu, bare feet, anklets, earrings, rings, false eyelashes, false breasts, expensive nine yard saris. In cultivating these roles, Gandharva was careful with his body. He would never walk barefoot, and would rub his palms and soles with stones when he bathed so that they remained soft. For the performance he would paint them with henna, choosing different shades in keeping with the character portrayed. He also took good care of his skin and teeth. A fair complexion, "classical" features and feminised gait were essentials for a successful female impersonator. Gandharva had them all. The tragedy of Gandharva, as the biographies present it, was an ageing body which gained weight as time went by, forcing him to take on male roles late in his career, at which he was unsuccessful. Anuradha Kapur, writing on another famous female impersonator, Jaishankar Sundari, whose theatre career as female impersonator, and director spanned from 1901–1932, notes that the female impersonator's iconic status as a charismatic performer, loved and consumed by the audience both for himself *and* his female role, presents a particular problematic for the actor. When realism becomes the grammar of an acting style, the demand is for total identification of actor with character. Within this mode of acting it is possible for the actor to divest him/herself of her stage character and become his/her individual self again at the end of the play. In the convention of female impersonation, however, where adulation and fetishising of both (male) actor and his (female) stage character have taken place simultaneously, there is no such "exit" possible for the female impersonator.[73] Bal Gandharva's anxiety over his obesity and baldness and his failure in male roles present such moments of entrapment.

But while feminisation was still possible, it was voluptuously reinforced on stage. At the height of his career Bal Gandharva's dresser, Dhondi Jamdar, would dip the sari Gandharva was to wear on stage in eau de cologne so that the wet fabric would cling to the actor's limbs.[74] Emulating Kalidasa's notion of *rasā* as scent, this was an index, too, of how vital it was for the actor to be as slim and as feminised as possible. The homo-erotic pleasures for a male audience in viewing such clinging drapery, of participating in the spectacle of the male in drag, of the bodily *authenticity* of female impersonation (many anecdotes of eminent female impersonators like Gandharva and Jaishankar Sundari relate how they gate-crashed "women only" parties in drag and spent entire evenings undiscovered by them) cannot be underestimated in understanding how the female character was received, fetishised and constructed on stage.

Gandharva self-consciously cultivated a cult of the exotic around his roles. He would choose saris from Benares and Indore—centres of fashion—and wear embroidered georgettes and silks from Bombay, fabrics and designs which became fashionable with middle class Maharashtrian women in the period between the two world wars.[75] He began to wear exotic accessories such as embroidered jackets over the sari blouse, perhaps to cover his male contours which also became fashionable with women at the time. He designed his own jewellery and wore the *nath*, the nose-ring worn by married women.[76] At his most extravagant, in a performance as Draupadi, he had the stage sprinkled with expensive French perfume,[77] linking olfactory sensory pleasure directly with the appearance of fe/male bodies. When necessary, however, he played female roles shorn of all such adornment. As Sindhu, the poor wife of an alcoholic husband in *Ekach Pyala* (1919) Gandharva wore a plain white sari; a photograph of him in that role shows him seated forlornly on the floor, at a grinding wheel. In an interview Bal Gandharva stated that his role models were his mother and sister, women with "natural grace, sincerity of character and lofty charm in action and thought".[78] His notion of the ideal woman coincided perfectly, then, with the prescriptive roles for the respectable woman that had circulated in literature, religious teaching and nationalist thought. They were the "fictions of, and about, women" that, as Anuradha Kapur notes, "the female impersonator gathers and models into and on himself to become an exemplar for real women who (in turn) produce themselves on the fictions of the impersonators".[79] If female impersonation has the potential to trangress dominant gender roles, such subversion is not possible in the nationalist theatre where s/he is "fixed" in her symbolism.

Bal Gandharva's stage poses were coy, shy, plaintive.[80] The portrayals were of feminised charm, of love and romance or enduring dutifulness as wife and mother, but he was equally adept at playing the siren and would use different styles of grooming to aid his portrayals. When playing a courtesan he would part his hair on the side and use the sweep of hair to denote a coquettish personality, while for mythological female heroines his hair would be parted at the centre.[81] Gandharva thus (re)created stereotypes of deportment and grooming for differing female characteristics. The actor's flexibility with female costuming would have contributed in no small measure to how s/he moved on stage and, in turn, influenced how women themselves began to walk and behave. What established itself was a dialectic between actor and audience, the consumption of each by the other. As noted above there were many sartorial trends that Bal Gandharva set amongst his women audience.[82] In turn, the female impersonator's "authenticity" of performance was judged in terms of current fashions and codes of female behaviour. It is this dialectic that is important in studying the construction of the Sinhala woman in John de Silva's plays, particularly as the number of women in the audience began to increase. It provides a clue to the process by which the normative ideal woman was constructed both on and off-stage and how she came to be a role model for so many Sinhalese women.

The Construction of the Arya Sinhala Woman[83]

In John de Silva's *Sinhala Parābhava Nātakaya*, two sets of women and their respective rural/urban settings are pitted against each other. The wife and daughter of Wanasinghe, a marriage broker, deeply rooted in village traditions, stand for the ideal Sinhala woman. A stage description stresses their femininity.[84] Dressed in traditional attire—saris, or cloth and jacket, long hair and basic jewellery (as the setting is the household), neither their dialogue nor plot (in which they are never agents), require them to move about hurriedly or in a confused way. They are calm in demeanour, the daughter is demure and they have not lost their "native" customs. They are hospitable to the old man, Romel, and the daughter, Leelawathi, is particularly (and suitably) respectful to him.

In contrast are the mother-daughter pair of the urban Deranasekera household. Their names, Regina Victoria Angelina and Leonora Matilda Wilhelmina, respectively locate the family's cultural slant and alienation from its indigenous roots. While Sinhala is spoken by the two women of the Wanasinghe household, the Deranasekera women speak more English than Sinhala, with extensive code-switching. Daughter Leonora is a product of the standard finishing school available for elite and middle class girls of the time. She is accomplished in music, drawing, French,

Latin and English and is about to sit for the Cambridge examination. The pillorying of her is a good indication of the anxiety felt by patriarchal nationalists over women's education, their commitment, if at all, limited to a *sufficient* modernity for their women. Other signifiers of the women's alienation are that they drink whisky and dance. Wanasinghe expresses shock and shame at the physical intimacy—promiscuity in his terms—allowed a man and woman in western dance, and Romel proclaims that infection can spread through the touching of palms during such contact! These metaphors of disease and contamination, of the native mind and body infected and polluted by western habit and culture is thus made clear in nationalist thought.

Given the ideological constructions in the play, within the exposition scene itself, the Wanasinghe mother and daughter are shown to be the credible, "authentic" carriers of Sinhala culture. Thus when Leelawathi expresses shame at a modern Sinhala woman of her generation, like Leonora, who has cut her hair and wears "*lansi*"[85]/western clothes (p.69), she carries the stamp of nationalist approval. When her mother Tarakajani adds her chorus of approval, lamenting the current state of the Sinhala language—the Deranasekera's "*thuppahi*"[86] language is a good example of this degradation—she voices yet another important nationalist concern. Central in the national imagining was the rehabilitation of the Sinhala language from its colonial denigration, its appraisal as a form of communication and culture, a window into indigenous traditions, customs, literary, religious and historical heritage. Both the Wanasinghe women in *Sinhala Parābhava Nātakaya* own such a sense of their heritage. Leelawathi alludes to the legend of Vijaya's advent on the shores of Sri Lanka and the beginnings of the Sinhala race (the unmarked irony of course being Vijaya's own "strange" hybridity), and not alien wedding ceremonies such as that staged by the Deranasekeras, as causes for authentic celebration.

The logic of the play dictates a plot in which their men end up bankrupt and ultimately in jail, because of the Deranasekera women's desire for wealth, westernisation, new clothes and fashion. This changing woman is both the index and the foremost culprit in the moral degradation of the Sinhalese. The women's life-style causes ruinous debt and their values are based on false premises. The grand event in the play is the marriage of Leonora to Harry Amaranayake. It takes place at night, there is dancing, and men and women in formal attire—tail-coats, gowns, gloves, hats, glittering jewellery. The event and guests (introduced quite deliberately in English) come centre-stage in pairs, as if in a pageant at a royal court. The gas lighting and dazzling costumes add colour and theatricality to the scene. The edge is taken off the grandeur of this spectacle by ironic public announcements, also in English, of the wedding presents which amount to mere trinkets. The comedy lies in the shaming of the Deranasekera family and in the householder's consternation as he realises that the worthless presents will by no means set off his substantial debts, as he had hoped.

The women of two households, the Deranasekeras themselves and the Satharasinghes (the latter a family "in between" classes, not quite "respectable" provincial middle-class as the Wanasinghes, nor rich like the Deranasekeras are believed to be), spend much time discussing the attire and jewellery they intend to wear for the wedding. Imitating western fashion and the purveyors of British colonial power, the women as well as the son, Crispin Satharasinghe, symbol of the alienated modern Sinhala man, aspire to western formal dress suitable for a ball.

Governor Hugh Clifford had this to say about the Sri Lankan middle class milieu in one of his dispatches (1926):

An essentially imitative people, they have adopted from their childhood the manner of living, the speech and as many of the social usages of the English as their means can make accessible to them. . . they delight in public banquets. . . and attend them clad in orthodox evening dress.[87]

It was the pressure to dress "up" in the white man and woman's clothes in colonial mimicry that, by extension, implied the (perceived) neglect of household duties, thrift and discipline—those Victorian values which for the nationalists, too, were the basis of good womanhood—that earned their ire. Their campaign against westernisation had to keep pace with its rapid spread even in the provinces and villages. By the early 20th century, men and women who would otherwise have worn sarong and cloth and jacket, or sari, dressed up in formal western attire for weddings and family portraits.[88] Western attire provided the respectability and status that indigenous dress could not; the nationalists' insistence on the sari—the *osiriya*, Kandyan, or Indian—for their Arya Sinhala women was, then, an instrument of resistance to colonial impositions on dress and habit. The sari became a signifier both of subversion and conservatism. On the one hand a signifier of nationalist resistance to colonialism and a leveller of class and caste, as its use became widespread, it remained nevertheless an instrument of male domination in its very prescriptiveness, impairing a woman's freedom of choice over her dress and body.[89]

The nationalist "ideal" woman therefore wore *osiriya*, cloth and jacket, or gown (on stage) if a regal personage, which clad her modestly. Her decorum was dignified and relatively static. In portraying her the female impersonator would be equally serene, concentrating on the voice, for timbre and tone were crucial in portraying pathos and anxiety, particularly in songs depicting a tragic heroine or a woman in love. As for the "bad" woman who, in contrast, sped giddily about the stage, we can reasonably assume that the female impersonator used camp body language, satirical gesture and exaggerated facial expression, for these characters were essentially the butt of satire and ridicule. When the era of the female impersonator was over, these demonised women were very often played by actresses from minority communities of "Other" ethnic origins such as Burghers and Malays.

How did actresses negotiate such character roles not only on stage but off it as well, given that on-stage female decorum had become a signifier of off-stage normative behaviour? In a theatre which was the site of ethno- nationalist formation, ethnicity was a key factor. Kathryn Hansen has noted the appearance of many non-Indian actresses on the Parsi stage, although this was not without initial resistance. Mary Fenton, of Irish paternity, who spoke Hindi and Urdu fluently and began performing in the 1890s, was one. Another was Patience Cooper, variously described as Anglo-Indian and Jewish; and many others like Ruby Myers, Renee Smith, Effie Hippolet and Winnie Stewart who broke onto the Indian stage with Sanskritised stage names such as Sulochana, Sita Devi, Indira Devi and Manorama, respectively.[90]

As Hansen notes, these actresses represented the "Other"

woman on stage. Their initial entrance was facilitated by the stereotype of the ethnic Other as already a loose woman, indifferent to, and not in need of, the moral/ cultural protection of the
males of the dominant community. But the different ethnicities
of these women also allowed the Indian male spectator "to possess the 'English' beauty, and in so doing, enact a reversal of the
power relations that prevailed in British-dominated colonial society".[91] It is no coincidence, then, that in Sri Lanka two renowned
early actresses were Lakshmi Bai and Gemini Kantha, both
Malays, descendants of a community that had arrived in Sri Lanka
from Indonesia and Malaysia in Dutch times. Hansen notes that
the ethnic Othering of the actress was both a means of entry on
stage when "respectable" women of the dominant community
were barred from it, and of enabling and encouraging an uninhibited male gaze, given that it was not being directed at one of
"their" own women. But how did actresses who did come from
the dominant community manage the circumstances of their entry on stage?

The Entrance of Annie Boteju

Annie Boteju entered the Tower Hall stage in 1917, playing the
role of Sita in John de Silva's production of *Rāmāyanaya*. She
was the first Sinhala actress to perform on that stage and was its
toast for over two decades, until the advent of film and the gradual
decline of the theatre in the 1940s. She was the first actress-singer
to have her voice recorded on gramophone[92] for labels such as
HMV, Parlaphone and Odeon.[93] Skilled in acting and singing,
she also played the *serpina* and was the only actress at the time
to be employed by two rival theatre companies. She was the highest paid actress in the 1930s, earning Rs. 600 per month plus
allowances (a salary higher than a state councillor's which was
Rs. 500 per month) from the Tower Hall and a fee of Rs.150 per
appearance for extra performances.[94] She was awarded a number of trophies and collected over 100 gold sovereigns from ap-
preciative audiences.[95] She was showered with gifts and tributes
by admirers; Charles Dias, another founding father of the Sinhala
nationalist theatre was amongst them. Later, she ran her own

theatre company with her second husband, Edwin Perera. Yet, when she died on 18 July 1982, reportedly at the age of eighty-two, she was almost a pauper, living in a wattle and daub house in Makola for which she paid a rent of Rs. 20 per month, forgotten in the world of theatre, a name that had no great significance for younger generations. Annie Boteju's story mirrors the rise and fall of the early Sinhala nationalist theatre, as much as the actresses' life and career, circumscribed by caste, ethnicity and class, a constant negotiation between the commercial and artistic demands of the theatre, individual needs and nationalist ideals of womanhood.

Born circa 1900, Annie came from a Sinhalese non-goyigama middle-class family.[96] She was the seventh child in a family of ten. Her parents were from different backgrounds. Her father, a transport merchant, was a Catholic from Kotahena; her mother a Buddhist. Her father died when she was quite young and her mother worked as a midwife to support the family. Although her mother was firmly opposed to Annie's career as an actress at first, she later gave up her own job to chaperone Annie on tours and was with her throughout her heyday on the stage.

Annie's stage entry was facilitated by John de Silva who lived in the same neighbourhood as her in Kotahena. Hearing her sing, de Silva persuaded her to have her voice trained and took her into his own household for the purpose. Annie's Catholic background had much to do with her initiation into theatre with its traditions of church drama and *Pāsku* plays, as well as early training in both choral and solo singing. Her teachers were renowned musicians, Kanthi Bai from Bengal and Appuhamy Master. Despite John de Silva's patronage, however, Annie's initial access to the stage was not uncontested. Romiel Perera, a renowned female impersonator of the time, was known to have scorned her for being non-goyigama and undercaste,[97] a slur precipitated no doubt by the threat to his own profession through the advent of actresses like her.

Annie had the classical good looks and deportment required for her roles on stage—long black hair, fair, poised and well-groomed. She played heroic figures even when, within the conventions of male/female impersonation, she played male roles.

She acted as Prince Kalinga in *Orison Palanthan* and, following Bengali theatre convention, rode a horse onto the stage.[98] She played Aladdin and the roles of both Romeo and Juliet on alternate nights in Shakespeare's play. For these male roles she learnt sword fighting, and said of the performances, "I just loved it".[99] She never took part in comedy but carefully cultivated the roles of tragic and/or romantic heroines. In John de Silva's plays she played Sakuntala, Madra Devi, Ratnavalie, Samudra Devi, Sita, Ehelepola Kumarihamy. She represented the ideal Arya woman and was a vehicle for middle class aspirations to "moral purification and national glory" through identification with such women.[100] She was a firm nationalist. She enjoyed having her sister read the nationalist novels of Piyadasa Sirisena and W.A. de Silva to her.[101] They had to be read to her because her education had progressed no further than the primary level, but this did not debar her from participating in the pleasure and nationalist pride the novels evoked.

It was a nationalism that would take on a distinctly communal flavour, not unrelated to the demography of Colombo and the ideological battle for the hearts and minds of the labouring class. The early 20th century was a time when the growth of manufacturing and service industries in Colombo resulted in a rapid increase in its working class population. Colombo was mainly a port city, providing warehousing and packaging of plantation crops central to the colonial economy, as well as being the administrative and commercial capital. Its population in 1921 was 244,163, six times more than other towns with municipal status. Of this, 16 per cent were engaged in industrial occupations, 37 per cent in trade and transport and 12 per cent in domestic service.[102] The manual workforce was concentrated in the harbour and the Colombo Ironworks, in coconut-oil mills and foundries. Tamils, Ceylon Moors and Malays formed an important segment of this workforce. In 1921, of the total population in Colombo, Tamils (both Ceylon Tamils and those of Indian origin) formed 22.1 per cent, Moors 16.2 per cent and Malays 2.3 per cent.[103] A large number of them lived in the areas of Pettah, San Sebastian, Maradana and Slave Island, where the first theatres in Colombo were situated.[104]

This was the nationalist constituency that coalesced around Colombo and the audience for John de Silva's theatre. But de Silva was selective in his address. For nationalists like de Silva, these people were a threat to Sinhalese jobs and livelihoods, and were therefore constructed as "foreign". John de Silva used to address his audience before his plays with "long and frequently abusive speeches (not only) condemning the aping of western manners, (but also) attacking Tamils and Muslims and extolling the virtues of the ancient Sinhalese".[105] Tamils, Muslims and Malayalis were stereotyped variously as shrewd and cunning, morally decadent, rapacious and lecherous.[106] In this way it was the Sinhalese who were picked out as the noble and legitimate heirs of the emerging sovereign nation. Their history and traditional customs were extolled with pride. What nationalists like de Silva contributed to was the eventual fragmentation of the working class into communal groups. In 1923 A.E. Goonesinha, leader of the Ceylon Labour Union, had been able to organise a multi-ethnic labouring class involving 20,000 workers, in a very successful general strike against British capital. But by the 1930s such a coalition had become untenable. The great depression had affected Sri Lanka's exports resulting in widespread retrenchment. An upsurge in unemployment followed in which the labouring class was the worst hit. Ethnic tensions flared. A boycott of foreign workers was called for and the Malayali community targeted. A.E. Goonesinhe himself adopted an anti-Malayali platform, appealing to Sinhala sentiment. At a public rally in 1936 he spoke of the disgrace to the nation "as a result of Sinhala women falling prey to the wiles of the Malayali", and joined the campaign calling for the boycott of Malayali workers.[107] Cultural ethno-nationalism in which, through theatre and literature, the Sinhalese were constructed as the sole legitimate subjects of the nation played its part in buttressing such discrimination.

Annie Boteju herself expressed strong anti-Tamil and anti-Muslim sentiments in her lifetime in keeping with the ethno-nationalist discourse of the Tower Hall itself.[108] It is significant that she played few comic roles enacting mostly tragic and/or romantic ones. If comedy, often carrying satire, was a site of pillorying the woman, Annie avoided such self-imaging, projecting herself rather, as an *ideal Sinhala* woman. In fact, ethnic mapping both on and off-stage as well as on actresses' bodies was such that, not un-coincidentally, the renowned comic actresses of the day were non-Sinhala women like Gemini Kantha and Lakshmi Bai who were of Malay origin. The roles of "bad" women were also enacted by them. One of Lakshmi Bai's famous roles was in *Sivammā and Dhanapāla* where, as the temptress Sivamma she seduces a village boy and runs through his possessions. King Dutugemunu banishes her for her bad deeds, and she is forced to beg for alms. A song Lakshmi Bai sang in this abject condition *"Tilo guru namayen memata"* while begging for alms, became very popular and drew large crowds to the play.[109]

Although Annie Boteju's stage roles reinforced the prescriptive of good Arya Sinhala women, her personal life flew in the face of such iconic figures. Her sexuality was trangressive when measured by the yardstick of bourgeois respectability. She never married, but had three children whose fathers she never acknowledged in public.[110] To the media however, she later affirmed two legal marriages. She first married a hotel owner who was a theatre fan of hers while still a teenager. They had a daughter but tragedy struck and this husband died when Annie was just 18 years old. She then married T.V.Edwin Perera, himself an actor.[111] They are reported to have run their own theatre company for a while, but records of this venture are scanty. Charles Dias, rival to John de Silva, was another ardent admirer of Annie's.

The real nature of these relationships, whether they were within the ambit of sexual favours and male patronage that actresses were dependent on, is a matter of speculation. What is significant is that Annie Boteju's sexuality contradicted the chaste image of Aryan womanhood she herself carefully portrayed/cultivated on stage. Why then did the Tower Hall patrons and playwrights, desperate to make the theatre "respectable" and acceptable to middle class morality, accommodate such transgression?

The answer lies in the fact that actresses had, by this time, become valuable capital. By the 1920s the touring Parsi theatre routinely used actresses who attracted large crowds, ensuring commercial success. In contrast, the continued use of female impersonation was a disadvantage to the entrepreneurs of Sinhala

theatre. Pressure mounted on them to compete with the Parsi
theatricals on the same terms. Following the performances of the
Olivali Victoria Parsi troupe which included actresses, at the
Tower Hall in 1921, there was a demand by local patrons that
they be hired for other Tower Hall performances as well.[112] Advertisements for plays during this period indicate just how important actresses had become to attracting an audience. Many of
them had the main actress's portrait at the top or middle of the
advert, with the title of the play, a short description, venue and
time of performance as text wrapped around the portrait. An
advertisement for *Aladdin and the Magical Lamp* (1928) is typical, with Sasadhi Devi, the main actress's portrait forming its
centrepiece.[113] The actress was promoted as the main attraction,
and her commodification was not coincidental to the capitalist
formation of the period. That the modern Sinhala theatre saw
itself as a commercial enterprise is clear. As early as 1885, John
de Silva had converted the Eastern Lanka Dramatic Society
(Pūrvadiga Lankā Nūrtiya Samagāma) into a limited liability
company, and sold its shares for Rs. 10 each.[114] The competition
that the theatre companies of Bastian Jayaweera, John de Silva
and Charles Dias entered into to produce bigger and better theatrical fare than foreign touring companies, requiring large
amounts of capital for stage sets and huge casts, was an investment designed to make profit from large ticket sales. If women
on stage could attract the crowds, the Sinhala theatre was under
pressure to do away with female impersonators and hire "real"
women.

Realism as the desired performative style of the time was
another factor that cleared the way for actresses, providing them
a vantage point from which to negotiate their terms. Realism
following western theatre traditions of the period, had taken hold,
transformed of course with an emphasis on spectacle. In the Bengali
theatre, live tigers and horses on stage were common attractions;
stages would incorporate earthen embankments to facilitate the
entry onstage of warriors or kings on horseback.[115] As already
noted, in productions like *Orison Palanthan*, in which Annie
Boteju as Prince Kalinga rode on horseback, the Sinhala theatre
followed suit, albeit to a lesser degree given that its theatre was

on a smaller scale. But there was a similar emphasis on props and stage settings. The retired Annie Boteju declared in an interview, "Two bits of cloth and no backdrops! In our time a palace looked like a palace. What is this modern drama? You don't feel like acting on a bare stage!"[116] Binodini Dasi described how the clothes and hair of actresses got singed when enacting the final scenes of a funeral at which the pyre on stage had real flames.[117] The acting styles of the day demanded a totally naturalistic performative language. Binodini Dasi again describes how, when playing various characters, she would literally faint during the performance, burdened by the pathos, or *bhāva*, of the situation and character portrayed. Reviews of the time praised actresses who had the audience in tears for the depth of identification with the tragic roles they played. What this emphasis on realism meant—the proscenium stage, which distanced the action from the audience, framed this illusion of realism admirably—was that it continually called for ever more credible performances by stage actors. Female impersonation became the one oddity within this paradigm.

It was for reasons of realistic representation that Lawrence Perera battled with the Catholic church to introduce actresses into his *pāsku* play. Peter de Silva, John de Silva's son, was also a vehement supporter of introducing actresses onto the stage and reportedly took issue with his father on this matter. John de Silva's position was more orthodox even though he encouraged actresses like Annie Boteju. He felt that actresses would bring indiscipline and disrepute to his theatre company. The son's concern was to make his father's plays both commercially competitive and artistically tenable in keeping with the new performative trends. When he began managing the Sri Lanka Natya Sabha Peter de Silva arranged for leading actresses like Annie Boteju, L. Jane Perera and Regina Perera to take part in the plays, and hired twelve female singers—drawn from the Sinhala and Burgher communities, with names like Aila and Florie a.k.a. Francy—to perform in them.[118]

In the beginning, the theatre only allowed actresses walk-on parts or small female roles, while the female impersonator (the box office attraction until then) continued to play the lead female role. Gradually however, the actresses took over but once they joined the stage, they were subjected to a regime of discipline that protected their own "respectability" and, by extension, their theatre company. Rehearsal hours were long. Annie Boteju's routine included a morning rehearsal that began at 8.00 a.m. and an afternoon one from 4.00-6.00 p.m. at the Olympia theatre (known then as The Criterion) before the evening's performance.[119] Shyamala Shiveshwarkar notes that actresses of the Parsi theatre were always chaperoned and made to live apart from the men, while the main actresses were given their own transportation of horse and carriage, and paid a salary. They were under the direct charge of the Manager so that there was no scandal.[120] That the managers were male and in a position of power over the actress would have given them the licence to control as well as exploit their employees' sexuality. When actresses married or had relationships with theatre entrepreneurs, fellow actors, musicians or stage managers (as Annie did with Edwin Perera and Charles Dias) it automatically set up a system in which the actress was under the scrutiny of her spouse or lover. Elsewhere, in polygamous cultures, a theatre owner/playwright/director like Nigerian Herbert Ogunde was able to marry his leading actresses, forming an extended theatre family that travelled around the country with each member of the household, including his children, contributing to the family's livelihood through theatre. In the travelling Lok theatre of Pakistan similar arrangements can still be seen. In such situations women often do not have individual power, as professional contracts and arrangements are negotiated on their behalf by their husbands or fathers. Legal marriage to theatre owners also ensures that leading actresses will not defect to other theatre companies. The extended family structure remains intact when the theatre owner recruits his wife/wives as female heroines, and her relatives as stage-hands or household servants. Thus in the Lok theatre each tent comprises a household, which in turn makes up an entire community whose occupation is the theatre.[121]

That many actresses were not empowered to manage their own finances—or did so without any idea of the future decline of the urban theatre to cinema, as happened in Sri Lanka in the

1940s—condemned those like Annie Boteju to a retirement of near poverty and neglect. Quite often actresses were paid only a monthly salary, not a percentage of the profits collected by the theatres they worked in, and attracted huge crowds to. This meant that when ill, or retired, their income ceased. In Sri Lanka, it was not until Prime Minister Ranasinghe Premadasa's inauguration of the Tower Hall Foundation in the late 1970s and of a pension fund for veteran actors and actresses, that artists like Annie Boteju received a small but regular monthly income.

Annie Boteju's story illustrates well the circumstances of women's incorporation into nationalism. She herself did not have to struggle much to enter the stage. The competition by touring theatre troupes and commercial interests paved the way for her stage debut. Moreover, the actress' feminised projections of sexuality and decorum, her portrayal of "good" and "bad" women became important sites of nationalist constructions of community, religion and tradition. The actress was instrumental in the acclaim that the productions she performed in received, but she never became an equal partner of this theatre. Her "star" status was located in the public adulation she received, dependent on the continuing success of her performances, the beauty of her body and the goodwill of her male patrons and theatre managers. An account of Annie Boteju in her heyday, written much later, is an example of the male gaze afforded the actress and how she continued to be appraised:

She had a luscious figure and also possessed a melodious voice. Milling crowds used to fight for admission to the Tower Hall to see this singing sensation, whose balcony song '*Banda ma deda piyano*' was a craze with drama fans, so was '*Pipila dasa man kusuman*'.[122]

Annie Boteju's life and career can be located at the very intersections within the Sinhala theatre of the time, as it responded to the needs of nationalism with its formulations of both tradition and modernity. These were requirements that were both conflictual and complementary. The nationalist need of the hour was to depict a glorious indigenous pre-colonial past, a proud history of which the ideal Sinhala Buddhist Arya woman was the emblem. In this project, Annie Boteju enacted perfect role models of dutiful, chaste, devout, dignified Sinhala women with great skill. When she played Sita and Sakuntala or the queens and good women of the Buddhist Jataka stories, she was also tracing a lineage from an Indian heritage of noble, aristocratic women for the Arya Sinhala woman. This archive was necessarily a historio-mythic one which the nationalists delved into for a re-valuing of the past. But the values these female characters stood for on stage were primarily those of self-sacrifice, including renunciation of excessive material wealth. This was in contrast to other paradigms of modernity, namely capitalist accumulation in early 20th century Sri Lanka, which made urban Sinhala theatre a self-consciously competitive commercial venture.

Yet, even as it commodified her, the actress was able to use her commercial value as a bargaining chip for greater empowerment within the theatre. After Annie's debut in 1917 in the Vijaya Ranga Sabha, she soon moved to the Arya Sinhala Sabha claiming that the Rs.40 per month paid to her by the former was inadequate. She was then able to negotiate contracts with two rival theatre companies and command a very high salary for the time. In making theatre companies themselves take note of their contractual obligations and heed the market value of their performers, actresses like Annie Boteju played a significant role in the modernising process of urban Sinhala theatre.

Moreover, Annie could negotiate her sexuality and choices in life precisely because the Sinhala theatre of the early 20th century offered her a dual possibility. Playing the good woman on stage Annie projected herself as the ideal woman. In a photo advertisement for the play, Thumpene Bandā, she is dressed in a cloth (lungi) and jacket with puff sleeves. Her waist is covered. She wears accessories of throatlet, earrings and bangles. Buxom by today's standards, her pose is decorous, attractive and "respectable" as she represents the "ideal" village lass. Thus, if her sexuality was transgressive, she could counteract its effect and the stigma of her profession itself by carefully choosing to play certain types of tragic/romantic heroines that foregrounded her as "respectable". Her stage/public image then symbolically veiled her private life and marked her as a woman of good repute. Ethnicity and class were also on her side, even if caste was not.

From a Sinhala-speaking middle class family, hers was not an abject position within the theatre. Indeed, her successful career is a testimony of her ability to negotiate the circumstances of her time—the rise of ethno-Sinhala Buddhist nationalism and its ideological construction within the theatre, the centrality of gender in this process, the shift in theatrical form from stylised to naturalistic, and the capitalist accumulation of the period—to her own advantage. Even if this fell short of pressing for equal partnership in ventures of which she was the star attraction, Annie Boteju's heyday reflected her own agency within nationalism and the possibilities available for women with outstanding talent such as hers.

Notes

1 Benedict Anderson, *Imagined Communities: Reflections on the Origin and Spread of Nationalism*. London: Verso, 1989.
2 For a discussion on some of these issues, see Kate Davy, "Fe/male Impersonation: The Discourse of Camp," in Janelle G. Reinelt and Joseph R. Roach (eds.), *Critical Theory and Performance*. Ann Arbor: University of Michigan Press, 1992. pp. 231–47.
3 Sudipto Chatterjee, "Mise-En-(Colonial)Scene: The Theatre of the Bengal Renaissance," in Ellen Gainor (ed.), *Imperialism and Theatre: Essays on World Theatre, Drama and Performance*. London & New York: Routledge, 1995. p. 23.
4 Ibid., p.21.
5 Ibid., p.23.
6 E.R.Sarachchandra, *The Folk Drama of Ceylon*. Colombo: Cultural Affairs Department. 1952 & 1966, pp.7–8.
7 Ibid., pp.19–23.
8 Ranjini Obeysekere, *Sri Lankan Theatre in a Time of Terror* op.cit., p. 85.
9 E.R.Sarachchandra, op. cit., p.9.
10 Ranjini Obeysekere, op. cit., p.87. Obeysekere sees the dictate by King Parakramabahu the second (AC 1236–71), himself a poet, author and noted patron of the arts, that monks should refrain from "poetry, drama and such despicable arts" as proof that even monks had begun to practice these art forms.
11 Ibid., p.86. In S. Paranavitana's chapter in *The History of Ceylon* Vol. 1 Part 1, which discusses religion, literature and art upto the Polonnaruva period, theatre is absent from the discussion of literary

and creative forms that existed, such as poetry, sculpture, architecture and painting. *History of Ceylon* Vol. 1 Part 1, Chapter 7. Colombo: Ceylon University Press, 1959.

[12] E.R.Sarachchandra, op. cit.

[13] E.R.Sarachchandra, "Sinhalese Drama," in *The Ceylon Observer Pictorial*. Colombo: Lake House, 1951, pp. 27–32.

[14] The Portuguese colonised the coastal areas of Sri Lanka from 1505 to 1658.

[15] Chatterjee, Sudipto "Mise-En-(Colonial) Scene" op. cit., p.23.

[16] Ibid., p. 24.

[17] Kathryn Hansen, "Making Women Visible: Female Impersonators and Actresses on the Parsi Stage and in Silent Cinema," *Economic Political Weekly*, 29 August 1998, pp. 2291–2300.

[18] Hapuarachchi, D.V., *Sinhala Natya Itihasaya 1860–1911* (History of Sinhala Drama 1860–1911). Colombo: Lake House, 1981, pp. 63–5.

[19] These were *Othello, Hamlet, The Merchant of Venice, Measure for Measure* and *King Lear*.

[20] Wimal Dissanayake, *John de Silva and Sinhala Theatre*. Colombo: Cultural Affairs Dept., 1974, p. 47. John de Silva printed 2000 copies of *Othello* in Sinhala in 1910 and sold them for Rs.1 each. The Register of Printed Publications, National Archives of Sri Lanka.

[21] For a study of the acting styles of Parsi theatre see Anuradha Kapur, "The Representation of Gods and Heroes: Parsi Mythological Drama of the Early Twentieth Century," in *The Journal of Arts and Ideas*, 23–24 January, 1993, pp.85–107.

[22] The term Parsi theatre is something of a misnomer. It is named after the Zoroastrian immigrants from Iran who settled in Bombay and began theatrical activity there around 1850. Two decades on however, its actors, directors, musicians, technicians, etc. were not exclusively Parsi but drawn from different communities and backgrounds. The financial capital and management of the theatres and productions were often still in the hands of the Parsis, particularly certain families such as the Madan family, until the 1930s. See Kathryn Hansen, op. cit.

[23] Kironmoy Raha, *Bengali Theatre*. Delhi: National Book Trust, 1978 & 1993, p.10.

[24] Michael Roberts, *Exploring Confrontation—Sri Lanka: Politics, Culture and History*. Chur: Harwood Academic Publishers, 1995, p.105.

[25] John de Silva, *Diary*, 7 April-11th May, 1904. Colombo: The National Archives, 25.30/3.

[26] Mudaliyars were originally translators for the British, and through

British patronage worked their way up the administrative ladder to become the highest-ranked local administrative head with attendant class and social prestige.

27 Christy Cooray (ed.), *Tower Hall: Theatre and Cultural Centre.* Colombo: Tower Hall Theatre Foundation, n.d., p.4.

28 See Kitsiri Malagoda, "Sociological Aspects of Revival and Change in Buddhism in 19th Century Ceylon," D. Phil dissertation, Oxford University, 1970.

29 L.D.A.Ratnayake, quoted in Wimal Dissanayake, *John de Silva and Sinhala Theatre*, op. cit., p.29.

30 Sudipto Chatterjee, "The Nation Staged: Nationalist Discourse in Late Nineteenth Century Bengali Theatre," Helen Gilbert (ed.), *(Post) Colonial Stages: Critical and Creative Views on Drama, Theatre and Performance.* Hebden Bridge: Dangaroo, 1999, p. 19.

31 Pradeep Jeganathan, "Authorizing History, Ordering Land: The Conquest of Anuradhapura," in Pradeep Jeganathan & Qadri Ismail (eds.), *Unmaking the Nation.* Colombo: Social Scientists' Association, 1995, pp. 106–36.

32 Frederick Dornhorst, Joseph Grenier and Richard Morgan were among de Silva's friends. Wilfred Gunasekera, "Life and Times of Dramatist John de Silva with Special Reference to his Hitherto Unknown Poetic Acumen," paper presented at the Royal Asiatic Society, Colombo, 26 January, 1998, p.2.

33 Wimal Dissanayake, op. cit., p.1.

34 Bengali theatre took a similar trajectory in the latter decades of the 19th century with the westernised "modern" women and their babus becoming an increasing target of attack in the farces of the day. Rimli Bhattacharya, *Binodini Dasi: My Story* and *My Life as an Actress.* New Delhi: Kali for Women, 1998, p.166.

35 Sunil Ariyaratne (ed.), John de Silva, *Collected Plays* Vol. 1. Colombo: S. Godage & Sons, 1992, pp.67–103.

36 Translated by Dr. Lakshmi de Silva.

37 See Manel Tampoe, *The Story of Selestina Dias: Buddhist Female Philanthropy and Education.* Colombo: Social Scientists' Association, 1997.

38 F.L.Woodward, "Girls, Wives and Mothers", *The Ceylon National Review* 1, January 1906. Colombo: Ceylon Social Reform Society, p.16.

39 Kumari Jayawardena, "Aspects of Religious Cultural Identity and the Construction of Sinhala Buddhist Womanhood" in Douglas Allen (ed.), *Religion and Political Conflict in South Asia.* New Delhi: Oxford University Press, 1993.

40 John de Silva, *Sri Vikrama Rajasinghe: Our Last King* in Sunil

Ariyaratne (ed.), *Collected Plays* Vol. 2. Colombo: S. Godage & Sons, 1992, p.48.
[41] Ibid., p.26.
[42] Syed Jamil Ahmed, "Female Performers in the Indigenous Theatre of Bengal," Firdous Azim & Niaz Zaman (eds.), *Infinite Variety: Women in Society and Literature*. Dhaka: University Press, 1994, p.264.
[43] Ibid., p. 266.
[44] Ibid., p.265.
[45] This is a legacy which has lasted for long; even in contemporary times educated women from the middle classes in India, Pakistan, Bangladesh and Sri Lanka are hesitant to join the professional theatre. That theatre performances are at night, interfering with family duties, is another contributory factor.
[46] In Madhusudan Dutt's *Shormishtha* on 16 August, 1873. Rimli Bhattacharya, *Binodini Dasi* op. cit., p.3.
[47] This was when Anna Perera took part in C.Don Bastian's *Romlin*, 26 September and 3 October, 1886. (Hapuarachchi, p. 297) It was not until the early 1920s, however, that the use of actresses in theatre became commonplace.
[48] *Binodini Dasi*, p.83.
[49] Ibid., p. 89.
[50] Ibid., p. 85.
[51] Tissa Kariyawasam, Introduction to W.C.Perera's *Eugene Nadagama*, Colombo, Cultural Affairs Dept. 1997, p. xlvi.
[52] Hapuarachchi, p.45.
[53] Ibid., p.46.
[54] Ibid., p.168.
[55] Ibid., p.166.
[56] Ibid., p.167.
[57] See E.R.Sarachchandra, *The Folk Drama of Ceylon*, pp.124–8.
[58] Ibid., p.126.
[59] Ibid., pp.126–7.
[60] Ibid., p.128.
[61] Hapuarachchi, p.117.
[62] Ibid., p.50.
[63] Anuradha Kapur, "Female Impersonation, Narration and the Invention of Desire," paper presented at the conference on "Mapping the Terrain: New Literary Histories", University of California, Berkeley, September 1999, p. 22.
[64] See Valerie Traub, *Desire and Anxiety: Circulations of Sexuality in Shakespearean Drama*. London: Routledge, 1992, and Marjorie Garber, *Vested Interests: Cross-Dressing and Cultural Anxiety*. New York: Routledge, 1992.

65 Although the inaugural plays of the nūrti tradition began at The Flower Hall, managed by C. Don Bastian, the genre later found its home in the Tower Hall theatre, opened at Maradana, a suburb of Colombo, on 16 December, 1911. Very soon, "Tower Hall plays" became the generic name given to the nūrti of playwrights like John de Silva and Charles Dias.

66 L.D.A.Ratnayake, *The History of Proctor John de Silva's Plays.* Colombo: private publication, 1963 & 1965, p. 74.

67 Garber, op. cit., pp.36–7. My emphasis.

68 See also Anuradha Kapur, "Female Impersonation," op. cit., p. 21.

69 Ibid., p.10

70 Kate Davy, op. cit., pp.236–7.

71 Ibid., p.233.

72 Dnyaneshwar Nadkarni, *Bal Gandharva and the Marathi Theatre.* Bombay: Roopak Books, 1988, and Mohan Nadkarni, *Bal Gandharva.* New Delhi: National Book Trust, 1988.

73 Anuradha Kapur, "Female Impersonation," p.2.

74 Dnyaneshwar Nadkarni, op. cit., p.99.

75 Ibid, p. 140.

76 Mohan Nadkarni, *Bal Gandharva,* op. cit., p.64.

77 Indrani Sawker, "The Living Legend Narayanrao Rajhans alias Bal Gandharva", *The Economic Times,* August 7, 1983.

78 Mohan Nadkarni, *Bal Gandharva,* op. cit., p.60.

79 Anuradha Kapur, "Female Impersonation", p.18.

80 Dnyaneshwar Nadkarni, op. cit.

81 Dnyaneshwar Nadkarni, op. cit., p.58.

82 See also Kathryn Hansen, "Making Women Visible," op. cit.

83 The term *Arya* as used by nationalists like Anagarika Dharmapala, following orientalists like Max Mueller and Wilhelm Geiger, conflated race theories with cultural traits. Taking the notion of Aryan as superior and noble, Dharmapala used the term to depict the uniqueness of the Sinhala race as opposed to "the Pagan Tamils and European Vandals".

84 John de Silva, *Collected Plays Vol.1,* op. cit., p.69. Pagination hereafter will be from this edition.

85 '*Lansi*' is the Sinhala term used for those of Dutch and Portuguese ancestry known as the Burghers. Although the dress codes adopted by the Sinhalese at the turn of the century were British, '*lansi*' is used generically as the Portuguese and Dutch were the first contacts the Sinhalese had with the West.

86 "*Thuppahi*" means mixed, and therefore, in this context, "debased".

87 Hugh Clifford quoted in Nira Wickramasinghe, "Some Comments on Dress in Sri Lanka", *Thatched Patio,* 5 No. 1, January-February 1992, p.6.

[88] Ibid.

[89] Ibid.

[90] Kathryn Hansen, op. cit., p.2297.

[91] Ibid.

[92] Turin Fernando, "Sri Lanka's First Stage Actress, Annie Boteju." *Janatha*, Colombo: Lake House, June 5, 1966.

[93] E.C.T.Candappa, "A Play a Week on the Road to Stardom". *Ceylon Observer*. Colombo: Lake House, March 3, 1974.

[94] Ibid.

[95] Carol Aloysius, "Annie, First Lady," *Ceylon Observer*, July 9, 1978.

[96] Goyigama or farmer caste is considered at the apex of caste hierarchy in Sinhalese society.

[97] Ranjith Perera, a close relative of Annie Boteju. Personal communication. Colombo, June 1998.

[98] Rimli Bhattacharya, *Binodini Dasi*, p.75. Binodini Dasi's martial role of Pramila in Madhusudan's *Meghnad Badh Kabya* required her to ride a horse and enact her role on horseback.

[99] Carol Aiyadurai, *Ceylon Observer*, October 3, 1969.

[100] Kathryn Hansen, reviewing *Binodini Dasi, My Story* and *My Life as an Actress* in *Theatre Journal*, Vol. 5 no.4, December 1998, pp.555-57.

[101] Ranjith Perera, personal communication.

[102] Michael Roberts, *Exploring Confrontation*. Geneve: Harwood Publishers, 1994, p.218.

[103] Roberts, *Exploring Confrontation*, op. cit., p. 219.

[104] The Flower Hall, the first commercial theatre in Colombo, was in Gintupitiya, and Tower Hall was in Maradana.

[105] Sarath Amunugama, "John de Silva and the Nationalist Theatre," *The Ceylon Historical Journal* October 25, 1978, p.288.

[106] Kumari Jayawadena refers to plays in which "the gloomy fate of Sinhala women who were enticed and later abandoned by Malayalis" were staged in the 1930s. *Ethnic and Class Conflict in Sri Lanka*. Colombo: Sanjiva, 1990, p.54.

[107] Ibid,. pp.54–5.

[108] Ranjith Perera, personal communication.

[109] Fiqo, *Ceylon Daily News*, Colombo: Lake House, June 16, 1966.

[110] Ranjith Perera.

[111] Carol Aloysius, op. cit.

[112] Christy Cooray (ed.), *Tower Hall: Theatre and Cultural Centre*. Colombo: Tower Hall Theatre Foundation, n.d., p.6.

[113] Tower Hall museum.

[114] Hapuarachchi, p.236.

[115] Binodini Dasi, op. cit., p.148.

[116] E.C.T. Candappa, *Ceylon Observer*, March 3, 1974.

[117] Binodini Dasi, op. cit., p.153.

[118] L.D.A. Ratnayake, op. cit., pp.197, 198. Other actresses of repute who entered the stage were Lakshmi Bai born in 1907, Annie Margaret Nona (1913), Susila Jayasinghe (1918), Letitia Mildred Pieris (1932) and Freda Aglin Parais (1935).

[119] E.C.T. Candappa, op. cit.

[120] Shyamala Shiveshwarkar, "The Rise and Decline of the Parsi Theatre", *The Hindustan Times*, 21 March 1976.

[121] Fouzia Saeed and Adam Nayyar, *Women in Folk Theatre*. Islamabad: Lok Virsa, 1991.

[122] Fiqo, op. cit.

Anil Marcia de Silva

2

FRAMING THE NATION'S RESPECTABILITY
Anil Marcia de Silva's Rite of Passage

"One should not be surprised, if in her next insane ramblings in the world of the East and literature, she advocated ardently the principle of Fusion of races, and herself delivers an object lesson, by precept and example. One cannot very well raise any material objection to what may be termed, 'her sincere learnings'.

But when this Marcia boldly ventures in the midst of her 'transcendental Moralizations' to kick her land of Birth and the good peoples therein, to fulfil her obligations to Beef and other Eaters in England, it is time that Ceylon said to her:—'Cut it off your programme, Marcia. You may wash your own dirty linen in England; if we have any, it is washed, in some quiet corner, by your kind in Ceylon, and they too are paid handsomely for the job.' But ours is pure Linen!"

From "Marcia De Silva In the Midst of English Beef-Eaters"
—*The Searchlight*, May 1932

"In her latest contribution to *The Queen*, a publication in London, Miss Marcia de Silva who had a lot to say against the seclusion of the Sinhalese women, in her sweeping statements to the press that amused a good many of us, has proclaimed that she is a disillusioned woman today. All that so-called freedom of the English girl which was Miss Silva's fascination that led her to abandon her home and seek one in that 'Land of Freedom' is nothing but unbridled license that is given expression to in the home, in society, and in other things that matter."

—*The Comrade*, September 1932

T HE SUBJECT OF the vitriol in *The Searchlight*[1] and *The Comrade*, two popular magazines of the 1920s, is Marcia Anil de Silva, journalist, biographer, art historian, founder-member of the Indian People's Theatre Association, a close associate of the Indian Communist Party and Bombay's avant-garde of the 1940s. She was the daughter of George E. de Silva, a prominent Sinhalese politician who rose to be President of the Ceylon National Congress and Minister of Health, and Agnes Nell, active in the campaign for universal suffrage, won in 1931. But Anil de Silva is not its only subject. In the attacks on her journalism, particularly when it was critical of Sri Lankan culture, on her political affiliations with her father's activism in the Ceylon labour movement, and on her choice of personal lifestyle are the dictates of a certain nationalist construction of "respectability" as it came to be typified for bourgeois Sri Lankan men and women. It signified, in particular, how a woman should behave in keeping with her class and caste status, and beyond that, how a Sri Lankan woman should conduct herself in the face of the challenges wrought by western influence.

Throughout her life we shall see Anil de Silva described, constructed and textualised in a particular way. The nationalist discourse on her hinges primarily on two facets: her caste and her sexuality. It foregrounds her "otherness" and her refusal/inability to conform to the tenets of respectability. It critiques her "rejection" of Sri Lankan values. In the construction of her sexuality, both right and left-wing criticisms coincide. We shall also see that, in turn, much of Anil de Silva's life and work was a response to these narratives, signifying that, despite her life's journey from provincial city and small island to the cosmopolitan worlds of Bombay, Paris and London, she carried with her a baggage of values with their own inflections of "respectability", cultural orientation and political commitment that crystallised in Sri Lanka in the early decades of the 20th century.

The Respectable Nation

George L. Mosse has shown how respectability is central to the very existence of modern bourgeois society.[2] It came to the fore

in Europe with the rise of the middle class, and religious awakenings such as Pietism in Germany and Evangelism in England.
Behaviour was taken to be an outward expression of inward piety, and these religious revivals had much to do with the construction of modern manners and morals in the late 17th and 18th
centuries. Moderation and control over the passions were stressed.
A life based on frugality, devotion, duty and restraint was valued. The middle class used these tenets to shore itself up against
both the "lazy" lower classes and the profligate aristocracy. It
used these notions to protect itself from the new challenges it
faced from industrialization and political upheaval. Thus, respectability as a defining category, which had become entrenched in
Europe by the first decades of the 19th century, not only provided
a code of conduct for the middle class but also gave it its basic
character, self-respect and sense of superiority, and therefore a
measure of *difference* from those outside its norms.

During national crises, respectability was reinforced as a signifier of patriotism. The elimination of vice became an integral
part of the defence of the nation. The Jacobins of the French
revolution, who decapitated a profligate aristocracy and prosecuted prostitution and pornography, were cited as having established "the connection between good morals and the proper
order and peace of society, more than all the eloquence of the
pulpit and the disquisition of moral philosophers have done for
many centuries". The Napoleonic wars in turn forged a new national self-consciousness in France, England and Germany where
patriotism was conflated with morality. English ballads written
during these wars, which failed to mention king and country,
were reprimanded as "impious and indecent".[3]

Nationalism in the colonies took the same route, forging alliances with bourgeois respectability to stave off challenges to its
dominance by colonialism. Largely derivative of European
thought, history and manners, it reinforced middle-class respectability in the name of religion and country. Anagarika
Dharmapala[4] was at the forefront of such a programme in Sri
Lanka. In the name of Buddhism he laid down a code of respectability that was metonymic of the emerging nation itself. Yet,
the bourgeois morality Dharmapala sought to reinforce had, in

the Sri Lankan context of the late 19ᵗʰ and early 20ᵗʰ centuries, come down from Victorian thought and Protestant Christianity. The missionary school played a pivotal role in channelling these norms of morality/respectability to native society. Supplementing core academic subjects such as English, Latin, mathematics, history and science, these norms included the tenets of cleanliness, obedience, industry and discipline.[5] While the qualities of leadership were further instilled for boys, for girls the virtue of modesty was paramount. By the late 19ᵗʰ century these values had been so instilled in a section of Sri Lankan society that even nationalists like Anagarika Dharmapala—who were derisive of western culture but whose early education had been in Christian missionary schools—strenuously reinscribed them in their template for national respectability.

But it was not only the Christian missionary impulse in the colonies that culled respectability. Richard Gombrich and Gananath Obeysekera point to an ancient Buddhist tradition which inscribed codes of acceptable/ethical conduct and demeanour.[6] This laid down rules of conduct for its priests and laity through its scriptures. While rules for the Buddhist clergy were carefully delineated, with great emphasis on personal decorum and good manners, those for the laity were drawn in broad ethical strokes. Anagarika Dharmapala found in the latter an opportunity to construct a new respectability for Sinhala Buddhists and filled the gaps with more carefully detailed prescriptions. In 1898 he published a pamphlet in Sinhala entitled *Gihi Vinaya*, or *The Daily Code for the Laity* which encompassed a set of 200 rules under 22 subjects, ranging from eating food, chewing betel, wearing clean clothes, to how to use the lavatory, behave on the road, at temples and in front of the Buddhist clergy. There were rules of conduct at festivities, ceremonies and funerals; what to observe when selecting Sinhala names; how servants should behave in the household and how children should treat their parents. It is not surprising that, given the symbolic embodiment of women as cultural signifiers, Dharmapala had no less than 30 rules on how women should conduct themselves. Prescriptions on how they should wear saris and dress modestly, keep their households, personal belongings and bodies clean, avoid indolence, avoid combing their hair or picking lice in the presence of others, on the proper form of address for children and servants, and on how to beautify their gardens with flowering plants, etc., formed part of his rules. As Gombrich and Obeysekera note, what Dharmapala was formulating here were new values and modalities of behaviour for an emerging Sinhala elite which drew on bourgeois western notions of propriety.[7] Cleanliness, for instance, was understood by Dharmapala as a coloniser's value that had to be emulated. In his diary he noted, "The Sinhalese people are treated with contempt by the English people on account of their dirty habits. . . The social rules and society etiquette preclude the civilised English from associating with them. We can't blame the English. We have to *rise* to their standard."[8] One sees here an anxious response to the harsh denigration of native culture by the British, which vindicated the nationalists' call for reforms and exerted pressure on them to keep to the received norms of respectability. At times this went to the extent of legitimising very alien manners such as eating with forks and spoons and the use of toilet paper before water during ablutions, which Dharmapala advocated. The *Gihi Vinaya*, then, became a site on which western norms of propriety and the needs of nationalism came together to reinvent traditions for an emerging Sinhala elite. Given that nearly 50,000 copies had been sold by the time of its 19th edition in 1958, it had clearly fashioned a code that was integrated into the fabric of indigenous society as "pure and ideal Buddhist norms".[9]

There were other ingredients that comprised Sri Lankan bourgeois respectability. Education was important. It paved the way for jobs within the colonial government service, opened up professional and political opportunities, placed the native in a good position to make profit from the economic expansionism of imperialism and acquire social status. For women, this education had to be modern, i.e., western-oriented. This is borne out by the fact that even when Buddhist schools for girls were started, many Buddhist elites preferred to send their daughters to Christian missionary schools. Clearly there was value placed on an English education, a knowledge of modern subjects and on qualities of discipline and industry instilled by the missionaries that would make their daughters not only good wives but *assets* to their husbands.[10] In any case, with the shift within missionary education itself in the late 19th century from Christian conversion to a greater emphasis on academic learning,[11] the non-Christian Sri Lankan bourgeoisie had less reason to feel threatened and anxious about their religio-cultural identities being swamped. Their support of the new style missionary school—which developed in response to their demand for a modern education for their children—reflected their aspirations as participants in an emerging modern bourgeoisie.[12]

Caste, class and ethnicity were other important rubrics of respectability. We have already seen how in the plays of John de Silva, the non-Sinhala polity was constructed as *illegitimate* heirs of the nation. Tamils, Muslims, Malays and Burghers had been the target of de Silva's racist vitriol and/or innuendo. In specific references to caste in his plays, it was the values and behaviour of the upper castes that were selected for legitimacy. The "true" sons and daughters of the nation were those who were also patriotic in terms of their *adherence* to Sinhala Buddhist cultural norms which included, for women, modesty, self-sacrifice and a sense of spirituality.

Anil de Silva was outside each of these categories. She embodied conflicting and contradictory subjectivities that simultaneously contained hybridity, dynamism and constraint. She was of mixed parentage, with a Sinhala Buddhist father and Burgher Christian mother and so, outside the "purities" of a race. She was Sinhalese by patrilineal descent and so a daughter of the nation, yet outside its elite due to her paternal family's low-caste origins. Sinhalese, but low caste, she took refuge in her maternal Dutch Burgher ancestry that gave her class status. Yet the Dutch Burgher community was being increasingly marginalised by the process of Sinhala Buddhist nationalism in Sri Lanka. Education and profession were not sites on which Anil sought to iron out these contradictory and ambivalent identities. She did not take her education at Bishop's College, a leading Anglican missionary girls' school, particularly seriously.[13] She did not aspire to a profession as an educationist or medical doctor—although her aunt, Winifred Nell, was Sri Lanka's first woman doctor who qualified in 1899 and went on for postgraduate qualifications to Edinburgh, and her sister, Minette, became a pioneering architect. She refused to conform to prevalent norms of sexual modesty and, in her journalistic writing, flouted the nationalist insistence on curbing criticism of the motherland. In supporting her father's political affiliations, she also challenged certain sections of the nationalist elite, particularly the Goyigama caste and the Kandyan aristocracy who were in anticipation of post-independence political prominence. Consequently, as a woman in the public gaze, a political daughter, a debutante presented at court in 1929 through the sponsorship of Beatrice Webb, an exotic and beautiful woman later photographed by Cartier-Bresson,[14] a woman prominent in the arts (she and her sister Minette took part in the controversial Pageant of Lanka in 1935), Anil Marcia de Silva was a figure who attracted nationalist interest and, when she refused to conform to its paradigms, nationalist derision.

A Life Through the 20th Century

A brief outline of Anil de Silva's life (1909–1996) which spanned almost the entire century, helps trace the trajectory she took and explain why a specific strand of early 20th century Sri Lankan nationalism influenced its course.

Anil had her schooling in elite Anglican missionary schools in Kandy where her parental home was situated, and later, in Colombo.[15] In 1928, at the age of 19, she left for England with her mother and sister, to be joined later by her father. Her parents were active in the campaign for universal franchise in Sri Lanka and both George and Agnes de Silva lobbied various British parliamentarians, and the British Labour Party in particular, for the concession of this right before the Donoughmore Commission visited Sri Lanka in 1931 to deliberate on the issue. On this visit Anil gave a piano recital at Whigmore Hall and was presented at court. Later, she worked as a journalist in England, writing for the *Sunday Express* and *The Queen*, with some of her articles reproduced in *The Times of Ceylon*. (This is how magazines like *Searchlight* and *Comrade* came across her writing.) She was also the first Asian woman to work in Alexander Korda's film studios, in the cutting and editing rooms at Pinewood. She returned to Sri Lanka in 1931 to help her father with his election campaign to the State Council for the Ceylon National Congress, in the first general election held in Sri Lanka under British rule.

Anil de Silva married Robert Nichol-Cadell, a friend of the poet Yeats, and lived in England from 1933–1938. Following the failure of their marriage, Anil travelled to Bangalore, and in 1940 went to Bombay to join her sister Minette, a pioneer in her own right, the first woman student at the School of Architecture there. Anil returned to England in the 1960s to settle down in a cottage in Cambridge where she lived until her death, at the age of 87, in November 1996. While in Bombay Anil became close friends with Mulk Raj Anand, a writer, an important member of the Progressive Writers' Movement, art historian, nationalist, member of the Communist Party of India. Through him she became assistant editor of the first few issues of the journal, *Marg*, devoted to an appraisal of both traditional and modern art and architecture. She was a founder member of the Indian People's Theatre Association (IPTA)—credited by two sources as having initiated its very idea[16]—which became a significant cultural movement in India in the 1940s and '50s. She was close to the Indian Communist Party based in Bombay, and well integrated in the avant-guard milieu there. She is credited with having written a book on women in China, published in 1945, and instrumental in the translation and publication of stories by Ding Ling.[17] She was keenly involved with promoting modern art and was responsible for facilitating, through *Marg* and various art exhibitions, the first appraisals of George Keyt in India.[18] She was also joint-editor with Pupal Jayakar of a children's magazine entitled *Toycart*.

In 1949 Anil left Bombay for Paris. There she married a Frenchman, Philippe Vigier, and followed a course in art history at the Louvre. She was the first Asian student to do so.[19] It is here that her exposure to Asian art, through her work with *Marg* and residence in India, led to an altogether more studied and mature appraisal of the Asian heritage, as she saw the art housed in the museums of Paris, specially the Musée Guimét. Here she saw linkages within the whole of Asia, not just the Indian subcontinent, through its religious, particularly Buddhist, art. This inspired her to produce a book entitled *The Life of the Buddha: Retold from Ancient Sources* (1955) illustrated with 160 works of art from all over Asia.[20] The book comprises a narrative from ancient sources, keeping to their ecclesiastical register of language, of the life of the Buddha; plates of sculpture and paintings from South and South-East Asia; an epilogue which traces the emergence of Buddhism in India, its elevation to a state religion during the reign of Aśoka (273–232 BC) and the factors that influenced the production of Buddhist art. In 1958, at a time when China was a "forbidden land" to the West, Anil travelled there with an all-woman team comprising Romila Thapar as research assistant, Dominique Darbois as photographer, and Mingo Wong, a Chinese woman translator, to research for two books on the cave paintings of Tun-Huang and Maichisan in the Kansu province of China.[21] Travel to China had been undertaken by women before, notably in the 19th century by British and American women like Constance Gordon Cummings, Isabella Bishop, Lucy Atkins, Alicia Helen Little, Julia Corner, Mary Geraldine Taylor. They wrote books on their travels in China while missionary women like Henrietta Shuck, Adele Marion Fielde and Emma Maria Anderson wrote about their missionary work and experiences there.[22]

But Anil's trip to China in 1958 was significant because it continued this line of women's travel to the country *after* the communist revolution which had closed China's borders to the West. Anil and her team also shifted the focus from British imperialism and Christianity in China to its Buddhist heritage. In Tun-Huang they visited 469 caves. Photographs of the caves they entered in Maichisan, climbing its sheer cliff on wooden scaffolds, tell of the team's sense of adventure and determination to fulfil their project. At Maichisan they lived in the spartan monastery. Guards were stationed to protect them from the leopard and bear prowling around at night. Photographing, measuring, annotating each mural proved to be an arduous task. Some of the caves were so low that the team had to crawl into them. Eye strain was an occupational hazard. Anil praises her team for tenacity and commitment to recording China's antiquity and heritage of the

Wei period, both for its own people and those outside, in show-casing Chinese art as part of the world's heritage. Earlier in 1956, this interest in Asia made her host a television show under the BBC series entitled, "Asian Club".

Later she was commissioned by Unesco to edit several books of art history in a series entitled, "Man Through His Art." This series was collected under several themes—"very Anil-like themes" according to archaeologist Seneka Bandaranaike whose first paid job was to help Anil with the series[23]—such as "Love and Marriage", "The Human Face", "War and Peace", "Music", etc. Bandaranaike considers them "Anil-like" because she was a romanticist; this epithet was also assigned her by Robert Knox, a friend who noted her interest in John of Gaunt and Christine de Pisan, on both of whom she wrote books when she was well into her eighties:

Her interest in the European grandees was an old one and based upon her abiding personal interest in Mediaeval history and its great characters. She was drawn to the remarkable and the intellectual in that period, and John of Gaunt and Christine de Pisan filled such a role wonderfully. Christine de Pisan was a great woman intellectual of overwhelming quality and huge strength of character. These issues attracted Anil and along with the idealised romanticism of the aristocratic mediaeval lifestyle she was a superb candidate for the sort of book Anil wanted to write.[24]

Anil was not only attracted to these figures for their courtliness, chivalry, grasp of diplomacy, battle and learning (as was the case with John of Gaunt) but also for their progressive outlook which struck a chord with her own liberal attitudes to life and society. This is borne out by the preface she wrote to her book on John of Gaunt. That John of Gaunt lived and oversaw a significant period of transformation in European society which encompassed "the development of the Commons, the first glimpses of the Reformation, the decline of feudalism and chivalry, the growth of secular learning, the emergence of educated women, and the rise of the vernacular language, with English replacing French and Latin as the language of poetry and learning"[25] is central to Anil's interest in his life and times. That his character held "a deep sense of compassion and care for his people", that he was just and "this great feudal baron (who) had the imagination to put himself in place of those he helped",[26] made his story one in which both personal integrity and progressive social revolution came together. Moreover, Anil saw links between Eastern cultures and those of medieval Europe and the renaissance that were compelling. She stated:

Underlying all this and connected with it was the notion of chivalrous love which was inseparable from poetry and music. Unlike modern western culture, where rigid demarcations are the rule, the inspiration for poetry and music was indivisible from the scheme of the universe; humanity was a part of it, and a part of the earth's creatures. . . We still get this sense of indivisibility in India and the East in general. Another striking similarity between the East and Europe of the Middle Ages was that the same allowance was given to impulse and unrestrained expression of feeling, in contrast to the modern world which is "excessive in its conventions for the repression of emotion".[27]

What Anil marks for us here is the suppression of emotional passion, sexual desire and a holistic approach to life which she saw available in the medieval and renaissance ages. Her own age is tethered to notions of bourgeois respectability that "restrain expression of feeling". We shall see later how Anil became a victim of its rigid standards and an outcaste of her nation, proving too that such constructions of respectability were by no means a modern European monopoly or invention, although its imperial project gave them decisive shape in the colonies.

This chapter, in discussing how and why Anil de Silva became a subject of the nationalist gaze, will pay special attention to her sojourn in Bombay in the 1940s. Although she had spent time in England in her early travels with her parents and during her marriage to Nicol-Cadell, it was in Bombay that she integrated with a milieu that facilitated the development of her interests in art and politics. There she would find close friends, a cosmopolitanness, and an exciting political ferment in the Indian independence struggle that she could relate to. In the reformist agendas of the Indian nationalists she associated with, she would find a dynamic search for modernity—all of which were liberating after the confines of Sri Lanka. Her exposure to the heritage of Indian art in particular would encourage her to lay claim to a pan-Indian identity that gave her a sense of being Asian, even as she rejected the constrictions of a Sri Lankan one. Bombay formed the transition to Europe where Anil came into her own as author and art historian, from where, significantly and contradictorily, she could, through her work in art history, return to her Sri Lankan roots to redefine them as part of a larger, more inclusive Asian heritage.

Making the Nation Respectable

Outcast(e) of the Nation

In the forging of bourgeois respectability the category of caste was an important signifier of legitimacy to the nation's power. By the turn of the century it was the traditionally upper Goyigama caste, and those such as the Karava, Durava and Salagama who had acquired socio-political eminence by taking advantage of the economic expansion under the British.[28] Anil de Silva's father's family which had its origins in the Rada caste, considered low in the caste hierarchy, came from outside this framework. Anil de Silva herself was, by and large, reticent on the subject of her caste nor did she publicly write about the issues surrounding the discrimination her family suffered because of it.[29] This response can be viewed in several ways. It was either too hurtful to confront; or she herself had, to some extent, internalised caste hierarchies and so remained silent on her "undercaste" identity; or by the time she arrived in London, Bombay and Paris, she had left a caste-conscious Sri Lankan society behind and integrated into more cosmopolitan societies where it no longer presented itself as an issue. Any of these reasons could have influenced her silence at one time or another, or indeed operated simultaneously. However, to those Sri Lankans who were close to her and knew her caste background, she would refer sardonically to the caste prejudice of upper class/caste Sri Lankan society.[30] It is also reasonable to assume that the caste bigotry she came across in Sri Lanka did influence her departure from the island, in that it contributed to the constrictions she felt in the land of her birth and from which, according to her sister Minette, she wanted to escape.[31]

Belonging to an undercaste was a fact that dogged Anil's father, George E. de Silva, throughout his life. In the unpublished memoirs he was writing at the time of his death, de Silva mentions being "greatly disturbed by the treatment meted out to his father" by both (upper) caste-minded Sinhalese and the class-minded British because of his caste/class origins.[32] The Rada caste, also known as Hena, was responsible for washing the linen of the upper caste families of the village.[33] It also had important ceremonial functions within the community: providing the linen for rites of puberty, marriage and death, and washing the white cloth used on these occasions. While the caste was of low status, its members enjoyed an ambivalently privileged position in the community for having access to the innermost chambers of upper caste families. Although low on the hierarchical scale, in actual treatment it was considered superior to many other low castes in the community.[34]

The growth of a market-oriented economy in colonial Sri Lanka offered this caste a certain mobility. In extending its services beyond the village to an urban clientele which could pay for laundry services, its members acquired an urban presence, became independent of the contractual obligations of the village, and soon ventured into other professions.[35] It is in keeping with such mobility that both George E. de Silva's father and grandfather came to be in the ayurvedic profession, commanding considerably more respectability than if they had stayed within the profession of their caste at birth. And yet, caste consciousness in Sri Lanka at the turn of the 20th century was such that families which had their origins in the undercastes were never allowed to forget it. This was particularly true in the political arena where Sinhalese nationalists belonging to different castes were jockeying for power and prominence. The traditionally privileged Goyigama caste, but also predominantly the Karava, Durava and Salagama castes, made full use of the new economic opportunities in the plantation, graphite, arrack-renting, export and import sectors that burgeoned with British economic expansion in the country. Consequently, elite members of these castes guarded and buttressed their turf through further economic expansion, expedient marriage alliances and entry through education, often abroad, into the professions of law, medicine and journalism. When it came to representation on legislative councils on the basis of education and wealth, therefore the Sinhalese elite of these castes were well-placed in their bid for power.

In such a scenario there was little room for "upstarts", and George E. de Silva was to bear the brunt of this competition and bigotry throughout his life. But it was not only from the Sinhalese that he received hurtful snubs. On the day of his first case before the Kandy law courts, the entire Kandy bar, dominated by Dutch Burghers, walked out in protest at the entry of a Sinhalese to its hallowed institution.[36] Malapropisms were attributed to him, pin-pointing his lack of a "sound" education in English and his family background. At a social level, conspiracies were afoot to ostracise and embarrass him. Jane Russell notes one such occasion: a dance in Kandy at which it had been planned to have each woman de Silva asked for a dance, refuse him. In his bid for election to the Ceylon National Congress he would repeatedly come up against the glass ceiling of caste, buttressed by the powerful upper caste Kandyan lobby.[37]

It is not surprising, then, that despite an association with the Ceylon National Congress of ten years (1916–1926), George de Silva left it to make alliances with A. E. Goonesinha, leader of the Ceylon Labour Union, which organised a series of successful labour strikes against British capital in the 1920s.[38] Goonesinha also came from a depressed caste. He and George campaigned fervently for universal franchise for Sri Lanka. This was both a campaign towards Sri Lankan sovereignty and a strategy to enlarge the vote bank, a considerable part of which was with their labour union. It is this constituency of Goonesinha's that the nationalist elite felt threatened by; in the *Searchlight*'s vicious attack on Anil quoted at the beginning of this chapter, its phobias about labour politics, denigration of the foreign, and anxieties of caste and sexuality come together.

Let us analyse its discourse: Anil is attacked, first, for consorting with the British. There is reference to a photograph of her with the Beefeater, "by whose hefty corpulence Marcia is supremely happy and deliciously snug". Her dress, described as having "just reached her from her laundress, commonly, perhaps"—a direct reference to her caste—is critiqued for its flimsiness ("perhaps this night was only a mild wintry night as far as

Marcia's English adventures are concerned".) Her inferred alliance with the foreigner is presented in the most xenophobic way, implying that she might advocate "the principle of Fusion of races, and herself deliver(s) an object lesson, by precept and example" in her next article. Continuing with metaphors of sexuality, lust and miscegenation, Anil is also made the very embodiment of her father's and Goonesinha's ties with the British. Both men were in England in 1928 to lobby British parliamentarians on the demand for universal franchise in Sri Lanka. Their actions are made to reflect her own denigration. "She, and her father, will then understand," intones the *Searchlight*, "that Ceylon is no place now for those who *prostitute* its noble ambitions for a rightful place in the great commonwealth of Nations for the Company of English beef-eaters and 'mutton-shop' grinders" (my emphasis). Given her behaviour, unacceptable in a respectable Sri Lankan woman, the *Searchlight* calls upon the nation to chastise her, because, "In these hard times, where all true and *well-born* in India and Ceylon are straining at the leash of liberty, Marcia de Silva is selling it through English mediums" (my emphasis).

It is clear from this tirade that the emerging nation required its women to be chastely accoutered conveyers of a normative bourgeois respectability, guardians of its culture and, in the light of the anti-colonial struggle, resist consorting with the colonising enemy. A populist nationalist agenda is clear. From this it can also be inferred that the *Searchlight*'s ideology is entrenched in the rhetoric of Anagarika Dharmapala and the Sinhala Buddhist nationalism associated with him that had gained ground by the early decades of the 20th century. It echoed the same anti-British rhetoric. In punning on the character of the Beefeater as a "beef-eater" it took its reference from Dharmapala's *Gihi Vinaya*, the rules of conduct, one of which was avoid eating beef. This was in keeping with the discipline of renunciation that Dharmapala advocated for the Sinhalese. He had in fact travelled around in a truck propounding the slogan, "Eat beef and become an outcaste."[39] The *Searchlight* differentiates the English "beefeater" from the indigenous, on the grounds of culture, religion and norms of civilisation it now assigns exclusively to Buddhist values. Of course it was not only the English who were denounced in this way. Sri Lanka's minority Tamils, Muslims, Parsis and Bohras were also the target of vicious attack.[40] Sinhala Buddhists were the chosen ones, picked out and given legitimacy in the land and nation. It followed then, that any Sinhalese who consorted with the "other" was inevitably accused of betraying Buddhist ethics and the ideals of the nation. To enact this betrayal through sexuality, as the *Searchlight* accuses Anil of doing, was to shame both Buddhist values and Sri Lankan womanhood. To be outside a respectable caste as she and her father were, was to have no place in negotiating or speaking on behalf of the emergent sovereign Sri Lankan nation.

The Command to Patriotism

The gleeful noting in the *Comrade* article of Anil's so-called retraction on the seclusion and cultural boundedness of Sri Lankan women, points to yet another rubric underpinning the formulation of respectability within Sri Lankan nationalism. The emerging nation should not be the subject of criticism, because this would jeopardise the nationalist call for sovereignty and undermine its strenuous reconstruction of a cultural and historical consciousness that Sri Lankans could rally to. It was not that the nationalists themselves did not possess a particular critical consciousness of their society; indeed the native reform movements in both India and Sri Lanka were launched as critiques of existing practices that were considered primitive and uncivilised in western liberal thought. In India, its English-educated nationalist elite campaigned to free its own culture from superstition, widow prejudice, casteism, illiteracy and practices such as sati. In Sri Lanka, Anagarika Dharmapala himself had been severely critical of peasant habits and the superstitions of the Sinhalese.[41] But to publish such critiques in British newspapers, as Anil de Silva had done, was the ultimate "toadyism", prostituting oneself for the benefit of the enemy. This was a struggle then about control over who gets to tell this particular story, and when and where.

And yet, Anil de Silva's "retraction" is also a site of her participation in the very nationalist discourse that vilified her. Here

is what she has to say about the difference between the eastern
and western woman:

I write this, feeling I am in a rather strange position. For you will agree
that an Eastern girl with a curiously Western outlook does not really belong either to the East or the West. Perhaps the fact enables me to look
through eyes that can see both sides with a detached, unprejudiced view.
Anyway, I find many things in the East and many things in the West that
surprise me. The Eastern woman's infinite capacity for devotion and self-
sacrifice does much more than surprise. It makes me feel rather humble.
With, at the same time, an inclination to pity, filled with admiration. Her
utter subjection of self and her whole-hearted concentration on her husband and children, cannot be gauged by standards that, if you will forgive
me, have become rather materialistic and perhaps a trifle unidealistic.
Perhaps some people would say. "How terribly monotonous—How dull
and uninteresting!" But is it? Is it such a very much more uninteresting life
to lead than that of those people who spend their life running about from
one night-club to another; which are eternally the same—or typing every
day in the same stuffy office? Monotony is the same whatever the cause—
and I must admit that your Eastern sister is far happier. . . .

Perhaps the strong sense of duty and honour is partly due to an Eastern
girl's upbringing. This, while being restricting, and almost deadening, in
some ways, has a great deal to say for itself.

                    Times of Ceylon, 4 September, 1932.

Granted the defensiveness of her tone when criticising the
western woman—the "if you will forgive me" to her English
reader—Anil de Silva's comments on the eastern woman in no
way reflect her unqualified support for the way she is gendered
in society, rather, a deep ambivalence. Even as she admires the
qualities of her eastern sisters, their devotion to family life, stead-
fastness and self-effacement, she admits to feelings of pity for
their boundedness. The lead quote when Anil's article was re-
printed in the *Times of Ceylon*, presumably by its editor, "Why
Western Life is Monotonous" erases this ambivalence; it con-
notes another nationalist agenda at work which seeks to trash
the West while implying the superiority of the East. It is clear
that Anil wishes to stand outside this enterprise by reiterating
her unbiased stand, that she belongs neither to the East nor the
West, although this itself causes her a certain anxiety that most
elite colonial subjects admit to.

Where she shares complicity with the nationalist project of

the *Times of Ceylon* is in her essentialist polarisation of East and West. Common in elite nationalist discourse was a manichean opposition between East and West to both reiterate essential cultural difference and foreground, as a controlling modality, the antagonism of one system towards the other. A favourite trope in this construct was the materialistic West opposed to the spiritual East; in the terminology of Négritude, it would be the mechanistic West opposed to the intuition, rhythm and spontaneity of Black culture. Anil de Silva recoups these stereotypes. Her critique of the western woman is that she lives in a society that is too materialistic and monotonous. In her generalisation of the western woman running from one nightclub to another is the denigrating of the latter as superficial, drunk, and alienated from family life and values. In her other journalistic writing, too, Anil chooses to foreground a particular type of high society—men and women who frequent the opera, the races, playhouses and bohemian pubs—that becomes a metonymy for the West and reflects her *own* privileged class and cultural orientation; this is never sufficiently problematised by her.[42] She participates then in an essentialist differentiation, embodied in the women, between East and West that posits the East as more spiritual, steadfast and caring than the materialistic West. In doing so, she adheres to the nationalist command to patriotism. This, as Partha Chatterjee has argued, is in keeping with the nationalist resolution of the "women's question" which, on the one hand, encouraged women through education and involvement in social service to break out of the confines of the home, but on the other, *culturally* circumscribed them ensuring their acceptance of their true role as nurturing wives and mothers *within* the home. It is this domestic/spiritual orientation that ultimately marked their superiority over western women.[43]

An Unbecoming Daughter[44]

Where Anil de Silva did flout the rules of middle class respectability and insist on a different ethic for herself, was in her attitude to sexuality. George Mosse notes how nationalism, and the society identified with it, used the example of the chaste and modest woman to demonstrate its own virtuous aims.[45] The religious revivals of Europe constructed virtue as a de-eroticised and chaste code of conduct. August Hermann Francke, a founder of German Pietism warned students in 1722, to avoid indecent posture, gestures and unnecessary laughter. Profane entertainment and personal ornamentation were condemned. In England, evangelism had preached a deep sense of sacredness in all things. Sins were to be atoned for through a single-minded concentration on one's vocation in life. Sexual relations between men and women were stripped of sensuousness, and marriage and the family were based on the ethics and practice of piety.[46]

As much as these strictures were reinforced from pulpits and in the classrooms, the iconography of Europe, particularly during the French revolution, exhibits significant tension between these dictates and the sensuous sexuality of figures representing the Revolution and the Third Estate. Needing to fill the vacuum at the centre of their national iconography, hitherto held by the now despised and deposed monarchy, the Jacobins turned to the female allegorical form. The figure of Liberty became a popular symbol. But from its depiction in Delacroix's painting in the 1830s as a feisty revolutionary leading the people, as time progressed she became abstract and sovereign, emptied of real individuality. Liberty was depicted standing or seated in an imposing posture, sedate and composed, symbolically pointing to the action that leads to liberty rather than herself being engaged in it.[47] However, as Liberty was always conceived as the *reward* for struggle, she is directly depicted in "relation to her male possessor who desires, acquires, cherishes and protects her".[48] This makes her the subject of an erotic gaze with her exposed or flimsily covered body, thighs and rounded breasts, invoking too the nursing mother of the nuclear family and the nation. It is an iconography in which, as Mosse notes, family ideal and public symbol reinforce each other.[49] It is also at the same time, decidedly erotic.

The values of chastity, modesty and accompanying rules of etiquette were handed down in the colonies by mission schools, but in the Sri Lankan context, as Michael Roberts has shown, a de-eroticised personhood, applying equally to both men and women, was also constructed in the name of Buddhism. The diary of Anagarika Dharmapala is a site of such formulation.

Imbibing central tenets of Buddhism such as self-denial and purity, Anagarika Dharmapala had personally striven towards sexual abstinence. As his diary entries indicate, he often struggled with himself to banish all thoughts of sex. One particular entry which Roberts has cited is telling: "Last night (my) mind was disturbed by polluting sensual thoughts. When will this filthy body become emancipated from low desires? There is no possibility of my ever taking the sensual life. Nevertheless disturbing tendencies at times overpower the higher nature." (14 June, 1907)[50] Chastity and sexual self-denial were linked to the attainment of intellectual and spiritual purity, and even as he struggled with his own masturbatory instincts, Dharmapala pointed an accusing finger at women "as sources of temptation leading to the downfall of male renunciants". He advocated avoiding "woman's touch as one avoids burning coal" (25 August, 1904; 20 November,1907) and wished that "all women appear to him either as mother, sister or daughter". (8 May, 1896; 15 January & 23 April, 1907; 25 July, 1908)[51] We see here a tremendous anxiety and fear of women's sexuality as having the potential to lead men astray from the path to purity and "Bosathood". Within this paradigm of respectability and religious attainment then, just as men had to curb their lust, women, too, had to be de-sexualised in order to make themselves safe for men.

Anil de Silva refused to be such a de-sexualised figure. She always dressed exotically with a view to stressing the sensuous and feminised in her personality. Uzra Bhatt, an actress with IPTA, noted how Anil always wore georgette saris in exquisite colours.[52] Quite often she would also wear a flower in her hair.[53] Her beauty and personality were always remarked upon. Raj Thapar described her as "rather remarkable and attractive".[54] In a letter of sympathy written to Anil's sister Minette, following her death, June Somasundaram said:

I feel so privileged to have known Anil, who was a most remarkable and accomplished woman, far ahead of her time in many ways.

I remember your mother telling me, while I was still a young girl at school, that Anil was (then) a newspaper correspondent in England and was known as Sunshine Sue. I realised, when I did eventually meet her and get to know her some forty years later, how fitting a name for her this was.

Anil was photographed by Henri Cartier-Bresson, who like June Somasundaram wrote of Anil as "an exceptional person who will always be in our hearts";[55] and sketched by the eminent Indian nuclear physicist, Homi Bhaba, with whom she had a close friendship at one time, as she did with Pablo Neruda. In Bombay she was quite a society figure who lived openly with Mulk Raj Anand although not married to him and, in Romila Thapar's words, had a "very open attitude towards sexuality which was a departure from the norm, although she was by no means a sex-kitten or a woman who slept around for its own sake".[56] Why, then, did Anil de Silva's sexuality become such a cause of speculation and concern for both right and left-wing sympathisers in Sri Lanka and Bombay?

We have seen how, a dominant strand of nationalist thought in Sri Lanka shored itself up by recourse to a rhetoric of racial and cultural purity, that made hybridity and inter-racial mixing taboo. For "mixing", as Ann Stoler writes in the context of European nationalism's engagement with the colonies, "called into question the very criteria by which Europeanness could be identified, citizenship could be accorded and nationality assigned".[57] Imperialism also produced an anthropological obsession about recording types, which became the criteria for exclusion and inclusion. These same criteria operated in nationalist thought in Sri Lanka. In the name of a "pure" Sinhala race and Buddhist culture, for instance, those outside their paradigms were considered less than legitimate heirs of the emergent nation. Anil's Dutch Burgher ancestry, her presence in the colonial metropolis of London, her writing for newspapers and magazines there, her marriage to a British citizen and her absence from Sri Lanka were all factors that contributed to her exclusion from this nationalist call. The fact that she was often the locus of opposition to her father's politics in magazines such as *Searchlight* and *Comrade,* or a newspaper like the *Times of Ceylon,* indicate both a shifting of the blame onto the woman and a sexist pillorying and chastising for consorting with the foreigner. That engagement as seen in the "beefeater" passage from the *Searchlight,* was cast in emphatically sexual terms.

In India there was another set of factors that influenced how people regarded Anil's sexuality. Mulk Raj Anand was a member of the Indian Communist Party in Bombay which, in the 1940s —the war years—was an underground party, hounded by the British colonial government for its anti-imperialist stance. Its members and their associates were regularly spied upon by the secret police. Theatre performances of the Indian People's Theatre Association (IPTA), affiliated to the Communist Party, were banned by the British, including by the interim government of which Nehru was vice president.[58] This persecution was used by the Communist Party to delineate strict rules about security, which included being selective about partners. Anil was, after all, an outsider, and considered a potential security risk. The gossip about her and the Party hierarchy was deemed damaging both to its security and morale.

Related to the issue of security was, as Romila Thapar sees it, "the strong streak of puritanism that attends all revolutionary parties".[59] The debate within the CPI was on whether a revolution could be attained without strong controls on sexual desire. What we see here is the absolute impregnation of bourgeois standards of respectability into socialist thought. The debate on the boundaries of sexuality has had a long history within the socialist movement. Scholars have pointed out that Marx himself did not radically examine the issue of sexuality when he dealt with the "women's question", the structure of the family or the issue of prostitution, and that both he and Engels examined the subordination of women within capital, *not* patriarchy, and that too from a contemporary Victorian standpoint.[60] Although pathbreaking in their apprehension of the emergence of the family as historically determined and fixed to the perpetuation of property, they foreclosed the possibility of engaging with the issues surrounding women's oppression in any progressive way by concentrating on the division of labour both within the family and in sexual reproduction. Equally important, was their Victorian attitude in their inability to radically re-frame the domestic space. For Engels, the Victorian family structure remained sacrosanct. He was shocked at what he saw as the dissolution of the family and the "complete reversal of normal social relationships" when women took on the role of breadwinners.[61] For Marx, prostitution was only "a *specific* expression of the *general* prostitution of the labourer" by capital; he believed that when the system of bourgeois capital was done away with, its evils would resolve automatically.[62]

The legacy of this conservatism translated itself into socialist state policy in the era of Stalin, although there were continued attempts to break out of its boundaries. For instance, the Soviet Union had experimented with new attitudes towards sexuality from 1917 onwards. Divorce was liberalised, public displays of nudity were no longer prosecuted, and equality between the sexes encouraged. Elsewhere, there were figures like Felix Halle of the German communist party who wrote *Sexual Life and Criminal Law* (1931) basing his arguments on earlier experiments in sexual liberation; Richard Linsert who advocated a development of individual sexuality unfettered to bourgeois marriage; Max Hodann who wrote for a popular audience, calling for an end to the sexual repression of adolescents. Contrary to the medical opinion of his time Hodann saw nothing wrong in masturbation and argued that it was neither a crime nor a vice. But these remained individual and isolated attempts at drawing up a new kind of sexual ethic within the socialist movement. With the triumph of Stalin, a return to conventional respectability was signalled and the link between socialist and middle-class morality was implicitly accepted by all communist parties.[63]

The Communist Party of India was no different. It witnessed a similar debate between proponents who wished to control and silence sexual desire and those who opposed its restrictions. Although the reality was that love affairs were going on all around them, the official version of party discipline reflected, in Romila Thapar's words, "a straightlaced puritanism as compared to other political parties which were not so secret and closed and were more relaxed about sexuality".[64] The fate of the Telugu writer, Chalam (1894–1979), a member of the communist party of Andhra Pradesh is a case in point, and foregrounds the terrain of the debate. Writing during a period which spanned the 1920s to 1940s, Chalam accorded centrality in his work to "female subjectivity and sexuality. . . (as) part of not just a debate on morality but on women's need for freedom from oppression (especially within marriage) and for the formation of an identity with its long history of self-denial, sacrifice and surrender of personal desires and needs".[65] The communist party, while supporting Chalam's denunciation of middle-class hypocrisy, fell short of accepting the argument that a woman has a right to her own body and sexual pleasure. For the Left, agendas of women's emancipation within male-female relationships were a matter of individual choice, not party policy.[66] Chalam refused to be silenced, however, and his own open sexuality and advocacy of free love, positions deemed threatening and dangerous, resulted in his expulsion from the communist party. From a contemporary point of view, it is possible to see Chalam operating entirely within heterosexual desire and therefore silent on the issue of women's choice of other women as sexual partners. But his views on the necessity to free women from sexual self-denial and his own transgressive sexuality were radical enough for him to be ostracised by his family in a manner that prevented him from acquiring suitable rented accommodation in "respectable" localities. It was only in the Dalit neighbourhoods that he finally found refuge.[67]

It is this same outraged sense of respectability that permeates the writing on Anil within the Indian Communist Party and its sympathisers. In Raj Thapar's *All These Years: A Memoir*, Anil's openness to sexuality is described in the following terms:

(Anil) kept me entertained with tales of sex, beginning with her experience in the Communist Party – the Indian one. She had applied for membership formally and, as was the rule then, she had to be on probation for three months. So, emancipated as she was, she moved into the commune which was overflowing with an assortment of all manner of males, all dedicated to the cause of the working class and all starved of women. In between intense discussions on the nature of the class structure, they would suddenly find themselves staring into Anil's rather gu-gu eyes. This obviously panicked them, threw them off guard. 'They looked so sorry for themselves, they had nothing else except their work, so what could I possibly do?' It was all in the plural and I could just about picture the kind of havoc she must have wrought in PHQ with her mere presence. The plurality finally zeroed in on Dange, the leader with the greatest personal charm, but his influence couldn't guarantee her membership and she had to finally leave. Mulk pulled her away from Dange but the two men bore each other a grudge for the rest of their lives.

All These Years, pp.58–9.

It is clear from this passage that it is Anil who is accused of causing "havoc" with party discipline. The responsibility for the breakdown of respectability is placed firmly on her shoulders while the men are excused on the grounds of the lack of availability of women. Anil is the vamp, and depicted as being self-consciously so. It is significant that in the entire memoir, Raj Thapar's description of Anil remains framed within the "trangressive" ethics of her sexual conduct. No other character in the memoir is foregrounded in this way. What is evident, as Thapar herself concedes are the author's own "prudish ways" which become the yardstick for middle class respectability. Accordingly, Anil's conduct in India is deemed to be outside its acceptable parameters.

A similar portrayal of Anil is found in Sudhi Pradhan's compilation of documents of the Marxist cultural movement in India.[6] In his introduction Pradhan describes the various figures behind IPTA and the Progressive Writers' Movement but chooses to introduce Anil mainly in terms of her sexual exploits and, that too, at second-hand. Quoting Hiren Mukherjee's book *Tori Hote Tir* (From the Boat onto the Shore), Pradhan reinforces the image of Anil as sexual vamp:

She was quite uninhibited when she narrated to me various intimate episodes of her life. One day she showed me a number of pencil portraits done by a famous scientist with whom she had continued an affair for a period and whom she found inadequate in the physical demands of the role. She had averred out of jest, that had she not liked my wife, whom she met in Calcutta, she might not have spared me as well. As if my opinion in the matter was of little consequence, and it all depend (sic) on how she wished things to happen. I have earlier mentioned the jesting remark of P.C.Joshi, that had it been anybody other than me, Anil's hospitality might have induced the Party to expel the recipient. (*Documents*, p.xxii)

Does this passage celebrate Anil's open sexuality by marking instead, the hypocritical conservatism of P.C.Joshi and his insistence on party discipline? If so, it is vitiated by Pradhan's later comment: "Happily I had no such experience with Anil" which announces his own need to be seen as distanced from her (im)morality. What is important to my argument however is that in Sudhi Pradhan's chronicles, too, Anil's subjectivity is *primarily* foregrounded in terms of a dangerous sexual desire that was discussed as threatening party discipline. No other figure of the CPI or IPTA was discussed in the *Documents* in this way. Anil's central role in IPTA as general secretary from 1942–1946 has to be placed side by side with her sexuality. Even Susie Tharu and K. Lalitha acknowledging Anil in a footnote as a leading ideo-logue and organiser of the Marxist cultural movement in India, mark her sexuality. This is what they write:

Anil D'Silva (sic) was one of the principal ideologues and organizers of the movement in its initial stages. In 1945 she wrote a book on women in China and was instrumental in the translation and publication of a collec-tion of stories by Ding Ling. In 1946 she was removed from the post of secretary of the IPTA, apparently on charges of sexual misconduct. A brief sketch of this spirited woman who was considered a problem by a predominantly male leadership is presented in Sudhi Pradhan, ed., *The Marxist Cultural Movement in India. . . .*"[69]

In the adoption of bourgeois respectability and the implemen-tation of its rules and regulations, then, there was no difference between the right-wing as in *Searchlight*, *Comrade* and the *Times of Ceylon,* and the left-wing as found in the CPI. Equally note-worthy is the fact that while Anil was flamboyant in her feminin-ity, nowhere in her writing did she use the issue of her sexuality to radically critique these notions of bourgeois morality or to transform it into a feminist politics.

Irreverent Citizens: Being Burgher in the 1920s

Another factor that contributed to Anil's exclusion from the "le-gitimate" nation was her Burgher ancestry. Her mother belonged to a renowned Dutch Burgher family in Kandy. From the time of 16th century Portuguese imperialism in Sri Lanka, the term "Burgher" has had many connotations including pejorative ones.[70] Its currency today has its roots in the Dutch settlements on the island in the 17th century, and afterwards in British colonialism—particularly its cultural colonialism—which transformed the island's bourgeoisie. The Dutch, more so than the Portuguese who married local women, brought their families out with them, or sent to Holland for prospective wives. The descendants of these families are today called Dutch Burghers. By the time the British arrived on the island, they were well placed to take ad-vantage of the new opportunities provided by British rule. To

begin with, as people of European ancestry, they were less subjected to the racial arrogance and prejudice of the British, although those Burghers of "mixed" ancestry were looked down
upon in keeping with the hierarchies of such prejudice. They had
already availed themselves of the educational opportunities facilitated by Dutch missionaries, were Christian, concentrated in
the urban areas and, as Dutch speakers, able to grasp the English
language more easily. These factors helped them access jobs as
clerks and middle-order bureaucrats in the British colonial ma-
chinery and agency houses.[71] Thereafter, as successive generations of Burghers became educated in British missionary schools,
they adopted an increasingly westernised outlook, entered the
medical and legal professions, became journalists and university
dons and created for themselves an elite milieu within the Sri
Lankan middle-class. Agnes Nell's family typified such professional achievement. Her father, Paul Nell, was a leading lawyer
in Kandy, her grandfather, Louis Nell, had been Deputy Queen's
Advocate—a post which later became that of Solicitor General—
and amongst her uncles were supreme court judge, Charles
Ambroze Lorenz, attorney general, Sir Richard Morgan and the
renowned eye surgeon, Andreas Nell.[72] Her aunt Winifred Nell,
as already noted, was the first woman medical doctor in Sri
Lanka.

Burghers played an important role within the local bourgeoisie which emerged in the mid 19th century to challenge British
rule. This bourgeoisie was a heterogenous and multi-valent group.
Recent work by Kumari Jayawardena shows the ways and means
by which this bourgeoisie emerged, unifying across ethnic, caste
and religious divides in a drive towards capital accumulation under
colonialism.[73] Of course, older and important caste and ethnic
identities did not disappear altogether with the new class formation. In fact, at times of socio-political crisis they came to the
fore to create disunity and dissension among the nationalists.
What Sri Lanka witnessed was specific to a colonial situation in
which capitalism was inserted into an older feudal system, with
both adjusting to new compatibilities in the interest of new capital. Nevertheless, grouped together for the first time under a common goal of capitalist accumulation, were Sinhalese of various

castes, Eurasians and Burghers of Dutch descent, Ceylon Moors who were descendants of Arab and South Indian Muslim traders, Tamils, and the Nattukottai Chettiars from Chettinad (South India), who had traded in Sri Lanka even before the advent of the Dutch in the island in 1656.

This class was essentially cosmopolitan in taste. As its members became educated in western thought and entered the professions available to them under colonial rule—as lawyers, academics, medical doctors, journalists and bureaucrats in public service, or business entrepreneurs or planters—many of them fitted into the colonial system as adjuncts of the British. Those who were loyal to the colonial government were rewarded with Mudaliyarships and land.[74] But a liberal nationalist sentiment also took hold from the mid 19th century onwards, most notably amongst the educated Burghers, which called for greater political autonomy for the people of Sri Lanka. The Burghers were amongst the first groups in Sri Lanka to come into contact with western liberal thought. Their community produced notable figures like Dr. James Loos, the first principal of the Ceylon Medical College, who advocated the entry of women into the medical profession as doctors, apothecaries and nurses,[75] and Charles Lorenz, a barrister and member of the Legislative Council from 1856 to 1868, who led a walkout of unofficial members from the Council in 1864, protesting the imposition of the colonial government's entire military bill on the people of Sri Lanka. Through publications like *Young Ceylon* (the first literary periodical to be produced entirely by a Sri Lankan) which Lorenz began in 1850 and *The Examiner*, a newspaper he edited with Anil de Silva's grand-uncles, Frederick and Louis Nell in 1859, Lorenz was at the forefront of shaping liberal nationalist thought.[76] These men supported girls' education in Sri Lanka (it is no coincidence that Sri Lanka's early women doctors, writers, students and teachers at missionary schools came from the Burgher and Eurasian communities) and espoused a secular, cosmopolitan outlook. Anil's mother inherited this liberal outlook and campaigned for universal franchise, girls' education and female healthcare. Her daughter, Anil, would live by the same tenets.

Of significance is the choice these Burghers made to situate themselves firmly within the Sri Lankan nation, no longer hankering for an European home, despite their westernisation and European blood; a spirited defence against British racism which assigned them pejoratives and denigrated the native Sinhalese, Tamils and Muslims; a converse appeal, informed by Christian sentiment and Enlightenment thought, for egalitarianism that dispensed with racist categories; a demand that Sri Lankans modernise and unite against divisions of ethnicity and caste to challenge British imperialism—the last informed, too, by the Burghers' need to integrate with a Sinhala-Tamil polity. Accordingly, the term "Ceylonese" became the appellative they used to describe the national polity incorporating diverse ethnic communities, and they called for the incorporation of more Sri Lankans into the Ceylon Civil Service in the late 19th and early 20th centuries.[77] But by no means were all Burghers united in these goals. For the poorer Burghers of Portuguese and Dutch-native descent, pejoratively called *thuppahi*, who worked as clerks, typists and railway hands, political, social and literary stardom were beyond their grasp. They were denigrated by elite Burghers themselves, and in the elite historiography of the Burgher contribution to the nation, they have no place.[78] The eclectic, cosmopolitan outlook of the Lorenzes and Nells differentiated them too from the exclusionary racism of other Burghers whose prejudice against the Sinhalese and Tamils was overt.[79] It also stood aside from the nationalism of those like Anagarika Dharmapala and John de Silva for whom the only legitimate heirs to the nation were the Sinhalese. It is not surprising then that, given Anil's early exposure to casteism and racism in the ethno-nationalism gathering momentum in Sri Lanka, it was her half-Burgher identity that provided her the most expansive spaces from which she could express herself as a "new" woman of her generation.

In as much as his caste was a handicap, the discrimination George E. de Silva suffered spurred him to "be as good as anyone of them", to acquire the social graces of colonial society, to dance, dress well, sing and play golf. It was Dr. Woutersz, a Burgher who lived in Nuwara Eliya, and his Scottish wife who provided

George the schooling in these social skills. In marrying Agnes Nell, George entered a social circle that set store by these accomplishments. At times, the combination of privilege and conspicuous consumption made some prominent Burgher families preordain their own destruction. Michael Ondaatje writes of this in his autobiographical novel, *Running in the Family*. Here is a scene of elite Burgher life far removed from the preoccupations of ordinary citizens, as enacted on the estate of one of the Ondaatjes' close friends, Francis de Saram:

People's memories about Gasanawa, even today, are mythic. "There was a lovely flat rock in front of the bungalow where we danced to imported songs such as 'Moonlight Bay' and 'A Fine Romance'." "A Fine Romance" was always my mother's favourite song. . . .

But for the most part it was the tango that was perfected on the rock at Gasanawa. Casually dressed couples, coated in a thin film of sweat, swirled under the moon to "Rio Rita" by John Bowles on the gramophone, wound up time and again by the drunk Francis. . . .

The parties lasted until the end of the twenties when Francis lost his job over too splendid a road. He was lost to them all by 1935. . .

The waste of youth. Burned purposeless.

Running in the Family, pp.46–7.

Ondaatje writes of the affairs, dances, drinking bouts and swagger of his family and its circle of friends. In doing so he chooses to foreground a milieu that quite blatantly flouted the rules of respectability. He was of course attempting to capture and create a particular ambience according to the narrative demands of his memoir. Although Anil was a classmate of Ondaatje's mother, Doris, and belonged to the same milieu, the de Silva family's engagement with society was of a far different nature. That engagement was deeply affected by the family's political beliefs—its involvement with the labour movement, the welfare of the undercastes, and Tamil estate workers. However, this was also a politics that, at another level, was deeply influenced by some of the tenets that elite Burghers, even as depicted in *Running in the Family*, lived by.

The most significant of these was a cosmopolitanness that was inclusive of different communities and, in its refusal to fall in line with colonial rhetoric, resisted harping on the purities of race. Although westernised, the Burghers were a separate social circle from the governing British. Within the boundaries of their class, therefore, they mixed with the English educated Sinhalese, Tamils and Muslims.

This was Nuwara Eliya in the twenties and thirties. Everyone was vaguely related and had Sinhalese, Tamil, Dutch, British and Burgher blood in them going back many generations. There was a large social gap between this circle and the Europeans and English who were never part of the Ceylonese community. The English were seen as transients, snobs and racists, and were quite separate from those who had intermarried and who lived here permanently. My father always claimed to be a Ceylon Tamil, though that was probably more valid about three centuries earlier. Emil Daniels summed up the situation for most of them when he was asked by one of the British governors what his nationality was—"God alone knows, Your Excellency."

Running in the Family, p.41.

It was this cosmopolitan, liberal and democratic spirit that Anil was influenced by, that drove George E. de Silva to campaign for a proposal such as the Mahendran Pact, and made Agnes speak eloquently for Indian estate Tamil women in her campaign for women's franchise. The Mahendran Pact was an accord between the Sinhalese and Tamils on seat distribution in the elected State Council, and the only successful agreement then between the two communities on political representation, a hotly contested issue between its leaders for 27 years.[80] George E. de Silva was a signatory to the accord and campaigned strenuously in 1925 for its adoption by the Ceylon National Congress. Jane Russell notes that one of his finest speeches was made on this issue. He stated:

Surely, it is clear that the temporary advantage which a few members of one community might gain over members of other communities is a mirage; a mere trifle which cannot count when considering larger national interests. What should it matter to vast masses of the Ceylonese people if a few Tamils should gain some slight advantage in terms of seats over the Sinhalese or if a few Muslims should gain some slight advantage over the Tamils? Let us forget this. Instead, let us ponder on the ennobling ideal of true patriotism where Christians, Muslims, Hindus and Buddhists stand shoulder to shoulder as brothers and work for the common good of all. No stable future can be built for our country on the foundation of racial hatred.

Our George, p.48.

Six years later, George E. de Silva would argue from a different position at the Donoughmore Commission hearings. "It will be destroying the essence of our common life by one stroke," he told the commissioners, "and I appeal to you not to introduce communal electorates in any shape or form. We are perfectly happy as we are and we are happy to make common cause with one another, Buddhist, Hindus, Christians and Muslims." Taking his municipal electorate as an example, George told the commissioners, "We have no communal seats; every seat is elected. You will find that elected members have not done anything to jeopardise the interests of the minorities; they have not created any ill-will amongst the various communities in the Municipal Council."[81] These statements appear contradictory given George's endorsement of the Mahendran Pact which solicited legislative seats on a communal basis. His commitment to that Pact indicated his acknowledgement that dialogue with Tamils and Muslims on their rights was important, that they did feel threatened by Sinhala dominance, and that affirmative action in terms of reserved seats was necessary to ease tensions and build a stable future for the nation. De Silva's stand at the Donoughmore Commission reflects then, a recapitulation of the Mahendran principles. Given that the conservatives in the Ceylon National Congress, of which George was President, were deeply opposed to the Donoughmore proposals and had boycotted the 1930 CNC sessions, it is clear that he had a hard balancing act to follow. His plea for non-communal representation could reflect, then, his need to placate this conservative lobby. On the other hand, his stance was within his consistent and deep *humanist* emphasis on compromise and tolerance, that was not pegged to ethnicity, religion and caste. Arguing for the Mahendran Pact he had said:

The basis of our nation must be formed from brother love and justice: a justice that will ungrudgingly recognise all claims that history has brought into existence, and a brother-love which knows no barriers of race and religion and embraces even those who dare to be adversaries from time to time.

Our George, p.48.

That in the first elections to the State Council under the Donoughmore reforms held in 1931, George was overwhelmingly voted in by the Indian Tamil estate workers as reward for his struggle in getting *them* the vote, proved his point.[82]

These were ideals shared by Agnes de Silva as well. Giving evidence before the Donoughmore Commission on the vote for women, she was asked if Indian Tamil women labourers on the estates should have the vote too. Her reply was, "Certainly, they are women, too. We want all women to have the vote." The Donoughmore recommendations went far beyond expectations. In 1931, every woman over 21, irrespective of literacy or property qualifications, was given the right to vote. As Jane Russell notes, this gave Sri Lankan women a headstart over their Indian sisters for, having won the battle for franchise, educated Sri Lankan women were able to enter public campaigns and parliament. In 1932 Lady Adeleine Mollamure entered the senate as the first Sri Lankan woman in the legislature, marking "an historical first in the annals of the British commonwealth".[83]

The radical stand of the de Silvas towards Sri Lanka's minority communities and estate labour of Indian origin, as well as their confrontation of caste and gender discrimination—in a speech to the Jaffna Youth Congress, George E. de Silva solicited the opening of Hindu and Buddhist temples to all castes, the abolition of dowry and education for women[84]—connoted a progressive liberalism that could not have failed to touch their daughter. She had returned to Sri Lanka from England to campaign for her father in the 1931 elections, and these would have been the principles she herself stood by. Of significance is the fact that their election platform signalled the existence of other, more inclusive and liberal strands of nationalist thought that went against the grain of the Sinhala Buddhist ethno-nationalism propagated by Anagarika Dharmapala and John de Silva. Anil's own ambivalence towards her Sinhala-Burgher ethnic identities would prove what a fierce site of contestation ethnic, class and caste identities had become in the nationalist debate. At a time of nationalist resurgence, with a father at the forefront of some of its campaigns and institutions, Anil took pains to stress her "Sinhala" roots.[85] Yet that "Sinhalaness" was also indelibly etched by a caste hierarchy that precluded her from its upper circles. Claiming her Burgher connections on the other hand would assure her of class prestige but marginalise her from the nationalist call. It was this call of Dharmapala's brand of nationalism that had gained ascendance in Sri Lanka by the late 1930s and '40s. Anil had to negotiate with its tenets of respectability and notions of caste and sexuality. She would comply with some of them through an admiring appraisal of the heritage of Buddhist art, but before that she felt compelled to go into exile.

The Passage to India

Anil de Silva's passage to India was determined by many factors that, in and of themselves, reflect the political energies and social ambience her parents had created for themselves in Sri Lanka. But beyond that, they also reflect the wider political orientations, the westernised and cosmopolitan life-styles of a certain section of the Sri Lankan middle class of the time. They explain her familiarity with elite India and easy integration into elite Bombay society.

The Indian nationalist movement which, as early as 1882 had united under the Indian National Congress and begun to agitate for home rule,[86] had been an inspiration to Sri Lankan nationalists demanding constitutional reform and a greater participation in the executive. These men had travelled to India for Congress conventions as early as the late 1890s, if not earlier.[87] Leading personalities of the Indian nationalist movement had visited Sri Lanka regularly from the late 19th century, whether inspired by their interest in promulgating theosophy and/or to show solidarity and solicit support for anti-British colonial agitation on the subcontinent. Annie Besant visited in 1893, Swami Vivekananda in 1897, Bipin Chandra Pal in 1918, Sarojini Naidu in 1922, a delegation led by Maulana Shaukat Ali in 1924, Mahatma Gandhi in 1927, Jawaharlal Nehru in 1931 and Kamaladevi Chattopadhyaya in 1931 and 1937.[88] Books by Indian authors on the Indian independence movement had been reviewed in journals like *National Monthly of Ceylon* and the *Ceylon National Review*, the journal of the Ceylon Social Reform Society edited by Ananda Coomaraswamy and W.A.de Silva. Begun in 1906 the latter echoed many of the concerns of the social reform movement in India and discussed a wide variety of interests ranging from women's education to vegetarianism and caste practices. (*Ceylon National Review*, no. 1, January 1906 and vol. 3, no. 9, March 1910).

The commonalities between British India and Ceylon were thus impressed in the minds of the Sri Lankan nationalist elite far more than their differences.[89] For instance, the real inspiration for confronting caste bigotry and injustice in the country came to George E. de Silva from the arguments of the Indian nationalist movement. Sarojini Naidu's visit to Sri Lanka in 1922, during which she spent time at St. George's, the de Silva home in Kandy, was to inspire both George and Agnes to political goals including Sri Lanka's independence struggle and universal franchise. For Agnes in particular, ameliorating the inequalities of women in society, eliminating the dowry system and arranged marriages, education for women, and their right to vote and engage in a profession. [90] Of particular significance to George was Sarojini Naidu's forthright attack on the Indian caste system, which struck a powerful personal chord given his own grievances. Recalling a speech by Naidu delivered while in Sri Lanka, George E. de Silva wrote in his memoir:

The most important point in Mrs. Sarojini Naidu's speech concerned the problem of untouchability. . . I realised that the problem of untouchability was not only confined to India. We had it here in Ceylon too. Although the educated class did not bother too much about caste distinctions, I knew that in the out-lying villages of the Kandyan provinces, this inhuman and degrading system was still being perpetuated. I realised that the British rulers wanted to continue the caste system in order that they should 'divide and rule'. They were shrewd enough to set one caste against another in Ceylon as they did in India. The townspeople did not realise what an inhuman system was being perpetrated by the privileged classes in the village. The headman and ratemahatmaya were appointed from these families; they controlled the parcelling out of Crown land to planters and to their own kith and kin. The poor villagers never got anything from the Waste Lands Ordinance. But it was only after I came to understand the conditions in India that this situation became apparent to me.[91]

From 1922 onwards George E. de Silva would attend every Indian National Congress convention. He met with Mahatma Gandhi, Nehru, Subhas Chandra Bose and Annie Besant, amongst others. When Nehru visited Sri Lanka with his daughter, Indira, in 1931, they visited the de Silva home in Kandy and Anil took on the role of Indira's companion. The anti-British nationalist struggle enabled the political elite of both countries to share in a sense of solidarity and commonality, despite the fact that in many instances the specificities of their situations were quite different.

This close connection with Indian politics and its nationalist leaders paved the way for Anil and her sister, Minette, who left for Bombay to study architecture, to be familiar with India and empathise with its socio-political struggles. It isn't surprising then that Anil would strike up a close friendship with Mulk Raj Anand, a member of the Indian Communist Party engaged in the nationalist effort to overthrow the yoke of western imperialism; who was himself a key figure in the modernist art and literature movement in India and had been the victim of caste prejudice.[92] It is telling that Anil who had turned her back on the Sri Lankan nationalist effort, could feel empathy for the Indian one. In India she did not experience the restrictions of caste and ethnicity, felt at home with the eclecticism of its Communist Party which repudiated caste and class and had attracted many Indian Muslims to its cause. Moreover, the dynamism of Bombay was refreshing after the stifling restrictions of Sri Lanka.[93]

Bombay: Gateway to India

Many factors had come together to make Bombay the most cosmopolitan Indian city in the 1940s. From the advent of the British in India, it had been looked on by the colonisers as the gateway to the subcontinent. Conversely, for the Indian elite, Bombay was a window to the West.[94] In the early stages of India's colonial encounter with Britain, by the late 17th century, Bombay had become an extension of the East India Company's trade with Gujarat, centred on Surat. Bombay was close to Surat and possessed a good natural harbour, which the British eventually used to establish a naval and commercial base.[95] In 1817–8, with the defeat of the ruler, the Peshwa of Pune, British political domination of the area became complete. By this time too, with the revoking of the East India Company's trade monopoly in 1813, private British commercial interests had established a presence in Bombay so that, by the 1850s, indigenous Gujarati and Parsi entrepreneurs were able to build on trade with the British and develop the production of raw cotton and cotton mills. By the end of the 19th century Bombay had been turned into the "Manchester of India"; its economic importance to the British was reflected in the fact that it was the first Indian city to have a railway system, inaugurated in 1853, which soon became the hub of a railway network that linked Bombay to all major cities in the country.[96]

Education and institutes of learning played a vital role in creating a cultural renaissance in Bombay during the first half of the 19th century. With the growth of British interests in the region, Christian missionaries were not far behind, opening up schools and mission centres in Bombay in the early 1830s. As in Sri Lanka, the products of this western education imbibed the ideas of the Enlightenment and took on the goals of western rationalist and humanist thought. They became a cadre of early indigenous reformists, denouncing the superstitious practices and backwardness of their people. Journalism became a prime vehicle for their ideas, and with the development of the vernacular press, newspapers were begun. The *Bombay Samachar*, a Gujarati weekly, was started in 1822. In 1832 Dadabhai Naoroji, who later analysed the economic bases of British imperialism and forwarded the "drain theory", began an anglo-Marathi newspaper called the *Bombay Darpan*. He set for himself the goal of opening "a field of inquiry for free public discussion on points connected with the prosperity of the country and the happiness of its inhabitants". The newspaper became an important vehicle of social criticism in Bombay and western India, although as a result of the conservatism of Jamhekar who ran the paper, it stopped short of critiquing the exploitative nature of British colonialism.[97] A space for such criticism was created with the inauguration of the *Bombay Gazette* in 1841, in which the British editor, who was considered a "nativist" and later sacked for his pains, invited readers to come forth with their grievances on British rule. He pledged to "unremittingly advocate measures which appeared likely to benefit the Indian people regardless of the source whence they emanate". A fierce debate ensued, with certain Indians denouncing British presence in India and the exploitative nature of its imperialism,[98] while defenders of the Raj took to another English newspaper, the *United Service Gazette,* to list its benefits to the country. What this did was to create a political ferment in which nationalist ideas came to the fore and a reformist agenda began to be debated. Govind Vithal Kunte, also known as Bhau Mahajan, epitomised this trend. In his newspaper, *Prabhakar*, begun in 1841, he voiced uncompromising critiques of British imperialism while being equally harsh on the "rotten Indian social structure which had made British imperialism possible". In keeping with his interest in educating Marathi society on the liberal ideas of the West, he introduced the history of the French revolution in a 25-part series and published literature on the French revolution in his paper.[99]

The commercial and industrial growth of Bombay supported the foundation of many learned societies during this period. The Royal Asiatic Society (Bombay branch) and Bombay Geographical Society were inaugurated in 1831, the Native General Library in 1845, the University of Bombay and the J.J.School of Art in 1857. The latter is a good example of how the native industrial elite supported institutions of modern science and technology. Its founding grant of Rs. 1 lakh had come from Sir Jamshetjee Jeejeebhoy (after whom the school was named) who had been a committee member selecting Indian goods for the Great Exhibition of 1851 held in London. Impressed by what he saw at the exhibition, and responding to the demand of a group of local elites for a school of art that would improve the quality of the arts and crafts and industrial goods of the region, Sir J.J.'s donation was meant to found an art institute that would teach drawing and design according to contemporary British criteria.[100] In fact such dynamism and enterprise ensured that Bombay was, in terms of technology and innovative commerce, far in advance of other major Indian cities. Cowasji Davar's Oriental Spinning factory begun in 1854, was the first modern factory of its kind. Bombay boasted the first Indian stock exchange in 1875. It was at Tata's Empress mills in Nagpur—a Bombay financed and controlled company—that the ring spindle was first introduced. The production of cement in India was first started at the Bombay firm of Khatau. In 1913 modern steel production commenced at a Tata company named Tisco. Automobile and aeronautics industries were started by the Bombay-based pioneer Walchand Hirachand, and a large scale hydraulic scheme was promoted in the Western Ghats by the Tatas–a Bombay-based family of Parsi magnates.[101]

If Bombay was, as popularly perceived, the rival of a city like Calcutta, this had much to do with Bombay's cosmopolitan population and its elite who were more western-oriented than Calcutta's Bhadralok class. Partha Chatterjee shows how, in the making of the Brahmo Samaj in Calcutta, its leaders such as Keshabchandra Sen, Ramakrishna, the latter's biographer, Saradananda, and playwrights like Girishchandra Ghosh critiqued the rationality of the West, trashed the reform movements initiated by those like Rammohun Roy and turned their nationalist energies *within*, to modify notions of spirituality and identity to suit their nationalist needs of *differentiation* from the West.[102] In doing so they reinscribed certain caste, class and gender practices that existed in traditional Indian society. So did the Calcutta Hindu nationalists who elevated advaita philosophy. By re-canonising the Vedas and Upanishads as the locus of authentic Hinduism they also served to reinforce the oppressive and hierarchical rubrics of caste/class, race and gender in those texts.[103]

The cosmopolitan elite of Bombay, on the other hand, by and large looked to Europe without any such anxiety, more excited by the hybridity that could be a metaphor for the identity they aspired to. Predominant in this elite were the Parsis who had settled in Bombay from the 8th century onwards, and the English-educated Gujaratis and Maharashtrians native to the region. There were also Hindu and Jain Banias who engaged in large scale businesses with the British,[104] and the presence in Bombay of European Jews fleeing Nazi persecution in the 1940s. Prominent among them were Walter Langhammer, who left Vienna at the outbreak of the war and became the art director of *The Times of India,* and Rudy von Leyden who came to India in 1938. They were both members of the Bombay Art Society committee, credited with introducing the latest trends in European modernism to the Bombay elite. There was a heady sense of inventing modernism for India, of a quest for new forms of expression in art and of a search for a hybridity that combined western forms with Indian traditions.[105] This was the milieu Anil entered. In a society as eclectic as the intellectual elite of Bombay she was readily accepted as one of their own. She was able to find ready acceptance in Bombay for the modernism of her friend George Keyt, whose first exhibitions of paintings in India she organised. Her interaction with Mulk Raj Anand, their editorial work on the magazine *Marg*, and her engagement with the Indian People's Theatre Association launched her own appraisal of the potential of indigenous cultural traditions, for a colonial society seeking its own sense of modernity to be emancipatory, not stultifying.

Marg

The driving force of the journal *Marg* was the self-conscious quest of a certain section of the Indian nationalist elite, to fashion a modernity for themselves that would both pay tribute to their Indian heritage and productively use "European innovativeness". Inaugurated in 1946, it was motivated by a commitment to an ideal of Indian modernity. Mulk Raj Anand approached the business magnate J.R.D. Tata for "7 ads and 2 rooms" with which to start a journal. *Marg*, signifying the path or way, was itself suggestive of a new direction; its main focus was on Asian art and architecture and, as Romila Thapar notes, it was considered a departure for its time in its presentation, self-conscious as it was in layout and format.[106] It featured many stunning black and white photographs of art, sculpture, buildings and architectural design on glossy paper, colour lithographs of modernist paintings and detailed articles on the traditional techniques of painting, sculpture and building construction. Mulk Raj Anand was its editor for many years and Anil, assistant editor from 1946 to 1948.

Marg provided Anil the space to write on Sri Lanka, feature its artists and retain her connection with the land of her birth. Its January 1947 issue had detailed articles with several photographs on various aspects of Sri Lankan life and its cultural heritage. There was an article on the peasant tradition in Sri Lanka by Andrew Boyd, architectural designs for two houses in Alfred House Gardens, Colombo, colour lithographs of "Rasa Lila" and "Prema" by George Keyt, a photograph of one of the Sigiriya frescoes for an article on "The Continuity of Indian art in Asia", a review of Ian Goonetileke's edition of George Claessen's (one of the 43

Group) drawings, and a note on the photographer, Lionel Wendt (also of the 43 Group) by L.C.van Geyzel. The issue also featured an article on "Better Medical Facilities for the Rural Population in Ceylon"; although no authorship is acknowledged, the article keeps so close to George E. de Silva's manifesto as Minister for Health on rural health care in Sri Lanka, Anil's hand in it cannot be disputed. It is accompanied by architectural designs for rural hospitals in the country. The next issue had a long article by van Geyzel on the paintings of George Keyt, with colour lithographs and black and white photographs of some of Keyt's paintings. After her departure from Bombay in 1949, Sri Lanka features less in *Marg*, although Anil's sister, Minette and the artist, Harry Pieris continued to be contributing editors. This indicates that it was important for Anil to include Sri Lanka in the appraisal of the pan-Indian cultural heritage that *Marg* was spearheading. It didn't quite matter that Sri Lankan art and folk traditions were seen only as *extensions* of the Indian. In fact a later special issue on Sri Lanka (*Marg* 5, no. 3) introduced the country and its connection to India in terms of a mother and child. While it did acknowledge difference, the emphasis was on the legacy of *Indian* traditions on the island. Of the sculptures at Polonnaruwa it noted that they "preserved the continuity of Buddhist culture, extending the inner spirit of Indian Buddhist art into a provincial accent which is in no sense parochial, but sometimes surpasses the achievements of the peninsula in the individual figures". It is both an index of *Marg*'s commitment to a pan-Indian identity and a reflection of its resistance to the growing inwardness of Indian nationalism that it criticised those "addicted to chauvinism" for not seeing "a much more fruitful relationship in the future between the two countries on account of their bias for the cultural affinities between India and Ceylon". (*Marg*, op. cit., pp.2–3).

The depiction of Sri Lanka in *Marg* is significant. As has been noted, there was an acknowledgement of Buddhist art and architecture as continuing traditional legacies from India. But equally central in the representation of Sri Lanka was its 43 Group. This group, named after its inaugural meeting on 29 August, 1943, was a fraternity of artists who worked in different styles and materials. It was united, however, in its commitment to the nationalist renaissance of indigenous art as found in the ancient cities of Anuradhapura and Polonnaruwa, the frescoes of Sigiriya and the temple paintings of the villages, but with a view to fashioning a new aesthetic which was eclectic, and drew as much from European, African and American sources.[107] This quest struck a chord with those within *Marg*. There were other connections with India as well. Two of the 43 Group's best known painters, Harry Pieris and George Keyt, had spent formative time in India. Pieris taught at Shantiniketan in 1935 and Keyt was a frequent visitor. He first went to India in 1939 and visited Anil and Mulk Raj Anand in Bombay in 1945 as their guest. Influenced by the Buddhist revival in Sri Lanka from the mid 19th century onwards, Keyt turned to Hindu mythology, iconography and sacred texts like *Gita Govinda* as inspiration for a style of art influenced, too, by Picasso, Matisse and Léger. William Graham noted in *The Studio* in 1954:

The genius of George Keyt lies in the wholly original manner in which he finds inspiration in ancient Eastern art. In Sinhalese and Indian mythology he has found themes capable of expressing a modern philosophy of life through his own emotional and poetic imagery. His work has a sensuous poetry, with frequent allusions to the ancient forms of song and dance, conveyed with a characteristically Oriental calligraphy.[108]

It was the recasting of traditional metaphors in a modernist idiom, using the distortions of expressionism, the geometry of cubism, etc. for a modern artistic expression that brought the Group to the attention of European art critics. John Berger, art critic for the *New Statesman* and *Nation* wrote the foreword to the catalogue of the 43 Group's exhibition at the Imperial Institute in South Kensington, London, from November–December 1952. He noted the Group's attempts to achieve a synthesis between the work being done in Paris by Picasso and Matisse and the ancient tradition of Sigiriya "which yet took into account the emerging power and equality of Asia in the contemporary world".[109] Justin Daraniyagala's work, Berger declared, he "would unhesitatingly place. . . alongside any of the 20th century masters of Expressionism."[110] He was less sure of Keyt's efforts stating that the latter "gathers together elements from Picasso, the Indian cave paintings at Ajanta and the Sinhalese at Sigiriya...(but) lacks the fire to fuse the elements together because his mood is too nostalgic and his observation too schematic."[111] Other art critics disagreed. A correspondent of the *Indian Express* reviewing a Keyt exhibition in Bombay in 1969 had this to say:

Classicist in thought but modernist in treatment, George Keyt first and foremost shows how tradition should be carried forward and interpreted. And the brilliance of his talent shines in every line as he cuts and sweeps in masterful style to recreate amorous couples in dalliance, or waiting with the weight of their passion for the hour of love.[112]

Marg echoed this view. In 1950 it published a monograph on Keyt's work by Martin Russell and had this to say about the 43 Group as a whole:

The peoples of Ceylon have already achieved a synthesis between the East and the West, far more intricate and more subtle in some respects than even that achieved in the mother country, India. I would venture the assertion that the small but energetic school of young painters in Ceylon is far more advanced in the range of their preoccupation, in their knowledge of handling paint and in their insistence on rhythmic vitality than the other painters in the East, even as the painters of Mexico have far outstripped the achievements of America.

Marg 5, no. 3, 1952, p.5.

It was the cosmopolitan eclecticism of the 43 Group that was being erased in concurrent nationalist projects in Sri Lanka. As we have seen, from the theatre of John de Silva to the formulations of Anagarika Dharmapala and the populist xenophobia of the *Spectator* and the *Comrade*, hybridity as a trope of identity was under fierce contest. The 43 Group may have soldiered on in Sri Lanka for a while, although artists like Ivan Pieris and George Claessen had migrated to England and Australia, seeking an artistic and intellectual ferment they found lacking in Sri Lanka. For Anil, it was Bombay rather than an increasingly ethno-nationalistic Sri Lanka, in which Tamil nationalism too had begun to emerge in response to the Sinhala one, by now referred to as the "tyranny of the majority" by Tamil politicians. A demand for fifty-fifty or equal political representation for the minorities was mooted by G.G.Ponnambalam in 1937, which infuriated the Sinhalese and a "large and influential section of the Ceylon Tamils and Muslims" as well.[113] Communal politics had become part and parcel of the socio-political fabric of Sri Lanka. The cosmopolitan and eclectic spirit that Anil and the 43 Group stood for had no place within this polity.

Raj Thapar wrote of Anil that she, like Mulk Raj Anand and Pupul Jayakar, recognized "in a vague, dreamy-eyed, almost mystic way, excellence in India's myriad aesthetic forms." (Raj Thapar, *ATY*, p.57). There was certainly a sense of excitement in their nationalistic reappraisal of their cultural heritage, but Mulk Raj Anand's editorials in *Marg* were by no means vague or romantic; they were a self-conscious intellectual search for a fusion of traditions relevant to India's modernity. His comment in *Marg* on the 43 Group quoted above, as well as his editorial interventions below bear this out:

When we turn to look with new eyes upon all that our past contains, we have not only to recover something of their ancient sense and spirit, long embedded and lost in the unintelligent practice of received forms, but to bring out of them a new light which gives to the old truths fresh aspects and, therefore, novel potentialities of creation and evolution. We can suffuse our modernism with much of ancient motive and sentiment; but we must have a better insight into the meaning of Indian things and their characteristics—*a free acceptance more of their spirit than of their forms and an attempt at new interpretation.*

Marg 3, no.1, 1950, p.10

The spirit Mulk Raj Anand celebrated is not a fixed, romantic essence of indigenous tradition, but a creative potential that can adapt to new needs and be unconfined by canonical forms. Obsession with and slavishness to traditional form was a nationalistic trend, whether of European or Indian extract, that Anand repudiated. On the one hand, he would complain of the buildings influenced by European styles:

Architecturally speaking, India has been unfortunate; during the last 150 years it has been overdosed with European eclecticism; Greek Revival, Gothic Revival, Italianate, European Saracenic, German Modernism, Cubism—buildings with all these labels can be found in any Indian city. The native genius has been swamped and the imported styles have been adopted wholesale.

Marg 2, no.3, 1948, p.6

On the other hand he was equally disappointed with a nationalistic revivalism that fetishised traditional forms of architecture:

There is. . . a demand from a section of the lay public that we should build in a recognised "Indian style" of architecture rather than in the hybrid "modern style". Building in an "Indian style" is understood. . . to mean that buildings should look like those in a particular period of the past in some particular area which is judged to have a character and merit of its own... The reason why such a course is fundamentally wrong is that the vital factors and forces which moulded such architecture and gave it meaning and beauty have changed altogether.

Marg 3, no.1, 1950, p. 5.

Here is an understanding that, with India's colonial encounter, its identity and needs changed inevitably; moreover, there was a *privilege* in creating a "new" aesthetic that would draw from its diverse inheritances. "What is required," he wrote further,

is a scientific outlook in our line of approach and our study of the glories of the past. Firstly, we must understand and appreciate its true significance. We shall then be in a position to evaluate it more correctly and sift the good from the bad, the truth and beauty in it from the spurious and superfluous. Unfortunately, such an approach is not in evidence in the realm of art and architecture in this country. We have at present no established character and aesthetic standards.

Marg 3, no.1, 1950, p. 5.

In this *Marg* shared a preoccupation with many other colonised writers and artists. Nobel laureate, playwright and poet, Derek Walcott of St. Lucia exemplified this quest when he wrote of the "Adamic" opportunity presented to the West Indian to forge a new identity. Referring to the history of deracination suffered in the Caribbean at the hands of conquering and colonising Europeans, its consequent loss of language, population and cultural roots, Walcott wrote "If there was nothing, there was everything to be made. With this prodigious ambition we began. . . We would walk, like new Adams, in a nourishing ignorance which would name plants and people with a child's belief that the world is its own age."[114] Looked at another way, it wasn't so much that there was an aesthetic vacuum to be filled, as that this was a site of contestation between different strands of nationalist thought, the one fetishising an essentialism of the past, and the other forging a modernity that was hybrid and sought to fuse both eastern and western inheritances.

Serious and committed too were the efforts of the Indian

People's Theatre Association of which Anil was general secretary from 1942–46. The idea of a people's theatre had its genesis in Romain Rolland's 1903 manifesto, *The People's Theatre,* in which he formulated a new approach in socialist populism. This was, first, to recognise the exploitation by capital of the working class, its brutalisation due to appalling work and living conditions, and its alienation from enriching forms of leisure and entertainment; and then, to facilitate its participation in a theatre and forms of popular culture of its own making. [115] Towards these goals Rolland brought theatre and music concerts into spaces congenial to the ordinary French citizen, such as schools, churches or town halls. The entertainment would have both a structure and ideology that raised people's awareness of their condition. Within the socialist movement this meant a consciousness about their exploitation by bourgeois capital. In the Indian context it was also to make the working class aware of the double bind of capitalism and imperialism.

In empowering the working class towards cultural emancipation, Rolland believed that the intelligentsia had to prepare the way. IPTA was primarily an organisation formed and run by the urban elite. It attested that its task was "to portray vividly and memorably through the medium of the stage and other traditional arts, the human details of these important facts of our people's rights and *enlighten* them about their rights and the nature and solution of the problems facing them." (My emphasis. *Pradhan,* p.151) IPTA kept close to Indian Communist Party doctrine. Its theatre was anti-imperialist, advocated an anti-Partition stance and Hindu–Muslim unity, called for the release of CPI leaders from jail, demanded a national government and was stridently anti-fascist. (*Pradhan,* p.*xvi*) Its executive committee was full of senior CPI members and it had branches in the regions and cities where the CPI was active. Its artistic success was largely due to the fact that it attracted good actors and directors who were finding other acting/directing jobs difficult to obtain because of the war. What little was being produced came under the umbrella of the war effort and purveyed imperialist propaganda. IPTA Bombay had the added advantage of being located in the capital of the Indian film industry, and was able to use actors, dancers and script-writers who were hovering around in search of jobs in the Bombay movies.[116]

In the 1945 Annual IPTA Report that Anil de Silva filed as its general secretary, she wrote:

> We have made but a slight contribution to the future of the drama. We have made no effort to seriously study our past classical Sanskrit drama and our folk forms of drama, so that our writers and producers could experiment in a synthesis of these two forms with modern stage technique and lighting. We shall have to make a serious study of these subjects; we shall have to compel our writers to help us experiment in the drama and to evolve a new drama; one that will be essentially Indian, bringing real creative talent that will base itself on both tradition and technique.
>
> Pradhan, p. 277.

This agenda of creating a new form suffused with both the old and the new resonated with that of *Marg* and reflected the thinking of a powerful faction of the CPI at the time. It also went hand in hand with the objectives of the All-India Progressive Writers' Association inaugurated in 1936. Many of its writers supported India's freedom struggle and were either CPI members or sympathetic to its cause. Mulk Raj Anand wrote of its goal:

> If we prefer to re-interpret old values, the cardinal virtues, so that they may come to be regarded not merely as abstract virtues or ends in themselves, but as related to the requirements of the *changing* society to which we belong and which we seek further to *transform*, that does not mean we have no morals. In the Progressive Writers' Association, therefore, the largest bloc of writers who, whatever difference in their standpoints, whatever their contradictions of philosophical, religious and cultural belief, join for common actions in the defence of our old culture and the development, through a proper criticism of the past, of a new culture. (My emphases.)
>
> Pradhan, pp. 15–6.

The search was on for new subjects and aesthetic standards which had an immediate engagement with the realities of the day. IPTA focused on the scandalous and tragic Bengal famine caused by, among other factors, a speculative hoarding of foodstuff lest the British divert food from the area to their soldiers in Burma—which they did. Approximately two to three million poor people starved to death. This blatant act of capitalist/imperialist exploitation became a rallying cry for Indian nationalists, and

IPTA was at the forefront of dramatising the causes and effects of the famine. *Navanna* (New Harvest) written by Bijon Bhattacharya ran for nearly 40 performances in Bengal. *The Hunger and Epidemic Dance* by Usha Dutta and Panu Paul was another creation on this theme performed in Calcutta in 1944. Many of these plays were performed at kisan (peasant) conventions, attracted huge crowds and moved the audience to contribute what it could to alleviate the suffering caused by the famine.(*Pradhan*, p. 287.) In Delhi, an IPTA production on the famine and aggressive intervention by its members elicited Rs.25,000 for famine relief from a Yagna Committee that had planned to burn thousands of tons of rice, wheat, ghee, sugar, etc., as offerings to the gods in a Mahayagna lasting 10 days in February 1944. (*Pradhan*, p. 302) The scourge of cholera that spread throughout Malabar in 1944 was another subject tackled by IPTA. K.A.Abbas's play, *Zubeida*, although set in Uttar Pradesh familiar to the playwright, was based on the story of a Muslim girl from Malabar who died for lack of an anti-cholera vaccine. Uzra Bhatt, dancer and actress from Lahore, was chosen for the title role. One of its performances, organised by the local trade union of Madanpura, was a novel experiment in street theatre at the time. A stage had been erected at a cul-de-sac, with spectators seated on the road and the balconies of the three-storied houses on either side. Ten thousand people watched the performance, of which at least a thousand were women who had never seen a play before. So moved was a poor woman member of the audience that she donated her earrings to IPTA which auctioned them on the spot, with the proviso that the earrings be returned to her. (*Pradhan*, p. 297)

What these productions achieved was a collective understanding and catharsis of the conditions surrounding Indian peasant life under capital and imperialism; under cultural/ caste/ religious rules; under regulations and neglect of welfare services such as education and health-care. In incorporating traditional theatre forms that included dance and song, and in experimenting with new ways of production and presentation, IPTA was forging a new aesthetic and theatre experience that it had understood as its goal in the first place. This was not without debate within IPTA itself. Writing of its role during the Bengal famine, Anil wrote:

There was need for unity against external danger and internal corruption; so the composers and playwrights poured forth song and plays to rouse the people to meet the exigency. (But, strange to say that even when we went to the masses, I mean the rural masses who form the bulk of the population of Bengal, it is always with forms of art that have come to stay in Bengal after our contact with the West.) No doubt they composed and wrote in the language of the folk...But what was not utilised to the fullest extent were the folk forms of art which would have taken us deep down to the masses. . . Whereas in Andhra we took pure folk forms and only put in themes on contemporary events, without changing the form in the least. In Bengal we spoke to the people in a language they did not understand, but mostly in forms more familiar to urban folk.

Pradhan, p.287.

Anil's statement is both puzzling and revealing. On the one hand, its insistence on evoking traditional folk forms alone goes against the grain of the goals of IPTA, *Marg* and the IWPA; on the other, it reveals a pragmatic approach which recognised that IPTA's ideological message could be best conveyed and in the quickest time, through traditional forms that village/working class audiences were already familiar with; that the fusion of style and aesthetic was a preoccupation and agenda suited, in the short term at least, to an urban elite.

Anil's Legacy

On leaving Bombay in 1950, Anil moved to Paris. There she entered a context in which orientalism had shaped certain expectations of the Asian. There were not many South Asians in the city. An aura of the exotic Asian beauty began to gather about her and Anil was photographed as one such by Cartier-Bresson. She continued to dress in exquisite saris, literally wearing her *difference* on her sleeve, and had a salon where South Asian students found encouragement and excellent food.[117] Once again her home acquired a cosmopolitan character. Now in the heart of Europe, she and her French husband, Phillipe de Vigier who was a member of the Communist Party, also hosted Americans who sought refuge in Europe from McCarthyism.[118] Anil was not defensive about her Asian identity, indeed she was proud of it; and her interest in Asian art history, deepened through exposure to the treasures at the Musée Guimét and her study at the Louvre, heightened her sense of pride in it. She was able to adopt an overarching "Asian" identity in which class and culture mattered, but not caste or ethnic origins. From this perspective she was able to view the land of her birth with nostalgia and a certain fondness. She dedicated *The Life of the Buddha: Retold from Ancient Sources* (1955):

To the memory of my FATHER who, when I was a child, taught me the Pali *gathas* of the monks and nuns of the Buddha as we walked at sunrise in the garden of our home in Kandy, Ceylon.

The close bond with her father, the Buddhism inculcated in her, and memories of her youth tempt the association of a (lost) childhood home as haven. Yet those who knew her are sceptical about her claim to the importance of Buddhism in her life,[119] and see such a recalling of Sri Lankan roots as nostalgia.[120] It is certainly the case that from her first long spell away from Sri Lanka in the 1930s, Anil wrote of the country in nostalgic tones. In an article published in *The Times of Ceylon* entitled, "The Scottish 'Invasion'" (15 May, 1932) she wrote wistfully of the hill-station Nuwara Eliya, recalling with irony the exodus to it of the Colombo elite during the April heat, while she experiences a British winter and longs for sunshine. In another article she refers to the "vivid beauty we always have around us in Ceylon".[121] She visited the country several times with husbands and partners and in 1967 commented:

I had forgotten how beautiful it all was—forgotten how Ceylon was the actual physical image of the legendary paradise island in the story books.
The Times, December 23, 1967.

The ability to express wonder and delight in the country's natural beauty was in keeping with Anil's sensibility, alert to art, nature and music. They represented "neutral" terrain, not the sites of casteism and abuse, ethnic chauvinism and sexual conservatism. By the time she returned to the country on short visits in the 1960s, the political climate in Sri Lanka had also changed. The UNP government was in power and George E. de Silva was Minister for Health. Caste as an issue of nationalist struggle was muted and criticism of George/Anil was absent in the local press.

The *Times of Ceylon* which had earlier vilified both father and daughter was now full of admiration for Anil. Her work on the heritage of Buddhist art no longer challenged nationalist ideology but coincided with it in its flattering appraisal of its unique manifestation in Sri Lanka.[122] There was, finally, no conflict of interest between her and the Sinhala/Buddhist nation.

Anil de Silva belonged to a small, but significant group of Sri Lankan women who, in the first half of the 20th century, challenged certain nationalist dictates through their lives and work, when they were at their strongest in their restrictive impact on women.[123] If casteism, ethnic exclusivity and rigid notions of middle class respectability were cornerstones of the rhetoric that mobilised the colonised to the anti-British nationalist call, they were the very boundaries that Anil de Silva defied through the choices she made in her life. Those choices were undoubtedly mediated by her class, privilege, and a cosmopolitan outlook that also provided her with the flexibility to travel and live abroad. Given her family background and its political affiliations, she was a committed nationalist—but of a different kind, and inevitably so, standing for a more inclusive, democratic and liberal modernity for her nation.

Notes

[1] In his fictionalised account of elite Burgher life in Sri Lanka in the 1920s and '30s, Michael Ondaatje writes of the power of *The Searchlight*: "If the crowd or the horses did not cause trouble, *The Searchlight*, a magazine published by the notorious Mr. Gomez, did. "One of those scurrilous things," it attacked starters and trainers and owners and provided gossip to be carefully read between races. Nobody wished to appear in it and everyone bought it. It sold for five cents but remained solvent, as the worst material could be toned down only with bribes to the editor." *Running in the Family*. London: Picador, 1984, p.51.

[2] George L. Mosse, *Nationalism and Sexuality: Middle-Class Morality and Sexual Norms in Modern Europe*. Madison: University of Wisconsin Press, 1985.

[3] Ibid., p.6.

[4] Anagarika Dharmapala (1864–1933) was born David Hewavitarana to a prosperous middle-class family—his father owned a successful

furniture business—and was educated at St. Benedict's and later St. Thomas's College, an elite colonial boys' school. When he was fourteen years old he came under the influence of the Theosophical Society (India) which he joined in 1884, becoming one of its most ardent members in Sri Lanka. When Colonel Olcott and C.W.Leadbeater toured the island to collect funds for Buddhist education, Dharmapala, who was a clerk in the education department at the time, accompanied them. Later, he resigned his post to work full-time for the spread of Buddhist education in the country. In 1891 he formed the Mahabodhi Society in Calcutta to propagate Buddhism and protect Buddhist sites in India. He travelled extensively, visiting Japan with Colonel Olcott in 1889, and represented Theravada Buddhism at the Parliament of Religions in Chicago in 1893. He was a fiery crusader for the Buddhist revival in Sri Lanka, speaking out against Christianity and western culture. His crusade took on nationalist tones when he urged the Sinhala people to repudiate westernisation and take pride in the Sinhala language and its customs, and in his call for temperance and Buddhist revival laid the foundations for an anti-British political struggle which "fired a whole generation of Sinhalese to refuse to accept the old world colonial mentality". See Visakha Kumari Jayawardena, *The Rise of the Labour Movement in Ceylon*. Colombo: Sanjiva, 1985, p.178.

⁵ For an excellent account of how these values were instilled in girls see Malathi de Alwis, "The Production and Embodiment of Respectability: Gendered Demeanours in Colonial Ceylon," in Michael Roberts (ed.), *Sri Lanka: Collective Identities Revisited* Vol.1. Colombo: Marga, 1997, pp.105–43.

⁶ Richard Gombrich and Gananath Obeysekera, *Buddhism Transformed: Religious Change in Sri Lanka*. New Jersey: Princeton University Press, 1988. pp.207–15.

⁷ Ibid., pp.213–15.

⁸ Michael Roberts, "For Humanity. For the Sinhalese. Dharmapala as Crusading Bosat," in *Journal of Asian Studies*, Vol.56, No. 4, Nov.1997, pp. 1020–21.

⁹ Gombrich and Obeysekera, *Buddhism Transformed*, op. cit., p.215.

¹⁰ Kumari Jayawardena, *The White Woman's Other Burden: Western Women and South Asia During British Rule*. London: Routledge, 1995, pp.38–9.

¹¹ Ibid., pp.38 and 47.

¹² Such was the demand for schools modelled on the British missionary pattern that when Buddhist Girls' College, the antecedent of Visakha Vidyalaya, was inaugurated as one of the first Buddhist girls' schools in the country in January 1917, it wholeheartedly emulated middle-class British school curricula and extra-curricular models. See Manel

Tampoe, *The Story of Selestina Dias: Buddhist Female Philanthropy and Education.* Colombo: Social Scientists' Association, 1997, pp.80, 98, 100.

[13] Kumari Jayawardena, personal communication, 1997.

[14] Of Anil's debut at Court, the *Daily Telegraph* wrote "The crowds pressed thickest around the car of a radiant little dark-skinned debutante dressed in a gorgeous sari of pink and gold, with wide eyes alight with excitement and the happiest laugh in the world. Again and again the blinds of the car had to be drawn and the crowds forced back on the pavement." Quoted in Minette de Silva, *The Life and Work of an Asian Woman Architect,* Vol. 1. Kandy: George E. de Silva and Agnes Nell de Silva Trust, 1998, p. 46.

[15] Hillwood Girl's School, Kandy, up to the age of 12, and then at Bishop's College, Colombo, till the age of 16.

[16] Sudhi Pradhan (ed.), *Marxist Cultural Movement in India: Chronicles and Documents (1936–1947)* Vol. 1. Calcutta: Santi Pradhan, 1979 & 1985, p.*xv*; and Joan L. Erdman with Zohra Segal, *Stages*, op. cit., p.122.

[17] Susie Tharu and K. Lalitha, (eds.), *Women Writing in India* Vol. 2. London: Pandora Press, 1993, p.79.

[18] George Keyt (1901–1996), Sri Lanka's best known painter of recent times. His work drew from Indian traditional and religious art as well as European modernism – a goal the 43 Group, a society of Sri Lankan artists of which Keyt was a founder member, was also committed to.

[19] Romila Thapar, personal communication, New Delhi, October 1997.

[20] Anil de Silva, *The Life of the Buddha: Retold from Ancient Sources.* London: Phaedon Press, 1955.

[21] Anil de Silva-Vigier, *Chinese Landscape Painting in the Caves of Tunhuang.* London: Methuen, 1964. The book on Maichisan was written by Michael Sullivan, entitled, *The Cave Temples of Maichisan: an account of the 1958 expedition to Maichisan by Anil de Silva.* London: Faber, 1969. Anil's own account of the journey and project forms a section of the book (pp.71–77.) The trip to China, adventurous and pioneering at the time, was made possible through Anil de Silva's friendship with S.K. Panikkar, distinguished historian from Kerala and then Indian ambassador in Paris. Panikkar was a friend of Chou En Lai, Prime Minister of China, and through this contact had arranged for her expedition to China. Romila Thapar, personal communication.

[22] Constance Gordon Cumming, *Wandering in China.* Edinburgh & London: William Blackwood and Sons, 1888; Isabella Bishop, *Yangtzee Valley and Beyond: An Account of Journeys in China* (1899), and *Chinese Pictures—Notes on Photographs made in China.* London: 1900; Lucy Atkins, *Recollections of the Tartar Steppes and their*

Inhabitants. London: 1863; Alicia Helen Little, *My Diary in a Chinese Farm.* Shanghai: 1898 and *Intimate China: The Chinese as I have seen them.* London: 1899; Julia Corner, *China Pictorial Descriptions and Historical.* London: 1853; Mary Geraldine Taylor, *In the Far East: Letters from Geraldine Guiness in China.* London: 1889. Books by missionary women include Henrietta Shuck, *An American Woman in China And her Missionary Work There.* Boston: 1874; Adele Marion Fielde, *Pagoda Shadows: Studies in Chinese Life.* Boston: 1884; Emma Maria Anderson (a Swedish missionary), *"Persecuted but not forsaken". . . the journey of three Swedish missionaries from Ho-nan to the coast.* London: 1900. I am grateful to Minoli Samarakkody for this information.

23 Seneka Bandaranaike, personal interview. University of Kelaniya, Sri Lanka, January 1998.

24 Robert Knox, personal letter, 22 June, 1998.

25 Anil de Silva-Vigier, *This Moste Highe Prince...John of Gaunt 1340–1399.* Durham: The Pentland Press, 1992, p.2.

26 Ibid., p.80.

27 *John of Gaunt,* op. cit., pp.45–6.

28 See Michael Roberts, "Elite Formations and the Elite 1832–1931" in *Sri Lanka: Collective Identities Revisited,* op. cit., for a discussion on the rise of the Karava, Goyigama, Salagama and Durawe elite in nationalist politics.

29 For instance, Anil never spoke about her caste to Romila Thapar who was her research assistant. Romila Thapar, interview, 1997.

30 Kumari Jayawardena, personal communication. Susil Siriwardhana who also knew Anil, noted that once she had achieved what she wanted in life, she was able to talk about the caste discrimination she suffered, with greater ease. Discussion following the presentation of this chapter at the Social Scientist's Association, Colombo, February 2000.

31 Minette de Silva, personal communication, Colombo, July 1997.

32 Jane Russell, *Our George: A Biography of George E. de Silva.* Colombo: *Times of Ceylon,* 1981, p.4.

33 Hence its members were commonly referred to as "dhobis".

34 Bryce Ryan, *Caste in Modern Ceylon: The Sinhalese System in Transition.* New Delhi: Navrang, 1993, pp.116–7.

35 Ibid., p.118.

36 Minette de Silva, *The Life and Times of an Asian Woman Architect,* op. cit., p.25.

37 Jane Russell, *Our George,* chapter 3.

38 On A. E. Goonesinha's advice, George E. de Silva formed a labour union in Kandy in 1923, which was affiliated in 1928 to the Ceylon Labour Union, founded by Goonesinha in 1922. The platform on which

both men campaigned was against "the caucus dominating not only Congress but the political scene in general by a shrewd utilisation of the power of the as yet-unmobilised masses" (Russell, p.52). De Silva and Goonesinha worked closely together, mobilising the labour unions against British capital in the country, and campaigning in London for universal franchise which came to fruition in 1931. A.E.Goonesinha's career was latterly, in the 1930s, mired in controversy however, as he increasingly resorted to a populist communalisation of labour politics (See Kumari Jayawardena, Class and Ethnicity in Sri Lanka. Colombo: Sanjiva, 1985, chapter 5), while his targeting of British capital, sparing the indigenous elite in capitalist enterprise, could be seen as complicit with the nationalist elite for his own political gain. (See Michael Roberts, Ismeth Raheem and Percy Colin-Thome, People In-between. Ratmalana: Sarvodaya, 1989, p.107. For an account of Goonesinha's politics woven into fiction, see S. Sivanandan, When Memory Dies. London: Arcadia Books, 1997.) George E. de Silva broke away from Goonesinha and rejoined the Ceylon National Congress as its president in 1930, a post to which he was re-elected in 1943, 1946 and 1947. (Russell, p.108).

[39] Gombrich and Obeysekere, Buddhism Transformed, pp.233–4.

[40] Roberts, "For Humanity. For the Sinhalese. Dharmapala as Crusading Bosat", p.1009.

[41] Ibid., p. 1014.

[42] Anil Marcia de Silva, "The Scottish Invasion,"; "When the Shakespeare Memorial Theatre Was Opened,"; "Marcia de Silva Meets More Celebrities,"; "Marcia de Silva at the Opera," Times of Ceylon Sunday Illustrated, 15 May, 1932, 22 May, 1932, 29 May, 1932 and 12 June, 1932, respectively.

[43] Partha Chatterjee, The Nation and Its Fragments: Colonial and Postcolonial Histories. New Jersey: Princeton University Press, 1993, chapter 6, "The Nation and Its Women".

[44] I borrow the phrase from a volume that foregrounds the personal testimonies of colonial women writers as path-breakers. Anna Rutherford (ed.), Unbecoming Daughters. Sydney: Dangaroo Press, 1994.

[45] Mosse, op. cit., p.90.

[46] Ibid., p.6.

[47] Monica Juneja, "Imaging the Revolution: Gender and Iconography in French Political Prints," Studies in History Vol.12, No. 1, Jawaharlal Nehru University, New Delhi, January–June 1996, p.19.

[48] Ibid., p.15.

[49] Mosse, op. cit., p.18.

[50] Michael Roberts, "For Humanity," p.14.

51 Ibid., p.15.

52 Uzra Bhatt, personal interview. Lahore, November 1997.

53 Kumari Jayawardena, personal communication.

54 Raj Thapar, *All These Years: A Memoir*. New Delhi: Seminar, 1991, p.12.

55 Henri Cartier-Bresson, sympathy card to Minette de Silva, December 3, 1996.

56 Romila Thapar, interview, Delhi, October 1997.

57 Ann Stoler, "Sexual Affronts and Racial Frontiers: European Identities and the Cultural Politics of Exclusion in Colonial Southeast Asia," in *Comparative Studies in Society and History* 34, No.3, July 1992, p. 516.

58 See Joan L. Erdman with Zohra Segal, *Stages*, p.123. The IPTA production of the Bengali play *Deep Sikha* which had become very popular, was banned by the Delhi government the night before its performance. Sudhi Pradhan (ed.), *Marxist Cultural Movement in India*, p. 302.

59 Romila Thapar, interview, Delhi, October 1997.

60 Lise Vogel, *Marxism and the Oppression of Women: Towards a Unitary Theory*. New Jersey: Rutgers, 1983, chapter 4; Juliet Mitchell, *Women's Estate*. New York: Vintage Books, 1973.

61 Lise Vogel, op. cit., pp.44–5.

62 Ibid., p.44.

63 George Mosse, op. cit., pp.185–6.

64 Romila Thapar, interview, New Delhi, October 1997.

65 U. Vindhya, "Comrades-in-Arms: Sexuality and Identity in the Contemporary Revolutionary Movement in Andhra Pradesh and the Legacy of Chalam," in Mary E. John and Janaki Nair (eds.), *A Question of Silence?: The Sexual Economies of Modern India*. Delhi: Kali for Women, 1998, p.178.

66 Ibid., p.179.

67 Ibid., p.180.

68 Sudhi Pradhan, op. cit.

69 Susie Tharu and K. Lalitha, Introduction, *Women Writing in India* Vol. 2. London: Pandora, p.79.

70 See Michael Roberts, Ismeth Raheem, Percy Colin Thoms, op. cit.

71 Ibid., p.90.

72 Jane Russell, *Our George*, p.18. "Uncle Andreas" supported Anil's sister, Minette, through her architecture course in Bombay. According to Minette, each month a cheque for £ 10 would arrive with a stern note warning against being spendthrift "like the Sinhalese, that is, like my father"!—Minette de Silva, interview, Colombo, July 1997.

[73] Kumari Jayawardena, *From Nobodies to Somebodies*. Colombo: Social Scientists' Association, 2000.

[74] Mudaliyarship was the highest position a native could aspire to in the bureaucracy. A Mudaliyar was responsible for the recruitment of labour, collection of revenue and maintenance of local law and order. Prior to 1833 Mudaliyars provided labour to the British government through *rajakariya*, a system of compulsory labour exacted from the peasantry. After the abolition of *rajakariya* the Mudaliyars acted as interpreters, translators, clerks, tax collectors and advisers to British officials. Land grants to Mudaliyars ended in 1833, but by that date over 50,000 acres had been allocated to them. Kumari Jayawardena, *From Nobodies to Somebodies*, p.22.

[75] Deloraine Brohier, *Dr. Alice de Boer and Some Pioneer Burgher Women Doctors*. Colombo: Social Scientists' Association, 1994, pp. 5–7.

[76] Michael Roberts, et al, *People Inbetween*, pp.152–59. See also Yasmin Gooneratne, *English Literature in Ceylon 1815–1878*. Dehiwela: Tisara Prakasakayo, 1968, chapter 8.

[77] Roberts, et al, op. cit., chapter 10.

[78] Carl Muller's *Jam Fruit Tree* (Penguin, 1993) and sequel *Yakada Yaka* (Penugin, 1994) which related the exploits of lower middle-class Burghers who worked for the Ceylon railways mark a refreshing change, contributing accounts of a community hitherto neglected in both history and fiction.

[79] We have already seen how George E. de Silva was the victim of such racism at the Kandy Bar. There were also many objections to his marriage to Agnes. Burgher respectability was thought to be undermined by someone of George's "obscure origins". However the respective parents of the couple were liberal and supportive of the alliance. (*Our George*, p.18) Michael Ondaatje writes of the adversarial relationship between his father and rather eccentric grandmother, Lalla. Reacting to her daughter's engagement Ondaatje writes, "Lalla turned to friends and said, 'What do you *think*, darling, she's going to marry an Ondaatje,....she's going to marry a *Tamil*!'" ...Lalla continued to stress the Tamil element in my father's background, which pleased him enormously. For the wedding ceremony she had two marriage chairs decorated in a Hindu style and laughed all through the ceremony. The incident was, however, the beginning of a war with my father." *Running in the Family*, pp.118–9.

[80] Jane Russell, op. cit., p.47.

[81] Ibid., p.56.

[82] Ibid., p.68.

[83] Ibid., pp.58–9.

[84] Ibid., p.69.

85 Kumari Jayawardena, personal communication, 1998.

86 S. Arasaratnam, *Ceylon*. New Jersey: Prentice-Hall, 1964, p. 166.

87 Michael Roberts, "Stimulants and Ingredients in the Awakening of Latter-Day Nationalism," in *Sri Lanka: Collective Identities Revisited*, op. cit., p.284.

88 Ibid., pp. 284–5.

89 Thus symbols of the Indian nationalist movement such as the charka, and its strategies of swadeshi and non-violence were absorbed into the Sri Lankan context whether they were appropriate or not. Following Gandhi's visit to Sri Lanka in 1927, George E de Silva was inspired to write, "We must follow the Gandhian inspiration and take up the charka. The spinning wheel will engage the minds of those who are lost today in the maze of fruitless chatter, idle gossip and wicked slander…The spinning wheel will spin out not only fabrics for our bodies and tapestries for our walls but happiness and love for our hearts." (Russell, p.65) This, despite Sri Lanka not being, like India, a significant producer of cotton! The Gandhian image was taken up by the young S.W.R.D.Bandaranaike in the 1930s. A speech by him published in 1938 as a pamphlet entitled, "Charkaya Saha Goyam Keta" (The Spinning Wheel and the Paddy Field) had a photograph of Bandaranaike in Gandhian fashion, behind the spinning wheel. (Roberts, "Stimulants and Ingredients in the Awakening of Latter-Day Nationalism" p. 291)

90 Russell, op. cit., pp.42–3.

91 In keeping with his commitment to lessen the inequalities of caste hierarchies, George E. de Silva successfully brought a motion before the Ceylon National Congress to have the village headman elected by the villagers in a secret ballot, rather than be appointed by the government —a practice which lent itself to favoured appointments. Russell, ibid., p. 75–6.

92 In an autobiographical essay entitled "Apology for Heroism: A Brief Autobiography of Ideas" (Bombay, Kutub-Popular, 1957) first published in 1946 during Anil's time with him, Mulk Raj Anand states that his early ambitions of a legal career ending in a high office, such as that of Chief Justice, were brought down to earth by the snobbery of other castes and classes that dominated Indian society. Anand's family had its origins in the coppersmith profession and although his father left this artisan caste for a career in the Indian army, social prestige never kept pace with his professional mobility thanks to casteism. It was the same in Sri Lanka. Although George E. de Silva's family had moved out of its original profession several generations earlier, the social stigma attached to it had been referred to and reiterated by the upper caste elite.

[93] A good example of the restrictions both Anil and Minette felt took place at a rehearsal for a pageant on "The Heritage of Lanka" to be staged in Kandy in 1937. Minette took part as Vihara Maha Devi, one of Sri Lanka's famous queens. But the *Times of Ceylon* mistakenly, and perhaps mischievously, reported an incident in which she, dressed in yellow robes for the role of Sanghamitta (closely associated with the arrival of Buddhism in Sri Lanka) was seen by an outraged crowd smoking a cigarette. Following this report and the outcry at such blasphemy, the pageant was cancelled. (*Times,*24 August 1937.) Minette was later paid compensation by the *Times* for its inaccurate description of her role in the entire fiasco. (Minette de Silva, personal communication, January 1998.)

[94] Alice Thorner, "Bombay: Diversity and Exchange" in (eds.) Alice Thorner and Sujata Patel, *Bombay: Mosaic of Modern Culture.* Bombay: Oxford University Press, 1995, p.*xii.*

[95] Meera Kosambi, "British Bombay and Marathi Mumbai: Some Nineteenth Century Perceptions" in Thorner and Patel, op. cit., p.4.

[96] Kosambi, op. cit., p.6.

[97] J.V. Naik, "The Seed Period of Bombay's Intellectual Life, 1822–1857," in Thorner and Patel, op. cit., pp.64.

[98] A series of eight letters written under the pen-name "A Hindoo" published in the *Bombay Gazette* in 1841 accused the British, even as he gave them credit for certain humanitarian achievements such as the abolition of sati and female infanticide, for being treacherous in their politics, deceitful in trade, engaging in extortion from peasants, ruining indigenous industry, draining India of her wealth, racial discrimination, withholding high appointments from Indians, judicial injustice, narrow educational policy, hypocrisy regarding religious neutrality, wanton imperialism in Afghanistan and China and lack of objectivity in their writings on India. Naik, op. cit., p. 66.

[99] Ibid., pp.68–9.

[100] Yashodhara Dalmia, "From Jamshetjee Jeejeebhoy to the Progressive Painters" in Thorner and Patel, op. cit., p. 182.

[101] Claude Markovits, "Bombay as a Business Centre in the Colonial Period: A Comparison with Calcutta," in Sujata Patel and Alice Thorner (eds.), *Bombay: Metaphor for Modern India.* Bombay: Oxford University Press, 1995. p.40.

[102] Partha Chatterjee, *The Nation and Its Fragments.* op. cit., chapter 3.

[103] Annapurna Garimella, "Engendering Indian Art" in Vidya Dehejia (ed.), *Representing the Body: Gender Issues in Indian Art.* New Delhi: Kali for Women, 1997, p.32.

[104] Kosambi, op. cit., p.7.

[105] Dalmia, op. cit., p.191.

[106] Romila Thapar, interview. Delhi, October 1997.

[107] Neville Weeraratne, *43 Group: A Chronicle of Fifty Years in the Art of Sri Lanka.* Melbourne: Lantana, 1993. The foremost artists associated with the group were George Keyt, Harry Pieris, Justin Daraniyagala, Geoffrey Beiling, George Claessen, Richard Gabriel, Ivan Peries, L.T.Manjusri and Lionel Wendt.

[108] Ibid., p.111.

[109] Ibid., p.26.

[110] Ibid.

[111] Ibid., p.111.

[112] Ibid.

[113] Jane Russell, quoted in Godfrey Gunatilleke, "The Ideologies and Realities of the Ethnic Conflict—A Postface," in Roberts (ed.), *Sri Lanka: Collective Identities Revisited* Vol. 2. Colombo: Marga, 1998. p.421.

[114] Derek Walcott, "What the Twilight Says: An Overture," in *Dream on Monkey Mountain and Other Plays.* New York: Farrar, Straus & Giroux, 1970, pp.4 & 6.

[115] David James Fisher, *Romain Rolland and the Politics of Intellectual Engagement.* Berkeley: University of California Press, 1988, p.25

[116] Uzra Bhatt for instance, was a dancer with the Prithvi Theatre in Bombay when she took part as Zubeida in the IPTA play of that name, written and directed by Ahmed Abbas, in 1945.

[117] Anil was an excellent cook, as was her mother Agnes Nell, and the author of a book, *Ceylon Cookery.* Her food was innovative and prepared without help or much fuss, but was excellent. Kishwar Jain, Romila Thapar, Kumari Jayawardena, personal communications.

[118] Kumari Jayawardena, discussion following the presentation of this chapter at the Social Scientists' Association, Colombo, February 2000.

[119] Kumari Jayawardena and Seneka Bandaranaike, personal interviews.

[120] Seneka Bandaranaike, interview.

[121] The *Times of Ceylon*, "Marcia Meets More Celebrities," 29 May 1932.

[122] Sri Lanka is unique for being the only country in the world where the Theravada form of Buddhism is practised.

[123] A significant contribution to an assessment of what women like Winifred Nell, Mary Rutnam, Doreen Wickremasinghe, etc., achieved at this time is now in progress through the Gender History series of the Social Scientists' Association, Sri Lanka.

Jean Arasanayagam

3

A QUESTION OF IDENTITY
Jean Arasanayagam's Landscape of the Nation

I have no country now but self.

—*Jean Arasanayagam*[1]

JEAN ARASANAYAGAM IS a Sri Lankan poet and short story writer[2]
whose work is a testimony to a ceaseless re-positioning of
herself within the changing and crisis-ridden language and
landscape of the nation. What makes her particularly sensitive to
contemporary articulations of nationalism in post-colonial Sri
Lanka is that her ethnic and class origins, religion, education and
marriage place her at the very interstices of the identities in con-
tention, that is, in the gaps and crevices where they both overlap
and displace each other. She is a Burgher of Dutch ancestry and
therefore a descendant of the agents of colonial rule.[3] Her colonial education places her amongst the English-speaking cultural
elite of the nation. Yet she lives in a society where such privilege
is a site of contest. Given the post-independence prominence of
Sinhala as the language of administration and medium of instruc-
tion in schools, and the adoption in state rituals of the cultural
practices of the Sinhala Buddhist majority which she stands outside of,[4] Arasanayagam belongs to a cultural minority which has
become increasingly marginalised. The command of the English
language however still carries with it social status, mobility of
profession, access to travel and the potential for cosmopolitanness,
unavailable to her fellow citizens who are outside the privileges
of class and the colonial tongue. She inhabits a further paradox
in an identity both dislocated and enriched by being a Christian
married into an orthodox Hindu-Tamil family from Jaffna, the

major city of the Tamil north of Sri Lanka. Occupying these indeterminate spaces, what are the cultural options that the Sri Lankan post-colonial nation has to offer her, in which she can find affinity?

The thematic and narrative discourses, the language and metaphors to be found in Arasanayagam's work are dictated by this question. They produce an interesting paradox. On the one hand they challenge the assertions of many postcolonial writers and critics, that cosmopolitanism and syncretism are the ultimate metaphors of the postcolonial condition.[5] Her writings imply that syncretism is never an *equal* mixing of diverse inheritances, that cosmopolitanism is classed and raced, and that identity is as much about political exigency dictated by the dominant hegemony. It is also gendered. On the other hand, they testify to the fact that a hybrid, cosmopolitan and secular space is the only one in which a postcolonial writer such as Arasanayagam can find a congenial home. In a nation that, in its postcolonial era, has taken a different route from these ideals, Jean Arasanayagam's work is about negotiating a legitimacy for herself within its terrain. In this negotiation and in choosing her cultural affiliations, she had a robust archive of (post)colonial debate to drawn on.[6]

Re-imagining (Post) Coloniality

In casting off the colonial yoke, as (post)colonial writers began to re-vision their identities of culture, community and nation, an influential body of post-Négritude writing and theory developed from the mid 1950s onwards, that forwarded a synthesis of European and indigenous traditions as the "authentic" identity for the colonial. The Caribbean, in particular, was a region which held rich promise of syncretism for its colonial subjects. Its particular colonial history of deracination, slavery, genocide of native populations and near effacement of indigenous epistemes produced what some writers saw as a tabula rasa where, "if there was nothing, there was everything to be made"[7]. Ironically, the notion of such a vacuum traced a genealogy to a colonial discourse which dated indigenous history to be only as old as the colonial encounter. The pre-colonial, if at all, was dismissed, nonup the position: "We have no adequate reference of traditional conduct. . . (and) are made to feel a sense of exile by our inadequacy and our irrelevance of function in a society whose past we can't alter, and whose future is always beyond us."[8] For the West Indian, only Friday's footprints in the sand remained.

How was this void to be filled, how could the future be claimed? The debates in the Caribbean resonate with those that took place elsewhere in the (post)colonial world, including Sri Lanka, although the specificities of each society, its particular history and temporal contexts dictated their nuances. By and large there were two distinct responses: one which sought to return to, and privilege, pre-colonial indigenous traditions; the other which argued for syncretism of the diverse inheritances the colonial was heir to, including the indigenous and European. That these arguments have taken place in different places and temporalities, and with differing emphases, yet have remained essentially the same throughout five decades of (post) coloniality, says much about their allure for the colonial redefining his/her society, as well as the fact that nationalism's closures are never complete. In the Caribbean, the "absence" of traditions endemic to the region pushed nationalists to look to Africa as their homeland of origin. In the 1960s this went hand in hand with the spread of black nationalism and the black power movement in Trinidad, inspired by the U.S. civil rights movement of the time. Many Caribbean writers and scholars looked to Africa as their legitimate cultural source which also offered models of political institutions that could be emulated. (Many African countries had gained independence in the early 1960s and adopted socialist policies.) Arguing that African traditions did survive the middle passage to be transplanted and transformed on Caribbean soil, these nationalists took to scholarship and re-intepretation of the African presence in the Caribbean.[9] (Later, Alice Walker would focus on the African legacy in North America as a central paradigm in her understanding and definition of Womanism.) But in their crudest and most extreme nationalist articulations, the legitimacy of all else (not just European, but other ethnic communities the colonial encounter had brought to the Caribbean) was repudiated in favour of the black African. On a tour of Guyana in 1971,

Stokely Carmichael declared, "Black Power means just what it says: Power to black people. Not for Indians, nor for Chinese, but black people alone."[10] While the definitive struggle was to free the region of Euro-American capitalist exploitation, this type of nationalist rhetoric, taking its cue from colonialist discourse, remained stuck at reiterating a particular trope of race as the defining paradigm for the Caribbean.

The counter argument insisted that the European legacy could not be wished away, that it had changed the course of Caribbean history, and contributed much to its culture. For the colonial whose ancestry derived from both Africa and Europe, whose education and cultural orientation were European, the fascination with Africa spelt a "romantic darkness", a futile urge for revenge and an escape from the reality of the region as cosmopolitan.[11] St. Lucian poet and playwright, Derek Walcott (later Nobel laureate) called for a celebration of the Caribbean writer as "the mulatto of style. . . the assimilator".[12] Writers like Wilson Harris of Guyana, George Lamming and Roberto Fernando Ratemar of Cuba—the latter two vocal against Euro-American exploitation of the region—nevertheless celebrated the Caribbean as a *culturally* rich site "where the world met",[13] a place unique for being a "vast zone for which *mestizaje* (racial intermingling) is not an accident, but rather the essence, the central line".[14] In the late 1970s when feminist scholars began to appraise the role of women's identity and writing in the Caribbean,[15] similar affirmations of heterogeneity were articulated, heterogeneity made all the more dynamic by its gendering. Elaine Savory Fido declared:

I am still primarily interested in the way in which Caribbean literature is a confluence of ethnic literatures, primarily African, but an African presence mediated through other influences so that it becomes Creole, Caribbean. The feminist lens, then, becomes another way of seeing this complex culture—women's culture and women's place in the world constitute another vital strand of consciousness here.[16]

These debates echoed elsewhere in the colonial world where nationalism solicited a redefinition of political and cultural identities. On the Indian subcontinent and the African continent, where a colonial history of deracination and transplantation was less pronounced and indigenous systems could be recouped more easily than in the Caribbean, there was a return to the myths of the immediate land and its gods,[17] to pre-colonial heroic achievements and the sophistication of indigenous cultures, architecture and languages. Language became a particularly fraught terrain of contestation, when whether to write in the native or colonial tongue became a significant question in redefining (post)colonial identity. In many of these "return(s) to the source", myth, and pre-colonial and contemporary histories were recounted as forming a chronological continuum.[18] The return to mythology was not without controversy. When Nigerian Nobel laureate, Wòle Soyinka interpreted the myth of the Yoruba god Ogun as an apt *metaphor* for (post)coloniality, his discussion was critiqued for occurring within the all embracing title, *Myth, Literature and the African World*[19]; this homogenised the "African World", privileged one episteme over the other and, in defining an archetype, effaced pluralities within Nigeria itself. He was also accused of a "mythopoeic narcissism" in his work.[20] Fierce arguments raged as to whether the myth of Ogun could accommodate Nigeria's modernity or not.[21] The alternative did not displace the importance of Africa itself as the prime focus and locus of (post)colonial redefinition, but suggested a materialist understanding of its societies' socio-political and religious structures and the possibilities of reform and regeneration within them.[22]

In India, the modern search for an authentic Indian history was signposted by Bengali nationalist elites like Bankimchandra Chattopadhyay (1838–94), who insisted that Indians must have a history and that it should be written by Indians themselves. In 1880, using Bengal interchangeably with India, Bankim declared "Bengal must have a history, or else there is no hope for it. Who will write it? You will write it, I will write it... Every Bengali will have to write it."[23] The British version of Indian history was inauthentic and to be discounted. As Partha Chatterjee notes, "In the mode of recalling the past, the power to represent oneself is nothing other than political power itself."[24] This was put to use both against the British and the Muslims in India. Bankim's version of "true" Indian history, with its glorious pre-British past, was one in which the heroic protagonists were Hindus who fought the invading and marauding Moguls. The story of this struggle and Hindu achievement therein were in keeping with an already declared challenge to British colonialism, and a warning to Muslims of their alien status in India. Indian nationalism was synonymous with Hindu nationalism.

In contrast was Rabindranath Tagore, who asserted that Hinduism carried the potential for hybridity, assimilation and eclecticism. He wrote, "We forget that Hindu civilization was once very much alive, crossing the seas, planting colonies, giving to and taking from all the world. It had its arts, its commerce, its vast and strenuous field of work. In its history new ideas had their opportunity."[25] Disillusioned with the Swadeshi movement's use of neo-Hindu symbols to garner nationalist support and passion, Tagore noted that this orthodoxy and its politics of nationalism were to blame, for constructing Hinduism as exclusionary in a sectarianism which militated against his ideal of a common humanity as a "federation of the races". He warned against the nationalism which both incorporated and provided the vehicle for such orthodoxy in these terms:

An education which can free the nations from this ungodly fetish of Nationalism is what is chiefly needed today. Tomorrow is to begin the chapter of the federation of the races. Any evil tendencies of thought and sinful habits which militate against the spirit of federation will unfit us to take our part in the history of tomorrow. I hope I can claim to be duly conscious of the glories of my own country, but my fervent prayer is that such consciousness may never make me forgetful of the earliest message of our seers, the message of unity, in which the forces of disruption can have no place.[26]

It followed that the ideal culture for achieving such a federation, was an eclectic one. Writing of his admiration for the Indian reformist, Rammohun Roy, Tagore noted:

The ideal I have formed of the culture which should be universal in India, has become clear to me from the life of Rammohun Roy. I have come to feel that the mind which has been matured in the atmosphere of a profound knowledge of its own country, and of the perfect thoughts that have been produced in that land, is ready to accept and assimilate the cultures that come from foreign countries.

Ibid., p.352.

Here was a recognition that re-visiting native thought and tradition was imperative for (post)colonial recovery, but that this re-visioning of native culture needed to be enriched (towards the project of Indian modernity itself) with the best from all cultures, including those of the West. In 1921 Tagore wrote:

It is the dream of my heart that the culture-centre of our country should also be the meeting ground of the East and West. In the field of business, antagonism still prevails; it struggles hard against reconcilement. In the field of culture, there is no such obstacle. The householder who is exclusively occupied with his domestic concern and is chary of his hospitality, is poor in spirit. No great country can afford to be confined to its kitchen, it must have its reception room where it can do honour to itself by inviting the world.

Ibid., p.437.

As noted in Chapter 3, Mulk Raj Anand added to this line of thinking when in the 1940s he forwarded a view of Indian society that captured a pan-Indian diversity and refused to fetishise tradition for its own sake. We also noted how a cultural association like IPTA drew its inspiration from Romain Rolland's *The People's Theatre*, and committed itself to heterogeneous theatre forms, including indigenous ones. By making a serious study of classical Sanskrit drama and folk theatre IPTA sought, in the words of Anil de Silva, to "experiment in a synthesis of these two forms with modern stage technique and lighting".[27] IPTA also drew inspiration from writers and intellectuals in America and Asia who had organised themselves during World War II to resist imperialism and fascism wherever in the world they occurred.[28] These ideals were close to the writers of the Progressive Writers' Movement and the work of its foremost women writers, Rashid Jehan and Ismat Chughtai brought gender nuances to those of class, religion and imperialism. In her short fiction and novels like "The Quilt" (1942) and *The Crooked Line* (1943) Chughtai foregrounded female narrators who negotiate the difficult and complex terrain of desire within the space of tradition/the nation.[29] Rashid Jehan took on the architecture of public/zenana spaces to work out a politics that sought to allow women under siege to live a better, though not necessarily different, life. Miraji, a male writer of the Progressive Writers' Association with a female name and, therefore, the hybridity of androgyny, demanded a syncretic reading of his work. He brought together in a complex way various strands of indigenous poetics to European ones like symbolism and modernism to fill the "void" produced by the deracination of the colonial encounter. His essays on local writers, using the mode of analysis offered by Roger Fry on Mallarme and published in *Adabi Duniya*, as well as his essays on Indian poetry and western poets, followed the PWA's adherence to forms of syncretism as a poetic, political praxis.[30]

The contemporary interventions of Salman Rushdie take this cosmopolitan politics further, aspiring to a world without borders, repudiating nationalism as a " 'revolt against history' which seeks to close what cannot any longer be closed. To fence in what should be frontierless," so that "good writing assumes a frontierless nation".[31] Rushdie's internationalism takes its cue not only from his individual biography of being born in Bombay, educated at Cambridge, domiciled in London, with family in India and Pakistan, but also his sense of belonging to an international family of writers, working with a literary form that is frontierless. He stated:

If you are an extra-territorial writer you select a pedigree for yourself, a literary family. . . Swift, Conrad, Marx are as much our literary forbears as Tagore or Ram Mohun Roy...We are inescapably international writers at a time when the novel has never been a more international form. . . cross-pollination is everywhere.[32]

This cross-fertilisation is valuable for Rushdie as it carries the possibilities of innovation. Following the fatwa which put a price on his head for defaming the Prophet and Islam, Rushdie wrote in defence of *Satanic Verses*:

The Satanic Verses celebrates hybridity, impurity, intermingling, the transformation that comes of new and unexpected combinations of human beings, cultures, ideas, politics, movies, songs. It rejoices in mongrelization and fears the absolutism of the Pure. Melange, hotchpotch, a bit of this and a bit of that is *how newness enters the world*. It is the great possibility that mass migration gives the world, and I have tried to embrace it. *The Satanic Verses* is for change-by-fusion, change-by-conjoining. It is a love song to our mongrel selves.[33]

Like Rushdie, Jean Arasanayagam would acknowledge her "mongrel" self and reject the myths of purity of race and culture. Yet, she would show that hybridity is not necessarily an easy identity to wear, particularly while living within the nation's territorial and ideological boundaries. Rushdie himself concedes that celebrating hybridity and secularism "may have been easier...to do from outside modern India than inside it".[34] The complex and contradictory pulls that Jean Arasanayagam has to negotiate from within the nation, as well as the violence that has become systemic in Sri Lankan postcoloniality, make her take both, a more guarded position on syncretism as the quintessential postcolonial condition, and express a pessimistic view of the nation's political and cultural landscapes. However, as will be discussed later, apocalyptic views of the nation are within the ideology of a cosmopolitanism that advocates syncretism. Moreover, the internationalism of writers like Rushdie and Walcott are both classed and gendered. The events of the 1950s in Sri Lanka, the ascendant cultural and linguistic nationalism of the period that set in motion the eventual displacement and de-centering of those outside the Sinhala language and its culture, the rise of Tamil nationalism in response to this and the migration of Burgher professionals and elites from its shores, were to have a profound impact on the nation's course and on how writers like Arasanayagam re-imagined its landscapes.

1956 and the Postcolonial Landscape

1956 marks a watershed in the story of Sri Lankan nationalism. Building on the Buddhist revival of the late 19th century which gave an impetus to the anti-British nationalist struggle, S.W.R.D. Bandaranaike led the Sri Lanka Freedom Party which he founded in 1951 to a sweeping mandate in the 1956 elections, and reinstated both the status of the Sinhala language and Buddhism as the foremost religion of the nation. Himself the son of a wealthy, westernised, Christian Sinhala aristocrat, Bandaranaike was educated at Oxford, but political exigency demanded a (re)conversion to Buddhism and Sinhala-ness on returning to Sri Lanka and entering national politics. The 'Sinhala Only' movement he gave direction to signalled a decisive "event" in the nation's postcolonial journey. It brought together both peasant and provincial middle class constituencies. Through the *Sinhala Mahā Sabhā* Bandaranaike made contact with villagers and peasants and inspired in them a cultural nationalism that reinstated the value of

Sinhala from its denigrated position in British colonial times. He was also able to muster crucial support for this agenda from the Sinhala-speaking bourgeoisie made up of village headmen, translators, registrars and clerks of the colonial government; school teachers, Ayurvedic physicians, Buddhist monks, planters and provincial entrepreneurs whose status in society had suffered under colonial rule. These "touchstones for the masses at large" called for a greater degree of social justice.[35] During British rule the language of administration, commerce and influential education was English, a language that 85-90 per cent of the population did not speak or write. The nationalist agenda of Bandaranaike and his supporters was to dismantle this system and replace it with one in which the Sinhala-speaking bourgeoisie would enjoy dominance. A coalition of the above forces together with Sinhala landed gentry and professionals, and a "no contest" pact with the main left-wing parties made this electorally possible.[36]

Jayadeva Uyangoda writes of these events and their re-visioning of the postcolonial state in these terms:

The state-reformist agenda of the Sinhala nationalist movement of the early Fifties posited that the independence of 1948 was an incomplete task since it did not restore the lost sovereignty of the Sinhalese-Buddhist nation. In order to complete political independence and make independence meaningful and relevant to the majority, a political re-constructionist vision was mapped out in a religio-political idiom. A defining feature of it was the pre-coloniality of its major expectations of sovereignty, duties of the state, paternalistic welfarism, relationship between the state and religion, and the role of the Buddhist religious elite in the affairs of the state. In other words, Sinhala nationalism re-imagined and re-conceptualized Sri Lanka's post-colonial state through a pre-colonial idiom of power. No other social or political force in Sri Lanka has so far been able to appropriate the state with so much vigour and vitality as radical Sinhalese nationalism. The only alternative it allowed to emerge, in a logic of negative dialectic, was militant Tamil nationalism to counter its own discursive categories of political power.[37]

In keeping with the desire for such a sovereign state, the political agendas of Bandaranaike and the SLFP stood for an equally radical nationalist politics. Once in power, defence agreements with Britain were cancelled, and the British air force base at

Katunayake and its naval base at Trincomalee transferred to the Sri Lankan state. Diplomatic links with communist countries such as China and the U.S.S.R. were forged and the doctrine of non-alignment was adopted as foreign policy. A Paddy Lands Bill of 1958 insured peasant cultivation, and the Colombo port and bus companies were nationalised.[38] It was, however, the 1956 Language Bill which moved to make Sinhala the only language of administration, that caused the first major upheaval in the postcolonial nation's history after the *hartāl* of 1953, and the mood and events that led to Bandaranaike's assassination in 1959.

During 1951-3, the SLFP stood for both Sinhala and Tamil as official languages of the newly independent nation. But by 1956 when Bandaranaike became Prime Minister, the right-wing faction within the SLFP which promoted a Sinhala Only policy, was in ascendance. Bandaranike, himself not averse to negotiating with Tamil politicians (as far back as 1929 he had expressed the conviction that "political power in Sri Lanka had to be shared by ethnic communities on the principle of political equality")[39] caved in to this constituency and mooted the Sinhala Only Act in Parliament. There was widespread dissent from Sri Lankan Tamils. The Sinhala Only agenda effectively pushed them out of administrative jobs in the public service. The Tamil Federal Party organised a satyagraha campaign. Bandaranaike, realising the danger and volatility of the situation, decided to negotiate with the Federal Party on devolution of power in the Tamil majority areas of the country and, through the Tamil Language (Special Provision) Act, make it the language of administration in those areas. But the communal enmity that all this had unleashed could not be contained. The Sinhala Only lobby militated against the negotiations. J.R.Jayawardena, a future President of Sri Lanka who oversaw the 1983 pogrom against the Tamils, led a march from Colombo to Kandy protesting against any concession to the Tamils. Ethnic riots broke out in 1958 throughout the country and in September 1959, Bandaranaike was assassinated by a Buddhist monk angered at his perceived conciliatory stance towards the Tamils. [40]

What was the impact of these upheavals on the Dutch Burgher community to which Jean Arasanayagam (née Solomons) belonged, and to its ideal (as expressed in literary journals like *The*

Examiner and *Young Ceylon*) of a Ceylonese nationalism that was cosmopolitan and inclusive of all communities? The Dutch Burghers have occupied shifting and often contradictory positions in Sri Lankan society. From colonial privilege during the Dutch regime (1658-1796) they became, in British times (1796-1948), not central players but a privileged marginal group nevertheless. As a distinct community, they were well placed to take advantage of the system the British put in place. They were already Christian, their elite had fair complexions,[41] were urban, westernised and possessed a language close to English. They joined the British administration as middle and lower rung bureaucrats while some, depending on their class status, availed themselves of British education and went on to serve in the legal, medical, academic and journalistic professions. Although they were by and large socially excluded by the British, they did not make an effort to integrate with the Sinhala, Tamil or Muslim communities either.

The Burghers in ethnic, political, and cultural terms occupied not so much a homeland as a nebulous borderland; they were a liminal people, neither there nor here, fully at home only within their created Burgherhood. Theirs was an attempt at exclusivity at the fringes rather than at the centre.[42]

With the upsurge of anti-British nationalism and the culmination of its political project in independence in 1948, the Burghers of Sri Lanka had to contend with a fast-changing order in which the choice was either to emigrate or re-negotiate their place within the new hegemony. The 1958 Sinhala-Tamil communal riots would significantly mark their marginality within the nation, outside the ethnicity of these two main communities, culturally alienated from the new dispensation and sidelined from administration when the Sinhala-speaking bourgeoisie took over.

Jean Arasanayagam describes the effects of the 1958 riots on her in a chapter entitled, "The Last Enemy" in the autobiographical account of her life, *A Nice Burgher Girl*:[43]

Each one of us was confronted with a sense of our separate identities and individual loyalties. For whom would we feel a sense of sympathy? For the other? For whomsoever was the victim? This kind of danger was new to us.

"The island will soon be in flames," someone declared. We tasted ter-

ror words on our tongue. Chill sweat crept under our armpits. The close-
ness, the intimacy we had shared with each other in this vision of the
world, so small, so limited, was now and for all time fragmented. Dissi-
pated in contorted shadows.

When I reached home I heard my parents listening to the radio. At that
time I was young. Unmarried. I had just bought a seven valve HMV Radio. I had an old gramophone on which I played a collection of old jazz
records....That evening I first listened to the voice of the Prime Minister.
His urgent tones sounded hoarse, weary. Two political parties were proscribed—the Federal Party and the Jathika Eksath Peramuna. Martial law
was declared over the whole island.

I began to think of my own contextual status in this crisis. I did not
belong to either of the two communities embroiled in the racial and communal tensions. All I knew was that I belonged, wanted, desired greatly,
to belong in this island where I had my roots. I was yet to feel myself
divided among the divided. (pp.3-4).

That sense of division and unbelonging would be experienced
most sharply twenty-five years later, in July 1983, when the UNP
government of the day, together with Sinhala gangs, mounted
attacks against the Tamils as reprisal for the LTTE ambush and
killing of 13 soldiers. The violence was severe, and signalled the
beginning of the separatist war that continues to blight the nation. Thousands of Tamils were affected. There was loss of life
and property and internal displacement, while many had to seek
refuge abroad as a result of the pogrom. Arasanayagam and her
family had to flee temporarily to a refugee camp close to their
home in Kandy. But even before this she had been alive to the
socio-political changes taking place and her own sense of unease
within the emerging postcolonial nation. That unease was heightened by the loss of what the liberal, middle class Burgher community stood for during Sri Lanka's bid for independence. As
noted in the last chapter, these Burghers had committed themselves to forging an eclectic polity within Sri Lanka itself, rather
than hanker after an European home. (Arasanayagam's statement, "All I knew was that I belonged, wanted, desired greatly,
to belong in this island where I had my roots", bears this out.) In
their spirited defence against British racism, the Sri Lankan
Burghers had refuted the category of race as a definitive paradigm in the nation's postcoloniality. They argued for a Ceylonese
nationalism that would repudiate communalism and casteism.

The legitimacy of eclecticism, as it imagined a secular, democratic, multi-ethnic Sri Lanka would no doubt best suit the
Burghers who could continue to play a significant role within the
nation as professionals, planters and managers of agency houses.
The events of 1956 greatly damaged these expectations and made
their vision of a cosmopolitan polity increasingly difficult to
realise.

Postcolonial Unease

The predominant images from Jean Arasanayagam's first collection of poems, *Kindura* (1973), reflect these concerns and are
those of unease, restriction, alienation, decay. The title poem
draws on the *Jātaka* story which tells of the Bodhisatva as a
kindura, half-human, half-bird. Its hybridity resonates with the
poet's own identity; but what is foregrounded is not a celebration of that duality, but a suppression of one part, that makes the
calm façade a deception:

> Feathers slice off your waist,
> Tail plumes splay the air,
> Claws grasp earth,
> Fingers touch flute,
> Music twitters from those human lips.
> Your imperturbable profile
> Does not suggest
> Discrepancy or disembodiment,
> Yet your folded wings
> Unruffled feathers
> Suggest an immobility
> Of flight arrested,
> And I see in my own
> Submerged personality,
> A strange, restless
> Ghost of Kindura.[44]

The *kindura* is caught, neither able to enjoy the freedom of a
bird—"slice" and "splay" alliterations that connote a laboured
flight and even immobility or damage in folded wings — nor
fulfil its human potential, for the music is not harmony but a
twitter not a song. The poem, carefully crafted, speaks eloquently

of a postcolonial condition in which the poet is restricted, haunted by the ghost of a bird with its feathers sliced, rather than at liberty to celebrate its flight/claim her diverse inheritances. Here is the challenge to the hybrid-multicultural argument that is not sufficiently cognizant of the lived, everyday realities at high points of nationalism, which determine which identity is to be foregrounded, which to be suppressed. In the aftermath of the 1950s, effects of which were seen in Sri Lanka well into the 1960s and 1970s, the poet's multiple and indeterminate selves provide a sense of strangeness and unease in a difference that is arrested rather than enabling. An unqualified politics of syncretism is not an option for her.

This difference comes not only from belonging to an ethnic minority and subscribing to a cultural entity under siege, but also from the poet's class position and urban milieu, all of which overdetermine each other. In "A Seasonal Adjustment" Jean Arasanayagam contemplates her alienation from the landscape and "its people". Watching men and women working the rice fields she is struck by the bond between them and the land:

> The sun with strong hands
> Strokes their breasts and burnished faces,
> Recreating each season,
> The body bends, then rises,
> A compulsion of the blood
> ...
> Living with earth,
> Their bodies passage
> Through this life
> A recurring ritual
> ...
> With earth and growing,
> There is no separateness.

Kindura, p.43

Romanticism, the attraction for the peasant attuned to the land, unambiguously possessing a sense of rooted identity – "Do I envy them their innocence?" the poet asks — and ready acceptance of life and body in syncopation with the seasons, while the city dwelling poet stands apart—"Wishing vain hope,/ Acceptance/ Of my own ages seasonal/ Adjustment"—are evident here. That urban life, education and class have a price to be paid in the alienation from the well "adjusted" peasant are echoed in other colonial responses too, for they traced a common genealogy to a western romantic tradition, its poetry and painting, imbued in the colonial through education. Accordingly, an urban/rural divide, current in European thought following the industrial revolution and its aftermath, was reconstructed in the colonies. Romanticism also anthropomorphised nature as an inner force so that the peasant body became abstracted through the naturalised movement of work. Derek Walcott was aware of these influences when he wrote with self-irony of the elite gaze on the St. Lucian fisherman:

Theirs was a naked, pessimistic life, crusted with the dirty spume of beaches. They were a sect which had evolved its own signs, a vocation which excluded the stranger. The separation of town from countryside and countryside from sea challenged your safety, and all one's yearning was to enter that life without living it. It smelled strong and true. But what was its truth?

That in the "New Aegean" the race, of which these fishermen were the stoics, had grown a fatal adaptability. As black absorbs without reflection they had rooted themselves with a voracious, unreflecting calm. By all arguments they should have felt displaced, seeing this ocean as another Canaan, but that image was the hallucination of professional romantics, writer and politician.[45]

It is the "unreflecting calm" of Walcott's fisherfolk that is echoed in Arasanayagam's finely controlled poem which listens to the rhythms of the villagers' work songs, and contemplates the recurring movement of the cyclical harvest and its repetitive *assuredness* that anchors the peasant to the land in a way that eludes the poet. A similar statement is expressed in "The Village" in which the poet's sense of estrangement from the village women who go about their daily tasks brings about a restlessness that "(Tears) a dream apart/ Scattering its fragments/ In my mind's vast, spatial vacuum." (*Kindura*, p.48)

As the poet stands apart, aware of difference, the villages are celebrated in rich, lush images of a bounteous nature and breathtaking landscape. Their rituals and the landscape which are the

178   WOMEN & THE NATION'S NARRATIVE

focus of her gaze encompass for her all that is wholesome and
untroubled by the angst of problematic identities. The villagers
live harmoniously with their environment, blest by "the river (that)
comes to meet them/ The trees grow close to their home/ The
fruit falls ripe for their food." (*Kindura*, p.48) Even when, as in
"Monsoon Rains", nature is on the onslaught, the emphasis in
the poem is on the monsoon's effect on the *landscape* rather than
the people. The exception is the persona of the poet, who becomes the only person in the lyric – "I creep into myself/ Away
from cold and wet/ Like a cricket in a leaf shelter/ And cease to
sing" (*Kindura*, p.53)). Her "I" comes into being through a Romantic vision of the colonial, the pastoral, the rural, which encourages an exotic understanding of the seasonal downpour. For
even while "Rank growth stretches roots/ Snaking its way through
sodden/ Moss and fungi" or "Parasitic creepers/ Twine rope ten-
tacles round/ Bark abraded trees", one also listens enthralled to
the "Syllables of water sound/ dripping from trees/ Utter melan-
choly dialogues", or looks on "Silver tributaries of water/ Streak
the rice-fields" and marvels at the image of "Leaves (that) flare
great green cobra heads." Such recoupings of the peasant and
village landscape come ironically close (ironically, because this is
not Jean Arasanayagam's political project) to nationalist
imaginings which forwarded the goodness of the village in contrast to the urban metropolis corrupted by colonial/alien ways.
Jean Arasanayagam's pastoral also stands in contrast to a kind
of past that produced itself as cultured, as having an ancient history, literature and body of aesthetic knowledge as promoted by
the nationalists. This disjuncture also recapitulated the one practised by orientalists who presented the village as separate and
oppositional to the "classical".[46]

The Mark of Cain

A primeval garden of Eden thus mapped, the systemic violence
of the nation's postcoloniality becomes an affront to the landscape. The beautiful and bounteous garden that evokes the Garden of Eden is an image which appears frequently in Jean
Arasanayagam's poems. Its origins lie in her father's garden in

the railway bungalow (he was an engine driver) that the family occupied in Kadugannawa. In *A Nice Burgher Girl* she writes:

My father created his garden, primeval in its innocence, a sanctuary for birds. At the same time it was the garden of his grief. He would ask me to touch the stems of thornless roses on the bushes he had planted. He did not want me to feel the pain of that stabbing thorn. Nor would he allow me to pluck a flower from that garden. The flowers bloomed and shed their petals in their natural season. But I plucked his flowers notwithstanding. Surely he would not miss a flower or two, but he did and up-braided me. There were certain rules that must not be transgressed. The garden was his Eden. The earth awoke and became a cradle in which he nurtured his roses, his Holy Ghost orchids, the hollyhocks and mugerine bush. At dusk the glow worms shone through the leaves in a nimbus of green phosphorescent light. Fireflies glimmered as they flashed their tiny lanthorns among the masses of dark leaves. Green chameleons impaled insects on their sticky tongues. The grey chickanellas were watchful among the flower-beds. And at evening the praying mantises and cicadas crept into the house when the lamps were lit...the birds and squirrels fed from my father's hands, they were so tame, so familiar with and unafraid of his presence... (pp.1-2)

Such a landscape, fecund, a safe haven for small animals and birds, even if it did carry its own "grief" and cycle of hunting and preying, is a garden that offers the poet safe sanctuary. Its primeval cyclical temporality stands against the linearity/fracture of present time provoked by violence. The post-independence violence from 1958 onwards changed the topoi of this Garden of Eden forever. With the 1971 JVP insurrection and its quelling by the SLFP government came another spell of brutal killings. In her poem, "April 1971" the poet's comment on that annihilation is located in the juxtaposition of two contrasting images. One is of breathtaking beauty, where "The paddyfields flow with the river/ Into the green wilderness of trees,/ Miasmic mists float over/ blue ranges", while "On the other side of the mountain/ thick blood flows from the jungle/ On the trampled grasses lie/ Scattered bodies like fallen trees". (*Kindura*, p.49) The closing stanza leaves us with the poet's apocalyptic vision—a later title of her anthology of short stories would be *All is Burning*—of a culture of violence that will permeate the nation's future.

Blue foliage trembles in the pelting rain,
Trees disappear in thick mists,
Now there are no mountains
Only falling rain
And bloated bodies
Casually drifting downriver.

Kindura, p.50.

The violent upheavals of the south have their parallels in the
north of the country, to which Jean Arasanayagam is linked
through marriage. Just as the changing landscape from lush primeval forests and Garden of Eden to damp and rank undergrowth
or arid desert[47] is an index of a way of life that is eroding, religious ritual and architectural grandeur are, in Arasanayagam's
poems, the markers of an elite Hindu lifestyle that is under threat
in a Tamil society in transition.

The ancient house   without echoes,
    an inner courtyard   filled with sand
            is strangely empty
            in the forenoon of your life.

The poet addresses her ageing Hindu mother-in-law here whose
domain, as for many women, is the inner courtyard—the title of
the poem. But the home and its courtyard are silent, shorn of
children and servants over whom the mother-in-law presided. It
tells of the old woman's loss of privilege, taken away at knife-
point by her own servants, demanding an end to caste and class
discrimination:[48]

                            All these voices
                    raised against you
        Gather with fury
                to strike
        the lingam and the stone naga head
            In Ganesh's temple.

        The knife in Kandan's hand
        Which severs the flower
                is the knife of the present

Which points
at your breast and those of your kinsmen
Who are alone,
left.

Kindura, p.75.

The awakenings of militant Tamil nationalism are discerned
in this poem written in the early 1970s. They will be the cries,
call to arms and bloodshed that, in Jean Arasanayagam's later
work, signal the fracture of the land and violent erasure of privileged, traditional ways of life. But there is also an irony here
borne out of personal vicissitude. Jean Arasanayagam herself was
as much a victim of orthodox Hindu caste hierarchies as the
Kandan who militantly demands a new dispensation. In poems
like "Mother-in-law", "Women, Goddesses and Their Mythologies", and "We See Each Other"[49] she writes of a tense, if not
openly hostile, relationship with her mother-in-law who had opposed her entry into their upper caste Hindu family, objecting
strenuously to the poet's Dutch Burgher ancestry and Christian
faith. This foreclosed for Jean, the normative de-ethnicising of
the woman who makes an inter-ethnic/religious marriage and
who, in taking on her husband's name/ ethnicity and religion,
suppresses her own. Deprived of the choice of entering a Brah-
min Hindu Tamil identity on the one hand, and a dominant
Sinhala Buddhist one on the other, the poet has few choices but
to insist on a secular, multi-ethnic polity that is her liberal/Burgher
predilection anyway. (This, notwithstanding the hierarchies within
the Burgher community itself and the prejudice of its elites to
those who were mixed, darker and of Portuguese heritage, or
Eurasian.) Jean Arasanayagam has always taken a firm stand
against such prejudice. The title of her autobiography, *A Nice
Burgher Girl,* affirms a retort she made to an elite Burgher who,
on meeting her after many years remarked, "But then, you were
a nice Burgher girl!" His implied lament was that in marrying a
Tamil she had sullied her *Burgherness.*[50] It is the repudiation, in
the tradition of Charles Lorenz and the Nells, of such racism and
their vision of a Ceylonese nationalism shorn of caste and ethnic
politics, that underwrites the poet's understanding of an ironical

situation in which the same haughtiness, casteism and consciousness of property which ostracised her, are now the cause of her
mother-in-law's downfall at the hands of her own (but undercaste)
people. However, as the poet contemplates her mother-in-law's
change of fortune and the passing away of a particular lifestyle,
her sympathy is for the defenceless woman in the evening of her
life, a sympathy heightened by a terror of those opposing the old
woman and the violence of that opposition. The repudiation of
such violence compels Arasanayagam, even as she acknowledges
the injustice of caste and class hierarchies in Jaffna society, to
deny the legitimacy of the demands for their dismantling. A poem
like "The Inner Courtyard" refuses to present in any great depth
the *people* behind the summons for a new order. They remain
mere voices which are, foremost, "strident", "clamour(ing)" and
"shattering" as they make their calls to violence, or hooded figures who sneak up in the night and melt away into the landscape
with their deathly booty once their ghoulish deeds are done, as in
"The Death Carvers":

> We talk as if it is another country
> The harsh rock of flesh hacked with hatchets
> The secret men with masks who belong to bloodnights
> The death carvers
> ...
> On the face of the sky a grimace of stars
> The moonlight congeals like fat
> Splattered over the darkening gouts
> On bodies lifted with their wounds
> Vanishing into the forest,
> Into night.
>
> *Reddened Water Flows Clear*, p.62

These people are without the subjectivity that accrues to the
poet's "I", and when violence is all, the causalities are de-
emphasised. The reasons that prompt the actions of another
generation, whether Sinhala or Tamil, and their re-visioning of
society and the state are ones that the poet wishes to stand outside
of. The militants are invested only with the capability of destroying, not creating a better, regenerative order. Their violence has

continuities from the past—both mythic and historical:

> Tied to the stake, these new martyrs ignite
> Like faggots and blaze away, burnt for their
> Heresies in this new witchcraft, worshippers
> Of the powers of darkness; decapitated too.
> Time turns over pages of history to show us
> Heads lolling off gibbets, bodies wrenched
> Apart by falling trees, elephant trunks
> Hurling you into the sands and flesh shreds
> Like votive flags fluttering among twirled
> Bones twisting in the sand.
>
> "Murals," *Reddened Water Flows Clear*, p.110

But their struggle is for a new mythology of nationalism, and in their cult of martyrdom they are the new heretics:

> Holed in within cracked tombs
> Hidden behind the sandbags and the battered walls
> Lie the sons of a different ancestry
> Bridegrooms of death
> That await the final consummation
> There's fire in the streets
> For the agni worshippers
> They tread on ash
> No sacred yaham's left
> For them, garlanded, three times to circumambulate
> The bullets chant the vedas
> And the bows of epic heroes
> Arc in the curving hand
> Of a flung grenade
> The sons of this family
> Do not ride the chariots to battle
> In these new mythologies.
>
> "His Family," *Reddened Water Flows Clear*, pp.53–4

It is of the LTTE militants, whose ideology and rhetoric most deeply enshrine and valorise the cult of martyrdom, that the poet writes. For her all forms of violence, whatever their justifications and temporal contexts, are self-defeating affronts to humanity. She is a firm opponent of any ethno-nationalism that excludes (democratic) plurality by its very nature, whether enunciated by the "death carvers" of the JVP, the LTTE or the state. Her own diverse identities demand the dismantling of the barriers of ethnicity, caste and class and the ideologies of nationalism that carry exclusion. These are nationalisms that leave her with no option but refusal of their projects.[51]

This stance, however, is not unconnected to the fact that what is most threatened by the militants—whether in the Tamil north or Sinhala south—are ways of life that the poet's families, by descent and marriage, have stood for. Her refusal to engage with the (creative) possibilities of a new order are implicated in her own negotiation for the maintenance of her liberal and privileged identity within the crisis-ridden postcolonial nation. She is aware of the ambiguity of her position. As Das, the school teacher in the short story "I Am An Innocent Man"[52] who wishes to remain impartial realises, neutrality is an untenable position in the context of war. His refrain is that he is innocent, neither a supporter of Tamil self-determination when, as the story shows, it comes at the cost of life and is propped up by corruption, self-interest and authoritarianism, nor of the Sri Lankan state which, in its bid to stamp out the guerrillas, sprays a schoolyard with bullets, harshly interrogates Tamil civilians and suspects all Tamils of being terrorists. Das has been witness to an LTTE ambush of army commandos near a prawn farm in the east of the country. Interrogated by the state's security forces on what he knows, he remains silent. Silence is his self-defence, yet it is a performance that carries guilt—the guilt of the witness, and the guilt of the survivor. At the end of the story he contemplates: "I am back in my school now. I have placed my fingers on the bullet holes that pit the walls. Looked out to the field where I saw death. I remember. Perhaps in time I will forget. But—an innocent man?" (AIB, p.42) A rhetorical question, but Das knows the answer—there is no such thing as innocence in this war, and impartiality is a performance promising only the illusion of safety. As he admits, "I *play* safe." (AIB, p.27, my emphasis.)

The Discursive Performance

Impartiality calls for a particular discursive performance through the subjectivity of the "I", when the discourses of nationalism available to writers like Jean Arasanayagam are inadequate to capture their postcolonial condition and unable to accommodate their political convictions. What are the particular discursive strategies with which Jean Arasanayagam negotiates her identity in her work? Erasure of privilege is one. Even as she writes of various oppressions and inequalities within Sri Lanka and locates herself within the hegemon (however indeterminate that may be), the *circumstances* that keep her there are erased. In the poem "A Question of Identity" she acknowledges, when pressed to do so (there is an honest self-irony here), the brutality of imperial conquest and the epistemic fractures wrought on the island by the Dutch coloniser/ancestor, as he spread the gospel and engaged in (unequal) trade with it:

> The talk comes up
> When I want to be separate
> When I have to defend myself against
> The conservative morals of other tribal groups
> The question of identity,
> We share the same guilt
> We were once invaders
> Whether Commandant, predikanten
> Conquistador or Koopman
> On our brows eating into skull
> We bear branded the mark of Cain.
>
> *RWFC*, p.85

But it is with reluctance and a note of exasperation—"When I have to defend myself against/ The conservative morals of other tribal groups"—that the poet is forced to talk of her colonial ancestry in this way. It is as if the nation needs her to atone for past colonial sins, and she is compelled to take on the collective guilt of *her* tribe. She thus poses a challenge to whoever insists on purity and "innocence" of race and history. No one has been exempt from the mark of Cain, neither the Burghers nor the Tamils, Muslims or Sinhalese.

Elsewhere in Jean Arasanayagam's writing, however, there is a discursive silencing of the violence of the colonial past. While in the poem "A Question of Identity" it was against conservatism alone that she deployed the defence of a narration of violent colonial culpability, in her other work the poet's subjective "I" is forced into acknowledging this past. But she does not narrate its culpability for she draws on and images the pastoral—itself a form of discursive erasure. The ambiguities of her subjectivities—socially privileged yet culturally marginal, born and bred in Sri Lanka yet alienated from its dominant socio-political visions, economically secure yet victim of ethnic violence—predicate this erasure. Recreating a Dutch ancestor in the poem, "*Domine dirige nos*" she writes:

> We are the epilogues he left behind,
> unfinished lines of history where yet
> > he set his seal for
> fleshly archives on the missives of our lives,
> our eyes, our ears carry, as memory rages
> > in the blood,
> a different sky and clime reeling with
> > galaxies and rent
> by storms; we clutch our rags, *flung*
> > on this shore,
> walk inland from the sea away from
> > fortresses and ghostly
> ships that sink and disappear.
>
> > *Shooting the Floricans*, p.8[53] (My emphasis)

The progeny of this Dutch ancestor are cast away, "flung" onto a foreign shore without choice, while the last images of shipwreck efface the complicity of the colonising Dutch in the purchase of the imperial enterprise. Sri Lankan born Michael Ondaatje, who traces Dutch and Indian (Chettiya) ancestry makes a similar discursive move in *Running in the Family*.[54] Celebrating the island's cosmopolitan hybridity, he makes full acknowledgement of its history of European invasion and colonisation:

The island *seduced* all of Europe. The Portuguese. The Dutch. The English.

And so its name changed, as well as its shape,—Serendip, Ratnapida (sic) ("island of gems"), Taprobane, Zeloan, Zeilan, Seyllan, Ceilon, Ceylon— the wife of many marriages, courted by invaders who stepped ashore and claimed everything with the power of their swords or bible or language (p.64, my emphasis).

Yet, even as Ondaatje notes this history of conquest, he writes:

This pendant, once its shape stood still, became a mirror. It pretended to reflect each European power till newer ships arrived and *spilled* their nationalities, some of whom stayed and married—my own ancestor arriving in 1600, a doctor who cured the residing governor's daughter with a strange herb and was rewarded with land, a foreign wife, and a new name which was a Dutch spelling of his own. Ondaatje (p.64, my emphasis).

The island seduces the European, and ships spill their European passengers onto it. In this way, the active agency of their colonising ancestors in undertaking voyages to the East, in the *conquests* that eventually made the coastal areas of the island into a Dutch colony, is erased. So, in Jean Arasanayagam's poem "I Have No Country" it is the sea winds that bring the Dutch ancestors to the island (*RWFC*, p.86), and in "A Journey into Exile" a boat falls out of the sun, drifts and is lost "In the high green wave/ From which we never returned."(*Kindura*, p.22) In "Ancestors" the poet writes of her Dutch ancestors' *tenantship* on the land (*RWFC*, p.25), implying a holding under a landlord rather than the imperial reality of forcibly subjugating and governing the native people; in the notion of tenancy, however, the poem anticipates the future dispossession of the Dutch Burghers in a post-colonial nation dominated by Sinhala hegemony.[55] This dispossession is evoked as an obliteration of roots, an elegy— even anticipating the poet's own death—to the insignificance of her current existence within the nation:

Out of the blindness of the sea where those unknown
Voyages began I was drawn through the sea nets
and flung among the coffee berries and cinnamon,
my skin is green with the verdigris of age
my insignia rubbed off the coin useful for
neither barter nor trade.
Soon the flag unfurled of that ghost ship
of my ancestors will curl

round me and flip me over into the sea of darkness
where it is no longer important to have roots.[56]

The Castaway

The metaphor of the castaway who, by pure accident, flounders
onto the shore—"Out of the blindness of the sea where those
unknown/ Voyages began I was drawn through the sea nets/ and
flung among the coffee berries and cinnamon" (my emphases)—
can be read, in effect, as a plea for reconciliation on the part of
the poet, a prelude to integrating into the contexts of the post-
colonial nation, unencumbered by a violent and exploitative past
whose guilt she is made to bear. In this Jean Arasanayagam shares
with Derek Walcott an investment in the figure of the castaway.
But while Walcott makes of the castaway an opportunity to create afresh, Jean Arasanayagam's response is muted to its empowering potential. These divergent approaches point to the differing personalities of the writers as well as the gendering of representation that gives Walcott an advantage as a male already
more in control of the directions of social change. Moreover, the
Sri Lankan civil war, its institutionalisation of violence and violent politics, presents Jean Arasanayagam with an altogether more
bleak postcoloniality than the West Indies does for Walcott, notwithstanding the poverty and underdevelopment that attends both
island-nations. However, the resonances in their use of the castaway as a metaphor for their postcolonial condition also indicate a path to cosmopolitanism. Cosmopolitanism requires reconciliation, also necessary for the negotiation of difference vis-à-
vis majoritarian politics and culture, which will bring these writers legitimacy within their respective nations.[57]

It is instructive, therefore, to pay attention to how the castaway figures in Walcott's writing and to see how Jean
Arasanayagam—quite unaware of Walcott's working of the castaway—replicates the discourse, albeit with different nuances, in
a different context. Identifying with the figure of Robinson Crusoe
who was cast away on a Caribbean island, Walcott holds up
Defoe's hero as an enabling metaphor for the West Indian artist
to create "from where nothing was", and through such an

"Adamic" task, emerge empowered from the negations of colonialism.[58] Walcott took issue with the more popular appropriation by Caribbean writers like Aimé Césaire, Roberto Fernando Ratemar and George Lamming, of Shakespeare's Caliban-Prospero relationship in *The Tempest,* as a paradigm for West Indian identity.[59] For Walcott, Crusoe's story had more in common with the West Indian experience, and the reasons he foregrounds for his choice are significant. Crusoe was cast away without choice on a Caribbean island just as the African slaves were forcibly transplanted onto that terrain. Crusoe's beginning on that island, stresses Walcott, was just as humble as these slaves. Unlike Prospero, Crusoe was "no lord of magic, duke, prince. He does not possess the land he inhabits. He is alone, he is a craftsman, his beginnings are humble." ("Figure of Crusoe", p.8) His survival resonates with the endurance of the West Indian slaves. The deserted island (symptomatic of Walcott's early readings of the Caribbean as having no pre-colonial culture and language of its own) offers a virginal landscape, "a green world, one without metaphors". In such a space Crusoe becomes the archetypal West Indian artist who learns "to shape the language of a race" from "where nothing was", his craftsmanship an inspiration to all West Indian writers, for with him, "even the bare necessities/ of style are turned to use/ like those plain iron tools he salvages/ from shipwreck, hewing a prose/ as odorous as raw wood to the adze".[60] Crusoe's journal becomes the first West Indian novel for Walcott, and the first Adamic example of the artist turning a loss of history into a privilege, as he names the landscape and its people with imagination and awe. But most importantly, the isolated Crusoe "howling for a human voice" mirrored Walcott's own alienated existence in the West Indies. Championing Crusoe in a climate of black nationalism ensured Walcott's ostracism. He felt betrayed by friends and colleagues. His identification with Crusoe's struggle for survival in the Caribbean took on a distinctly personal tone.

Unlike the autocratic Prospero, Crusoe, the more benevolent of the two, offered Walcott a model that enabled reconciliation with the coloniser. This was crucial to the writer's vision of the Caribbean as a multicultural society that acknowledged the importance of the colonial heritage, and its European and Creole descendants domiciled there. Walcott, himself of mixed Euro-African heritage—"I'm just a red nigger who loves the sea/ I had a sound colonial eduation/ I have Dutch, nigger, and English in me/ And either I'm nobody, or I'm a nation"[61] —had both a personal and ideological investment in the nation as eclectic, and cosmopolitan. The figure of Crusoe also paved the way for an easier integration with the Afro-Caribbean constituency, given Crusoe's less conflictual relationship with Friday than the Prospero-Caliban one. Crusoe, shipwrecked on an uninhabited island (amazing , as Peter Hulme notes, for a land so fertile[62]) did not have to wrest away land from the natives, as Prospero did. Friday is the accommodating slave, unlike Caliban. As he is rescued· from a dire fate at the hands of cannibals by Crusoe, he is bound by gratitude to his master, somewhat more like Ariel to Prospero, although again Ariel is far more rebellious than the gentle Friday.

In his book *Colonial Encounters,* Peter Hulme convincingly shows that Defoe's 18th century narrative is shaped and tailored for the consumption of colonial territories and their conquests by Europe. It is to this end that the conflict in Shakespeare's *The Tempest,* between European conqueror and native subject, is by and large suppressed in the story of Robinson Crusoe. Here the empty island facilitates an utopian paradise, and the benevolent commercial world Crusoe encounters effaces the tensions and inequalities of competitive commerce. It also finesses Crusoe's own previous accumulation of the capitalist European self through his plantations. By having Friday volunteer his services to Crusoe, Defoe circumvents the need for Crusoe to force Friday into servitude and call him "slave". It is not that the violence and inequalities of the colonial encounter are altogether absent. Crusoe may not call Friday "slave", but he has no qualms about teaching the latter to call him "Master". Friday conforms to a regime which gives him little opportunity of expressing a will of his own – the nostalgia with which he remembers his own people is proof of his loneliness. In fact the only way he can alleviate his loneliness is through this nostalgic memory, which is all that is left of his humanity. And while the name Friday itself serves, each week to remind the servant of his rescue and the gratitude owing to his benefactor, the name itself (not accidentally) serves to totally depersonalise the native inhabitant of the Caribbean. Friday's humility then is far from the forced servitude of Caliban, but it also follows that Crusoe's benevolent patronage (like the imperial civilizing mission) is both more sophisticated and insidious than Prospero's overt despotism.

Walcott is aware of these imbrications in Defoe's narrative. In "The Figure of Crusoe" he writes of a Crusoe who is no harmless hermit on the beach, but a man "self-righteous on subjects such as God, civilization, art and human nakedness. And of course, race." ("The Figure of Crusoe", p.10.) But in focusing mostly on Crusoe as the *isolated* castaway, Walcott's emphasis is on his bereft beginnings in the Caribbean, his determination and courage, his use of an "Adam-like" opportunity to create a language and culture from the bits and pieces of his wrecked ship and past cultural baggage.

For Jean Arasanayagam, on the other hand, flung onto a shore "in a different sky and clime *reeling* with galaxies and *rent* by storms" (my emphases) the metaphor of the castaway is a far less empowering one. Living in a postcolonial Sri Lanka punctuated by communal violence (see the poems "1958..'71.. '77..'81..'83" and "Nallur 1982"), and outside the language of the majority, her sense of security is at best "a taste on the tongue/ Remembered, lingering where it once blent so/ Easily with that other language to bubble milk-/ Frothing at our lips" ("Metaphors of History," *RWFC*, p.119); the castaway-poet has not found a congenial home. She is constantly reminded of her strangeness, the locus of which is her own body. In "Exiled Childhood" she writes:

> I too was born out of speckled egg, an embryo
> swimming in its golden yolk, with this strange
> crop of feathers, streak flash of red and burnished
> russet threaded through a clump of black and on my
> brown skin wires filigreed of golden hairs traced
> patterns on my wrist and arms, my mother had blue veins
> threading her milk white skin glimpsed as she pulled
> up stockings fixing her garters with a snap

> straitjacket corsets constraining her alabaster flesh,
> that bird, myself from migrant breed, overstaying
> its summer, cohabiting with native kind now grown
> into this rare genus...
>
> *Floricans*, p.13.

There is an anomaly here of the poet's mother dressed in the constraining bounds of garters and corset; white flesh held in tight and shaped to suit western taste, while her daughter becomes the strange hybrid whose golden hairs have been transmuted and miscegenated out of her mother's blue veins.

This sense of strangeness, of having to wear the names their colonial ancestors gave them uneasily on their limbs (*Floricans*, p.14), of having overstayed their welcome, is heightened for the colonised elite by the deeply polarised world of a postcolonial nation premised on divisions of ethnicity, class, caste and gender. In such a context Jean Arasanayagam's only response can be to re-visit herself as an exotic, lone survivor. "Shooting the Floricans" is a poem written on a visit to a heritage country house in England. On its walls are the trophies and instruments of hunting. As the owner of the house recalls his experiences in the colonies and the hunting of the florican there, the bird—"A most delicious bird for the table/ Superior to pheasant, game, partridge" —resonates in the poet's mind as an apt metaphor of herself: a dying species, hunted, frozen in time, exotic.[63] The stress in the poem is on the lone survivor, "the shrill moan of the dying florican" (*Floricans*, p.64). What this sense of a castaway produces in Jean Arasanayagam is not a determination to take up the challenges of the future but a nostalgia for a more secure past. From such a past, it follows that the nation's path to its contemporaneity can only be a slide from relative orderliness to chaos and destruction. In "Exiled Childhood" she writes of past certainties, even if they did produce a certain colonial panache close to arrogance, that foretells a doomed future:

> We were part of an Empire's glory, ourselves
> loomed in its rich tapestry, tilting low upon
> our brows pith hats and khaki helmets, twirled our
> brollies impudently against the gong face of

the burning sun that flashed its bronze light
across the clouds until the thunder crack
reminded us in louring skies of stormy destinies
                                        Floricans, p.10.

In the temporality that Jean Arasanayagam articulates, the nation is without a commendable future. The only time available to her therefore is an utopian, primeval, nostalgic past, or a doomed past of colonial glory with all its oddities and paradoxes. The gloomy skies of the present foretell the loss of the Edenic utopia; in keeping with this vision, Jean Arasanayagam writes of women whose bodies are sites of sexual passion (in itself refreshing, given the taboos of representing female sexuality) but which suffer the bloody traumas of childbirth, signifying fracture, loss and intense pain. Lines like, "The wounds half-healed still festering and bloody on my knife/ Slit, handstitched body that had given birth"[64] refuse to romanticise childbirth/motherhood and in doing so, challenge one of the most desired roles for women within nationalist patriarchy. For the nation the woman begets is not a heroic one but a monster child. In this context the poet's post-1983 dispossession, following attacks on Tamil households, is shocking but inevitable, although the choice of whether to leave or remain is fraught:

You tell me to pack up my bags and go
But where? I turn my face towards
Country after country
Silently I lipread their refusal
What do I call myself?
Exile emigré refugee?
The sunlight is a web
That silent weaves through
Light caught within its spokes
The delicate seeming threads
Strengthen draw tight
Noosing whats left of life
If I remain [65]

Here is the harshest critique of the vision of cosmopolitanism forwarded by writers like Salman Rushdie, reminding us that the allure of the cosmopolitan is for the privileged, the celebrities who can travel with easy access across borders, mingle freely with their high cultures, and whose primary homes are in the Euro-American metropoles. For Jean Arasanayagam, those borders are not as expansive, tightly regulated as they are by visas and racist immigration policies that are unwelcoming. This is not a position from which she can feel at home in the world, or play the role of an intermediary native informant interpreting Third World culture and politics, best situated in the West. If the blurring of the vocabularies of nationality and race is a founding strategy of the modern nation-state, [66] Jean Arasanayagam's work makes clear that state formation is inherently anti-cosmopolitan.

Where she does share affinities with what Tim Brennan calls "new cosmopolitanism" in an essay problematising its positionality, is in her own leanings to the West. Jean Arasanayagam argues for a national consciousness that is plural and diverse. A long history of interaction with foreigners through migrations, trade and imperialism has bequeathed the nation with multiple tongues, religions and cultural praxis which have also transformed native idioms and ways of seeing. But in her own writing she makes little effort to borrow from, re-inscribe and thereby create afresh the native literary and oral traditions within Sinhala or Tamil culture. The inter-textuality in her work almost always refers to the history and literatures of the West, the masters of Flemish art, the exotic foods and costumes of her Dutch ancestors, celebrated as vibrant and dynamic.[67] This in itself is a courageous articulation, when radical ethno-nationalism in Sri Lanka as manifested in *Jāthika Chintanaya* (indigenous thought/ ideology) brands the western corrupt and irrelevant. But, as Tim Brennan notes, the "cosmopolitan embrace" is not unconnected with the order of global politics today which privileges the West:

The cosmopolitan embrace—its articulation of a new world literature designed to capture the global juxtapositions that have begun to force their way even into private experience—involves instead a flattening of influences which assemble themselves, as it were, on the same plane of value. By stressing the global nature of everyday life, they consciously allude to the centre-periphery conflicts raised by decolonisation, and modify them by enhancing the role of the 'West' as, alternately, foil and lure. And this is, after all, the real distinction between the new cosmopolitanism and what Barbara Harlow, for example, calls 'resistance literature', the literature of the independence movements. That distinction has to do with the role of the image of the West. It is not the older concept of influences alone that is at work—say, the attractions for Peruvian or Nigerian novelists of French symbolism, imagism or *nouveau roman*—not, in other words, the attractions of high capitalist, city culture as filtered through its art, but the image of the West as receptacle of 'democracy'. [68]

As the West is idealised for democratic models of multiculturality (this can only occur when its inequalities of class, gender and race are levelled off, and as Brennan points out, socialist alternatives of Cuba and Vietnam for instance are dismissed), it follows that nationalism has to be parodied, and the project of independence itself at best, drawn ambiguously. The Sri Lanka Jean Arasanayagam writes of is a nation embroiled in narrow ethno-nationalisms and internecine warfare. The landscape she writes of can no longer be a Garden of Eden but a primordial forest of writhing serpents, preying spiders and throttling vines.[69] She has to disavow her privileges on this terrain by writing of herself as a castaway while elsewhere, particularly in the poems set in Jaffna, the stress is on destroyed, unpeopled landscapes in a Crusoesque emptying of the land of its people, so that only devastated architectural monuments remain. The same quality of eerie silence and "dim elegiac notion of decay"[70] are recouped in the short story, "The Cry of the Kite".[71] As Arasan, the poet's husband, takes his family on a visit to his ancestral home in Navaly, a populous town in the Jaffna district, the reader encounters an abundance of nature, unutilised for lack of people:

We turned towards the tall gates. Arasan opened them slowly. They had not been locked but were heavy and difficult to move. People seldom went in and out of them these days. We began to walk through the grove moving out of the darkness and light of shade and sunlight. In a stone trough margosa seeds were piled closely together. The ground was thickly strewn with margosa flowers and fallen palmyrah fruits, their blue-black skins shot with a crimson sheen. The yellow flowers were bright on the alaripoo trees and their green fig-like fruits a tender yellow green, transparent lanterns through which light shone pale gold. Clusters of green firm-skinned mangoes hung from laden branches. No one plucked them...There were no human voices, no whispers, cries or echoes, there was a stillness in the air as of time suspended, patterns of sunlight stretching tenuously across the grove in cobwebs of light from tree to tree. (p.17)

Depicted here, perhaps, is the "calm before the storm" of the civil war. The reality, however, of what the north and east of the country are today belies this eerie quiet, in which only the birds and a few old people remain to enjoy the fruits of the earth while time itself stands suspended. These landscapes have been the theatres of war since 1983, the terrain of bombings, ethnic cleansing, institutionalised militarisation and displacement, while its people have suffered distorted and ruptured lives. At the same time their societies have undergone radical transformations. New social orders have come into being. The LTTE, known as "the boys", have replaced the old hierarchies and Tamil women have taken to arms. Others, as war widows and consequently, heads of household have had to take on public roles, negotiate with the military forces and seek jobs outside their immediate communities. The landscape no longer yields the bounties of nature but the harvest of injustice, authoritarianism and a bitter war.

In the final analysis, it is these ellipses that make Arasanayagam's work important in the Sri Lankan literary and national contexts. Her poetry is always rich in its use of rhythm, although she is not a poet who experiments innovatively with language, or forges for herself an alternative discourse in the tradition of magic realism favoured by Rushdie, Marquez, Carlos Fuentes and Himilce Novas, in which images and metaphors constantly shift and destabilise to form new combinations and meanings in a performance resonant of cosmopolitanism. Nor does she show a consistent discipline in line and length. Some of her poetry suffers from overwriting and repetition, but its value lies in how it defines the condition of postcoloniality itself as worn by the nation. This is where the personal becomes the political, where the private and public meet. "In (the) banalities," says Homi Bhabha, "the unhomely stirs, as the violence of a racialized society falls most enduringly on the details of life: where you can sit, or not; how you can live, or not; what you can learn, or not; who you can love, or not."[72] Jean Arasanayagam's testimony of precisely these details, signifying an uneasy indeterminacy within the nation, carries the potential of being empowering by bringing to crisis the ethnic, religious, cultural, caste and gendered rhetoric of exclusion of our times. Her refusal to conform to such boundaries can be read as an agentive re-visioning of her hyphenated, hybrid identities. That it is only in the landscape of colonial memory that security exists for the poet, that the present is doomed and the future requires an altogether new imagining, is where her poetry challenges the dominant nationalisms of her time.

> I have no country now but self
> I mark my boundaries extend demesnes
> Even beyond the darkness of those regions
> Still to be explored, chart my ocean voyages
> In blood or stay becalmed watching a gull
> Impale its shadow on a thorn of wave.
> Waiting for the winds to blow to set once more
> In motion the pattern of the sea, a ripple stir
> Into a wave that sweeps, tidal, wide horizons,
> Rises above a cloud to drench the sky
> And pours its deluge on the stars to drown
> All lights and in that darkness find again
> New brightness from a self-created firmament

RWFC, p.86.

Notes

[1] Jean Arasanayagam, "I Have No Country," *Reddened Water Flows Clear.* London & Boston: Forest Books, 1991, p. 86.

[2] While Jean Arasanayagam has written many short stories and novellas and is now working on her autobiography, she is best acclaimed as a poet. It is as a poet therefore that I will refer to her in this chapter.

[3] The Dutch took possession of Sri Lanka's maritime boundaries from the Portuguese between 1638–58, and governed them until the advent of the British in 1795–6. The progeny of Portuguese men and indigenous women are also known as Burghers, but with considerable difference in status. The Dutch Burghers, as descendants of Dutch parents, consider themselves superior to the Portuguese 'half-castes'. For an account of early Burgher settlements in Sri Lanka see Michael Roberts, et al., *People In-between*, op. cit., chapters 3 & 4.

[4] Buddhism is the religion of the majority in Sri Lanka and enjoys constitutional primacy. All state institutions, without exception, foreground its privilege. The state-run Rupavahini (TV) Corporation commences its daily programmes with the recitation of Buddhist *gathās*, and many state institutions commemorate anniversaries and important events with the chanting of *pirith*, etc.

[5] Bill Ashcroft, Gareth Griffiths, Helen Tiffin, *The Empire Writes Back*. London & New York: Routledge, 1989. The authors state, "Both literary theorists and cultural historians are beginning to recognize cross-culturality as the potential termination point of an apparently endless human history of conquest and annihilation, justified by the myth of group 'purity', and as the basis on which the post-colonial world can be creatively stabilized." pp.36–7.

[6] The word "post" is in parenthesis because many of these debates occurred before the colonies gained independence. They were in the line of cultural decolonisation, a precursor to independence and post-coloniality.

[7] Derek Walcott, "What the Twilight Says: An Overture," in *Dream on Monkey Mountain & Other Plays*. New York: Farrar, Straus & Giroux, 1970, p.4.

[8] George Lamming, *Pleasures of Exile*. London: Allison & Busby, 1984, p.24.

[9] See Edward Kamau Brathwaite, "Timehri," in Orde Coombs (ed.), *Is Massa Day Dead?* New York: Anchor & Doubleday, 1974, pp. 29–44; *The Arrivants*. Oxford: Oxford University Press, 1973; "The African Presence in the Caribbean Literature," *Bim* 17, no.65, June 1979 and nos. 66,67, June 1983; Errol Hill, *The Trinidad Carnival*. Austin & London: University of Texas Press, 1972.

[10] Stokely Carmichael, quoted in Joseph Manyoni, "Emergence of Black Power," in Robert Moss (ed.), *The Stability of the Caribbean*. London: Institute for the Study of Conflict & Centre for Strategic & International Studies, 1973, p.112.

[11] Derek Walcott, "What the Twilight Says: An Overture".

[12] Ibid., p.9.

[13] George Lamming, op. cit., p.36.

[14] Roberto Fernando Ratemar, "Caliban: Notes Towards a Discussion of Culture in Our America," *Massachusetts Review* 15, Winter-Spring 1974, p.9.

[15] *Savacòu* 13, 1977, a special issue on Caribbean women's literature inaugurated the discussion on women's writing in the Anglophone Caribbean. See Carole Boyce Davies & Elaine Savory Fido, "Women and Literature in the Caribbean: An Overview," Carole Boyce Davies & Elaine Savory Fido (eds.), *Out of the Kumbla*. Trenton: Africa World Press Inc.,1990, p.13.

[16] Davies & Fido, *Out of the Kumbla*, op. cit., p.*xvi*.

[17] Wole Soyinka's recuperation of the myth of Ogun as a post-colonial metaphor is an example. See Neloufer de Mel, "Responses to History: The Re-articulation of Postcolonial Identity in the Plays of Wole Soyinka & Derek Walcott 1950–76," Ph.D dissertation, University of Kent at Canterbury, U.K., 1990.

[18] Such a continuum was reinforced in the recent millennium celebrations on Sri Lankan Rupavahini television, when the legend of the arrival of Prince Vijaya on the island, signalling the "beginnings" of the Aryan race here, marked the origin of Sri Lankan history in the last thousand years.

[19] Wole Soyinka, *Myth, Literature and the African World*. London: Cambridge University Press, 1976.

[20] Femi Osofisan, "The Alternative Tradition: A Survey of Nigerian Literature in English since the Civil War," *Presence Africane* 139, 3rd quarter, 1986. p.164.

[21] See the counter-arguments to Soyinka in Biodun Jeyifo, "Tragedy, History and Ideology: Soyinka's 'Death and the King's Horseman' and Ebrahim Hussein's 'Kinjeketile'," in Georg Gugelberger (ed.), *Marxism and African Literature*. London: James Currey, 1985, pp.94–109 and Femi Osofisan, "The Alternative Tradition: A Survey of Nigerian Literature in English since the Civil War," *Presence Africane* 139, 3rd quarter, 1986.pp. 162–84.

[22] The work of Nigerian novelist, poet and essayist, Chinua Achebe, is most frequently compared to Soyinka's in this regard.

[23] Partha Chatterjee, *The Nation and Its Fragments*, op. cit., p.77.

[24] Ibid., p.76.

[25] Rabrindranath Tagore, "East and West," in Susir Kumar Das (ed.), *The English Writing of Rabindranath Tagore* vol.3. Delhi: Sahitya Akademi, 1996, pp. 353–54.

[26] Rabindranath Tagore, "The Union of Cultures," in *The English Writing of Rabindranath Tagore*, op. cit., p.437.

[27] Anil de Silva, quoted in Sudhi Pradhan (ed.), *Marxist Cultural Movement in India: Chronicles and Documents*, op. cit., p.277.

[28] Susie Tharu & K.Lalitha (eds.), *Women Writing in India* vol.2, op. cit., pp.79–80.

[29] Female desire as portrayed by Chughtai was considered so transgressive for the time that "The Quilt", which humourously sketched a lesbian relationship from a child's perspective, and foregrounded suppressed and illicit desire as well as child abuse, got Chughtai into trouble with the authorities. She was charged with obscenity and underwent a trial in Lahore. The trial lasted two years before being dismissed for want of indecent language in the text. See Tahira Naqvi, Introduction to *The Quilt and Other Stories* by Ismat Chughtai. New Delhi: Kali for Women, 1990, pp. *xi–xii*.

[30] Geeta Patel, *Lyrical Movements, Historical Hauntings: On Gender, Colonialism and Desire in Miraji's Urdu Poetry*. Berkeley: University of California Press, forthcoming.

[31] Salman Rushdie, "Notes on Writing and the Nation," *Index on Censorship* 3,1997, p.36.

[32] Salman Rushdie, cited in Tim Brennan, "Cosmopolitans and Celebrities," *Race and Class* 31, July–Sept. 1989, p.3.

[33] Salman Rushdie, "In Good Faith," *Imaginary Homelands*. London: Granta,1991, p.394.

[34] Salman Rushdie, "Imaginary Homelands", op. cit., p.16.

[35] S.J.Tambiah, *Sri Lanka: Ethnic Fratricide and the Dismantling of Democracy*. London: I.B.Tauris & Co. Ltd, 1986, p.134.

[36] Michael Roberts, et al., *People Inbetween*, op. cit., p.132.

[37] Jayadeva Uyangoda, "A State of Desire? Some Reflections on the Unreformability of Sri Lanka's Post-colonial Polity," unpublished paper. Colombo: Social Scientists' Association, 1999.

[38] A.J.Wilson, *Politics in Sri Lanka 1947–1979*. London: Macmillan, 1974 & 1979.

[39] Jayadeva Uyangoda, op. cit., p. 9.

[40] For accounts of this period see Howard Wriggins, *Ceylon: Dilemmas of a New Nation*. New Jersey: Princeton University Press, 1960; Yasmine Gooneratne, *Relative Merits: A Personal Memoir of the Bandaranaike Family of Sri Lanka*. London: 1986; James Manor, *The Expedient Utopian: Bandaranaike and Ceylon*. Cambridge: Cambridge University Press, 1989; Godfrey Gunatilleke, "The Ideologies and Realities of the Ethnic Conflict—a Postface," in Michael Roberts (ed.), *Sri Lanka. Collective Identities Revisited* vol. 2, Colombo: Marga, 1999.

[41] Unlike the Portuguese who had children by local women, the Dutch brought their own women from Holland. Elite Dutch Burghers are descendants of these unions and consider themselves superior to Burghers of mixed parentage.

[42] Charles Sarvan, "Carl Muller's Trilogy and the Burghers of Sri Lanka," in *World Literature Today*,p.530.

[43] Jean Arasanayagam, *A Nice Burgher Girl*, manuscript.

[44] Jean Arasanayagam, *Kindura*. Kandy: Godamunne & Sons, 1973, p.2.

[45] Derek Walcott, "What the Twilight Says: An Overture in *Dream on Monkey Mountain and Other Plays*." New York: Farrar Straus and Giroux, 1970, p.16.

[46] A disjuncture which presented the Indian village as separate from the "classical" India of the Gupta period, for instance, can be found in the writing of scholars like Ananda Coomaraswamy and Tagore. Geeta Patel, "Desire/Violence and Tradition in writing by South Asian Muslim Women: The case of Ismat Chughtai" paper presented at the University of Pensyluania, 1998.

[47] Jean Arasanayagam, *Peacock and Dreams*. New Delhi: Navrang, 1996. The stories in this collection evoke Arjuna's childhood in Jaffna and

are based on Jean's husband's boyhood there. They abound with rich
imagery of various landscapes of tropical fecundity or aridity, evident
in the dryer north of the country.
48 In the short story "The Cry of the Kite", Kand(i)an appears as the
non-Vellala, undercaste servant of the poet's husband's family. In this
story too, Kandian, the toddy-tapper carries, and threateningly
brandishes when drunk, a gleaming knife. Jean Arasanayagam, "The
Cry of the Kite", in Ashley Halpe (ed.), *Contemporary Sri Lankan
Short Stories in English*. Colombo: EASL and the British Council,
1990, pp.13–31.
49 In Jean Arasanayagam, *Reddened Water Flows Clear*. London and
Boston: Forest Books, 1991.
50 Jean Arasanayagam, personal communication.
51 See Fiona Giles, "The Softest Disorder: Representing Cultural
Indeterminacy," in Chris Tiffin and Alan Lawson (eds.), *De-Scribing
Empire*. London: Routledge, 1994, pp. 141–51. Giles discusses the
work of Tasma, an Australian woman who, in 1891, wrote the novel,
The Penance of Portia James. Tasma's heroine refuses the identities
on offer, whether colonial Anglo-Australian, nationalist Australian
or colonising Anglo-Saxon. Giles argues that she occupies an
indeterminate state, situated "obliquely between" all these positions.
52 Jean Arasanayagam, 'I Am an Innocent Man,' in *All is Burning*. New
Delhi: Penguin, 1995.
53 Jean Arasanayagam, *Shooting the Floricans*. Kandy: Samjna, 1993.
54 Michael Ondaatje, *Running in the Family*. London: Picador, 1984.
55 At the last-held 1981 census, Sinhalese comprised 74% of the
population, Tamils 18.2% and Muslims 7.1%. Burghers were under
2%.
56 Jean Arasanayagam, "Roots," cited in Wilfred Jayasuriya, *Sri Lanka's
Modern English Literature*. Delhi: Navrang, 1994. p.109.
57 St. Lucia gained independence only in 1972, but Walcott's work from
the late 1950s onwards, influenced by debates on Negritude, Black
Power, ideologies of assimilation and cosmopolitanism, has engaged
directly with cultural de-colonisation as a precursor to political
independence.
58 Derek Walcott, "The Figure of Crusoe," paper presented at the
University College of the West Indies, St. Augustine, Trinidad, 1965.
59 For an excellent analysis of these see Rob Nixon, "Caribbean and
African Appropriations of *The Tempest*," *Critical Inquiry* 13, Spring
1987, pp. 557–578.
60 Derek Walcott, "Crusoe's Journal," *Collected Poems: 1948–1984*.
New York: Farrar, Straus & Giroux, 1986, p.93. Walcott reiterated
this analogy in his Nobel prize acceptance speech when he referred to

the Caribbean poet "making his own tools like Crusoe, assembling nouns from necessity"–"The Antilles: Fragments of Epic Memory," *The New Republic*, 28th December 1992, pp.26–32.

61 Derek Walcott, "The Schooner Flight," *Collected Poems*, p.346.

62 Peter Hulme, *Colonial Encounters: Europe and the Native Caribbean 1492–1797*. London: Methuen, 1986, p.186.

63 Jean Arasanayagam wrote in a letter to me (27 February 1993) "I'm sending you the first poem I've completed since I returned (from England.) I shall have to go back to search for the florican. Perhaps I am that florican too. It is a fascinating search for a new identity out of the colonial one..."

64 Jean Arasanayagam, "Women, Goddesses and Their Mythologies," *Reddened Water Flows Clear*, p.31.

65 Jean Arasanayagam, "Exile" in *Trial by Terror*. Hamilton: Rimu Books, 1987.

66 Radhika Vyas Mongia, "Race Nationality, Mobility: A History of the Passport", *Public Culture*, 29, 1999, p.529.

67 See the poems "Ancestors" pp.23–6, "Mother" pp.102–6, "Metaphors of History" pp.119–23 in *Reddened Water Flows Clear*, and "*Domine Dirige Nos*" pp.5–8, "Exiled Childhood" pp.9–14, "My Mother" pp.19–22, "Those Childhood Games" pp.23–7 in *Shooting the Floricans*.

68 Tim Brennan, "Cosmopolitans and Celebrities," *Race and Class* 31, July-September 1989, p.4.

69 Jean Arasanayagam, "Histories" in *Out of Our Prisons We Emerge*. Kandy: Ariya Printers, 1987, p.6.

70 Thiru Kandiah, "This Language and These Women," in Rajiva Wijesinha (ed.), *An Anthology of Contemporary Sri Lankan Poetry in English*. Colombo: British Council & EASL, 1988, pp. 137–40.

71 Jean Arasanayagam, "The Cry of the Kite," in Ashley Halpe (ed.), *An Anthology of Contemporary Sri Lankan Short Stories in English*. Colombo: English Association of Sri Lanka, 1990.

72 Homi Bhabha, Introduction, *The Location of Culture*. London & New York: Routledge, 1994, p.15.

Dhanu, centre, preparing to garland Rajiv Gandhi

composure. Dressed up for a wedding or festival, with flowers in my hair, I have pretended not to notice male eyes looking at me, but have felt warm in my womanhood; felt happy, felt even a touch of pride and power. I may not be a beauty but I was, have been, a woman. My heart and pulse; my breasts and full thighs have told me so unmistakably. But now I feel neither fear nor courage. I no longer know or care whether I am beautiful or ugly; good or evil. On this morning of marriage and death, I can't seem to make them matter. . . Charles Sarvan, "Appointment with Rajiv Gandhi"

This woman's act of terror is an empowering one. Through it she will break with an oppressive tradition. Unlike the usual arranged marriages, *she* will choose her bridegroom; unlike the traditional virgin bride, she will be touched by men before her "wedding"; unlike the modest woman who shuns publicity, her photograph will be flashed in the world press; unlike other Hindu women, she will walk to the site of numerous funerals, including her own. And within the ambit of Sarvan's story, in his juxtaposition of the woman's childhood reminiscences with the ruthlessness of the present, the "cold-blooded terrorist" is given her individuality.

But even as the woman militant transcends the bounds of traditional female identity, is there a price, other than death of course, to be paid for such "freedom"? I hope to show that there is—a loss located in significant ways within the domain of gender constructs and in particular, the forms of female sexuality and reproduction that are valued within it. This in turn reflects the wider issue of a militant's loss of individuality—whether male or female. For the militant's individuality can only be creatively fictionalised as in Sarvan's treatment of Dhanu's story, glimpsed in the discursive contradictions of his/her martial poetry or caught at a moment of hesitancy in conversation. The politics of self-representation otherwise denies the militant a personality and emotional expression of his/her own; the reality of his/her driving impulses lies in complete obedience to the will of the militant leadership on whose behalf s/he struggles. These losses in turn mark the paradigms and cornerstones of the anticipated state, and/or social order that militant groups like the LTTE and JVP struggle for. From these, other important questions arise that have significant implications for feminist struggles within militant nationalism and/or revolutionary movements. Do women who participate in militant armed struggle enjoy full agency? Does their recruitment to the struggle spell autonomous, individual choice? If so, why and how has there been, historically, an instrumentality with which nationalist/militant patriarchies have enlisted women? How radically have women militants been able to transform their societies to ensure greater social justice and gender equality? And even if, as a result of patriarchal containment within their chosen militant groups, they enjoy only agentive *moments* in an interregnum where normalcy is suspended and there is license to transform taboo and social convention, should these women not be held accountable for loss of life and destruction of livelihoods? For condoning the undemocratic practices of groups like the LTTE and JVP which resort to summary killings, prevent the return to civilian rule[2] and sustain themselves through the ideology of militarism? If, on the one hand, violence draws on the most noble of human qualities such as sacrifice for a collective good, on the other it "expropriates agency" as it acts to silence both an individual and a majority, and speak on their behalf.[3] How should the woman combatant who participates in such an expropriation of agency, even as she transforms her own life through agentive moments *in* violence, be looked at? This is the challenge for feminists in Sri Lanka, as well as in South Asia, in which militarism is fast becoming an organising principle in many countries, buttressing increasingly authoritarian state and non-state actors, supporting various cross-border, cross-ethnic conflicts, and where women's participation in violence has taken a significant turn.[4]

Shifting Sites

Women Fighters of Liberation Tigers (Jaffna: 1989) is a book by Adele Ann, the Australian wife of LTTE theoretician, Anton Balasingham. She was a regular spokesperson for the women's wing of the LTTE, which began as an autonomous unit on 1 July, 1987, although women combatants had fought side by side with the men from 1986.[5] Her function as spokesperson was not at first, unconnected with her foreign nationality, which gave the LTTE a certain credibility, particularly in the eyes of the western media. As in Sarvan's short story, it is the breaking of new ground for the women of Jaffna that is stressed in Adele Ann's book, particularly in the projection of LTTE women cadres as equal to those of men. In a chapter which describes the military training undertaken by the women, its rigorousness is emphasised and the endurance of the women admired.[6] The woman combatant is presented as no different to the male in terms of the combat situations she is chosen for, and the ideology and attainment of martyrdom that sanctifies a LTTE combatant's death is as much within her reach as it is for the man. In fact, given a woman's symbolic role as nurturer of society, her participation in violence signals the ultimate moral sanction that can be accorded to it.

In the struggle for the anticipated state of Tamil Eelam the socio-cultural role of its women has undergone, and continues to undergo, a radical transformation. From that of a conservative, feminised ideal, the LTTE woman combatant is transformed into a public figure engaged in "masculine" activities and repudiating patriarchal norms of womanhood. In the historical construction of a Tamil identity, peopled by men as male warriors, leaders, poets and philosophers, the LTTE struggle offers women a chance to take their place beside these men. Rajani Thiranagama, co-author of *The Broken Palmyrah*, pointed to the attraction of such a change for the women of Jaffna:

One cannot but be inspired when one sees the women of the LTTE, two by two, in the night with their AKs slung over the shoulder, patrolling the entrances to Jaffna City. One cannot but admire the dedication and toughness of their training, seen in the video films put out by the LTTE. One could see the nationalist fervour and the romantic vision of women in arms defending the nation. This becomes a great draw. . . our social set-up, its restrictions on creative expression for women and the evils of the dowry system, are some of the social factors that led to their initial recruitment.[7]

The dedication to change which, in this phase of the struggle for Eelam, is almost surely also a call to death, is borne out in a poem by Captain Vanathi of the LTTE women's wing, who died in 1991 in the battle at Elephant Pass at the age of 27. The poem is entitled "She, the Woman of Tamililam!"

> Her forehead shall be adorned not with
>   *kunkumam* (but) with red blood.

All that is seen in her eyes is not the sweetness
    of youth (but) firm declarations of those
    who have fallen down.

On her neck will lay no *tali*, (but) a
        Cyanide flask!

Her legs are going and searching,
    not for searching a relationship with relatives
    (but) looking towards the liberation of
        the soil of Tamililam.

    Her gun will fire shots.
No failure will cause the enemy to fall!!
It will break the fetters of Tamililam!!
Then from our people's lips a national anthem
        will tone up!! [8]

While the bridal imagery of traditional poetry remains, there is
an eroticising of the martial; parenthetical emphases in the poem
which make it clear that the LTTE woman has rejected the conventional world of feminised identities, and embraced a language
of death and militancy where there is no place for squeamishness
and coyness. Her sexual energy is directed at ushering in a new
state and dispensation, not preserving old familial ties.

It is a shift Adele Ann is eager to stress. She writes:

The very decision by young women to join the armed struggle—in most
cases without the consent of parents—represents a vast departure of
behaviour for Tamil women. Normally young women remain under the
control of the father and brother. Male control follows them throughout
their lives. The decision to break out of this cycle of suffocating control is
a refreshing expression and articulation of their new aspirations and independence. It could perhaps be one of the biggest decisions of their lives.
Such a decision makes a social statement about the characters of the young
women. It tells society that they are not satisfied with the social status
quo; it means they are young women capable of defying authority; it means
they are women with independent thoughts. . . Such young women fly in
the face of tradition, but they are the women who are the catalysts for
social change. Entering into the military programme represents an extension of the social challenge that young women have made by making a
decision to join the national struggle.[9]

The implication of this statement is clear. There can be no

emancipation for Tamil women without the attainment of a new state and social order in the first place. The 1991 manifesto of the Women's Front of the LTTE makes this explicit, in the priority given to "Secure the right of self-determination of the people of Tamililam and establish an independent democratic state of Tamililam" as its first clause, after which are listed the specific demands of women. These include the dismantling of caste and dowry systems, equal opportunities in employment, the dispensation to control their own lives, and legal protection against sexual harassment, rape and domestic violence. [10] The state as they know it today, administered by the Sri Lankan government, is inadequate and repressive. It has to be re-drawn; women have the potential and will to play a central role in that recasting. Prabhakaran, the LTTE leader, acknowledged this even as he further elicited the commitment of women to the movement. In a statement issued on 8 March, 1992 to mark International Women's Day, he stated:

Today, young Tamil women are there, carrying arms to extricate this soil in the battlefield. They have performed an immense sacrifice (*arppanippu*) of a kind that amazes the whole world. With pride I can say that the origin, the development and the rise of the women's military wing of the Liberation Tigers is one of the greatest accomplishments of our movement. This marks a revolutionary turning point in the history of liberation struggle of the women of Tamililam. Women can succeed on the ideal path towards their (own) liberation only through joining forces with a liberation movement. (Women) can change into revolutionary women who have heroism (*viram*), abandonment (of life) (*tiyakam*), courage and self-confidence. Only when women join forces with our revolutionary movement that has formulated (a path) to liberation of our women, shall our struggle reach perfection.[11]

A synergy between women's empowerment and revolutionary struggle is established here, but in the line that the "liberation of *our* women" has already been determined by the movement, the Tamil woman's agency continues to be suspended. By whom was the path to women's liberation determined? Were there women involved in its formulation? And in the possessive "our women", does patriarchy not rear its head in a collective control and protection of Tamil women by the male?

Growing up in the JVP

Juliet (a pseudonym), joined the JVP movement in 1969 as a schoolgirl of 13. The JVP or People's Liberation Front was a group comprised largely of university and school-going southern youth. Its inaugural meeting was held in May 1965, and it came into prominence in the late 1960s with an agenda directed towards the establishment of a socialist state. It has had two phases of militant uprising to date. Starting in April 1971 with attacks on several police stations, the first JVP insurrection was defeated by government forces some time in June that year. The second phase ran from 1987-89, when the JVP took on the UNP government of Ranasinghe Premadasa in a particularly brutal fashion. It conducted summary killings of government officials who disobeyed its orders and of security forces personnel who hounded it, at times wiping out their entire families. These were tactics of terror, through which it was able to successfully call for stoppages of work and boycott of elections which nearly brought the government down.[12]

Despite these violent campaigns there are many differences between the JVP, particularly in its first phase, and the LTTE that must be noted at the outset.[13] Such an emphasis helps us guard against a flattening out of all militant groups into a homogeneous set, while serving as an illuminating approach to the self-appraisal and representation of the women cadres within the two groups. For instance, unlike the LTTE, the early JVP never saw itself as a nationalist movement. Its rhetoric was that of class struggle; the ideology of militarism was not central to its make-up. A JVP woman member like Juliet would, therefore, inevitably see and represent herself differently, and far less militantly, than Captain Vanathi. Again, the JVP never considered itself as an army in its own right, unlike the highly militarised LTTE which has waged a war with state forces since 1983. The 1971 JVP insurrection was fought with relatively less loss of lives and property; an indication that it could be quelled more easily than the on-going separatist war. The JVP cadres that did survive were easily "rehabilitated" into the mainstream, even after prison sentences, and its leaders now hold important positions in the state and NGO (non-government organisation) sectors. The LTTE combatant, on the other hand, is often killed in battle or, when captured, bites a cyanide capsule that s/he wears round his/ her neck. The ferocity of the LTTE challenge and its dedication to the ideology of violence, then, cannot be matched in the efforts of the early JVP, although in its later phase the JVP mirrored the LTTE in its nationalistic call, and had the south gripped in terror. Because of the high visibility and efficient organisational structure of the LTTE, the like of which the JVP never had, its international presence through the Tamil diaspora, as well as international media interest in the 1990s on the issue of women combatants, LTTE women cadres have had more visibility than the JVP women ever did.[14]

Although there had been a tradition of significant women's participation in militant left-wing, anti-colonial campaigns such as the Suriyamal movement, the 1953 hartāl and other trade union protests in Sri Lanka, the JVP failed, because of its patriarchal bent, to foster and enlist large-scale female participation for its cause. The 1970s JVP had only five or six women at action committee level; there were no women JVPers on the district committees or the decision-making politbureau.[15] Even when the Samājavādi Kānthā Sangamaya (SKS) or the JVP women's wing was formed in 1976, it was assimilated into JVP patriarchy. Rohana Wijeweera, leader of the JVP until his death in 1989, himself admitted that it was the weakest wing of the organization. When, in 1982, the SKS organized a large international conference, it was the all-male politbureau of the JVP that was invited to its governing board, and its inaugural song chanted the praises of the martyred brothers (sadā samramu sohoyurō).[16] No woman militant sits on the LTTE politbureau either, but as a more sophisticated movement of the 1980s and 1990s, the LTTE has been alive to the political potential of a women's wing and its ability to capture international funding available for women's struggles and empowerment.

A full-length feminist study of the JVP movement in Sri Lanka has yet to be written, and the experiences of its women cadres yet to be recorded. But Juliet's voice within the first phase of the JVP struggle is instructive, as it resonates with the statements and silences of the women in the second phase of the JVP. Juliet's family belongs to the Sinhala-speaking bourgeoisie (although her father, a businessman, was conversant in both English and Tamil), domiciled in the town of Kegalle about 48 miles from the capital, Colombo. Her involvement with JVP politics and recruitment to the group took place through her brother, Sarath Wijesinghe, who was the JVP district leader for Kegalle. After the JVP's first strike on the Wellawaya police station on 5 April, 1971 and the subsequent rounding-up or killing of its cadres by government forces, Juliet regrouped with other JVP members in the jungles of Wilpattu. She lived in and around these jungles for five years helping with the JVP re-organisation. In fact, for about a year after the April insurrection, lawlessness continued in the North Central Province that encompassed these jungles. Public transport was disrupted, communication lines destroyed and banks robbed. Many of these disturbances were credited to the JVP. However there were also other gangs and thugs who took advantage of the situation for their own ends.[17]

In an interview with me about her experiences during those five years, Juliet stressed the breaking of new ground. She enjoyed a new-found freedom through her involvement with the JVP. She had been one of seven women chosen to retreat into the jungles because of her adaptability, and although in one sense she was on the run, a fugitive from the law, in another sense she enjoyed communal living. "We were a group of young people" she told me and "everyone helped with the chores, so it was enjoyable".[18] The relaxed tone of such reminiscences reflects, of course, the differences between the JVP then and the LTTE today, but the lack of ferocity of the early JVP campaign, compared to the LTTE, should not detract from the significance of the resistance of women like Juliet. The spurning of middle-class cultural norms that Juliet took on when she joined the JVP— actively recruiting for the movement at the University of Peradeniya, retreating to the jungles, always at the risk of personal safety, living with men, against the establishment, switching dress codes (wearing trousers where previously she would in public at least, have worn a frock or skirt and blouse as worn by young Sinhala women) was pathbreaking in its own right.

Empowerment and Containment: Duality in the Interregnum

The taboos and impositions of female identity that these women turned their backs on are those that acquire particular significance during national crises. It is ironic that at a time of upheaval, "when in reality social norms are being broken and old values begin to crumble, a stronger effort is made to visibly and vocally reiterate faith in the old morality".[19] This reflects the backlash by the established order, whether it be the state or class/caste interests, which digs its heels in when challenged, and in doing so reinforces the most conservative aspects of its cultural and political praxis—including the sexual division of labour. What is also of interest is how, on the terrain of gender, those fighting the establishment, mirror it, conforming to a received conventionality despite their pronouncements to the contrary, in moves that hardly distinguish them from the order they seek to dislodge.

For in the interregnum, as they engage in armed struggle towards the anticipated state, there is a containment of women within the LTTE and JVP at the very moment of their most innovative empowerment. It is a containment seen most graphically on the sites of female sexuality and reproduction. Motherhood is a key construct within female sexuality, a powerful sanctioning symbol of nation-building. Much feminist scholarship exists on the powerful configuration of the mother-figure as a signifier of national and communal identity in South Asia.[20] In its continuity as a recurring motif in nationalist/revolutionary discourse, lies the control of women by patriarchy in the name of combating a larger terror called state repression, or, if one is on the side of the state—separatist nationalism, or revolutionary anarchy. In this trajectory can be found both an internalising of feminised ideals by women, as well as resistance to them; and, most importantly, the complex and *protean* containment of women that reflects the shifting goal-posts and resilience of patriarchy itself.

Partha Chatterjee's understanding of elite Bengali nationalist discourse as formulating oppositional domains through which it constructed a gendered framework for modern Indian society, still remains useful to an understanding of women's containment, although it has been pointed out that many women challenged and subverted its impositions.[21] Chatterjee's arguments remain valid in understanding the moves made by patriarchy to contain women even at moments of their greatest empowerment. His analysis posits a discourse of elite Indian nationalism that constructed a framework of the material and spiritual—which became analogous to the outer and inner domains—in its forging of an independent modern indigenous society. In the context of early de-colonisation, if the West, through its technology and political practice has superiority in the material or outer domain, in the spiritual or inner spheres the East and its indigenous cultures enjoy primacy, and therefore sovereignty. The way gender operates in society, the public is typically the domain of the male, and the home or inner space, which "must remain unaffected by the profane activities of the material world", is represented by women.[22]

So, where elsewhere, sovereignty has been ceded women must compensate for this acquiescence by becoming the symbols of the inner, independent terrain. As such they are constructed by patriarchy in *relation* to the moral corruption and materialism that the public sphere is invested with. Given a woman's biological and gendered role of motherhood, in which she nurtures a younger generation and imbues it with specific cultural values, it is the trope of the mother—mother as fertile nurturer, chaste woman, spiritual and dutiful housewife—that women are most often co-opted into for symbolising this inner and sovereign cultural space of the emerging nation.

A brief reference to a medium of popular culture—the Sinhala theatre—illustrates this point and shows how important a symbol of authenticity and nation-building the woman is, particularly at times of crisis. *Bhashmantaragata* (In the Ashes, 1993) is a play by Amarakeerti Liyanage, written in response to the Sri Lankan separatist war. It is the story of a young woman, Pavithra, who lives in a refugee camp guarded by a Sinhala soldier, with whom she falls in love. It is primarily the role of mother that this young woman is invested with. She is made into "a mother of us all" and her maternalistic aim is to unite her family. It is significant, however, and entirely symptomatic of contemporary nationalist Sinhala theatre, that the family she refers to excludes the Tamil, Muslim and Burgher communities—they do not figure in the play. With this effacement, the implication is that the family Pavithra wants to collect and protect is wholly Sinhala.

As an object of appropriation, as a mother-figure, Pavithra is characterized by three key elements that underline all such co-options. First, she is enlightened, and this is related to the relatively high educational aspirations modern Sri Lankan women have. Through her insights Pavithra is able to lay bare the oppressive structures of society. In this play she accuses the state and its entrepreneurs of being dogs of war, for while the play remains within Sinhala Buddhist ethno-nationalism, it is critical of the alliance between global capital and the neo-colonial state. Secondly, she is de-sexualised. Her love for the soldier is coded in the usual de-eroticised discourse of courtship, in which male and female refer to each other as brother and sister, which may have its roots in the marriage alliances between cross-cousins that take place commonly among Sinhala Buddhist families. It also reflects the influence of Buddhist ethics which advocate restraint. The chastity of a woman, like the so-called purity of language, becomes a code for the nation's honour in nationalist discourse. The protection of this chastity is so important that Pavithra—her name itself projects her sexual purity and, therefore, virtue—rejects the sexual advances of another soldier and pays with her life for preserving her chastity because she is killed by the spurned lover. Thus, thirdly, and most importantly, women like Pavithra are shown to be interest-less in themselves. They do not seek self-preservation and advancement, but are maternalistic and altruistic. Because of this they are in a position to elicit sacrifices on the part of other characters and the audience, for the well-being of the nation, and of religion and cultural values they embody.[23]

In the interregnum, a period in which there is a suspension of normalcy, gender roles challenge the type of containment that Chatterjee and Liyanage delineate in their formulations. The LTTE and JVP woman militant, who is willing to both kill and be killed for her cause, participates in the public domain in a way that flies in the face of traditional patriarchal containment

designed for her. It is the exigency of the interregnum that the
LTTE was responsive to, when by the late 1980s with the war
taking its toll on males, it actively recruited women into its cadres. The early recruitment campaign took a familiar image from
revolutionary groups world-wide, and combined the role of
mother with that of the warrior woman. The woman guerilla
with a baby in one hand and a gun in the other has been used in
revolutionary recruitment and iconography from Latin America
to Asia and Africa.[24] Given the gendering of nationalist discourse,
its call on women to mother/nurture and birth a new nation
through sacrifice and courage, makes the collapsing of mother-
warrior an easy elision. The LTTE publication, *Women and Revolution: The Role of Women in Tamil Eelam National Revolution*
(1983), carried a prominent photograph of a Palestinian woman
holding a gun with one hand and a baby in the other.[25] But the
notion of warrior-mother did not displace deep-seated notions
of normative female identity which, through popular culture, the
media, educational texts and family conditioning, continue to
instruct the Sri Lankan woman on her symbolic value as a sexually chaste, enlightened, altruistic and maternal being. As Cynthia
Enloe comments, "interweaving the images of woman as combatant and mother so tightly suggests that as soon as the immediate threat recedes, as soon as the 'war is over', the woman in
the picture will put down the rifle and keep the baby".[26] It is
clear from the case of the LTTE that, instead of waiting until
"the war is over", its patriarchy puts strictures on women in
place during the interregnum that contain her even as she is invited to step into the public sphere as a combatant. The most
bizarre manifestations of such containment were the so called 10
commandments for women pasted on the walls of Jaffna in late
1984. The dictates were that all young women should wear traditional dress (sari), that married women should not be seen in
public in housecoats (Jaffna housewives often buy fish, early
morning, from vendors on the road and come out to do so in
their housecoats), that women should wear their hair long and
not ride bicycles (which have traditionally been the mode of transport in Jaffna, all the more important because there has been an
embargo on petrol in the war situation). Women who did not

abide by these commandments were threatened with being whipped.

The LTTE denied responsibility for the poster. It was signed by a group that professed interest in Tamil culture—the guise of collective authorship is a strategy whereby an impression of popular support for the dictates is created. Despite the LTTE's denial, these commandments were entirely in keeping with a statement issued by it in *Mukamoodikal Kilihinrana* two years later (1986), which declared:

It is important for women to take care in their dress, in their *pottu* and make-up. It doesn't mean that we are enslaved if we dress according to tradition. Some married women say that it is expensive to wear saris. This is not acceptable. Women should dress simply, and they should not attract men by their way of dressing. Some women say that it is difficult to maintain long hair. These pretensions are wrong...We are engaged in a struggle for national liberation. But, the changes which have been taking place in our culture will only demean our society.[27]

What is significant about this statement is its reflection of a growing unease on the part of the LTTE to changes taking place in Tamil society, and therefore a real ambivalence towards some of the social forces which it has itself unleashed. That women contested these imposed identities and fashioned their own resistance to them are significant indicators of such transformation. The 10 commandments were not taken too seriously; but what they stood for was serious enough for the Jaffna Mothers' Front which was formed in July 1984, modeled on the Mothers' Fronts of Northern Ireland and Plaza del Mayo,[28] to protest against them through a written submission published in the Jaffna daily newspapers. The concern of the Jaffna Mothers' Front was that, if such impositions of female identity were not challenged and nipped in the bud, they would grow to form the basis of a dangerous "fundamentalism" which would be particularly inimical to women.[29]

If, then, the women who joined the JVP and the LTTE as armed combatants were able to shift the parameters, it is abundantly clear that patriarchy responded by shifting its goal-posts within these groups. The LTTE tack of combining the roles of mother and warrior, thereby creating a kind of supernatural woman liberation fighter, is an illustration of such a shift. It ushers the woman from private to public and empowers her in an idea of militancy. But these shifts also always incorporate the continuing subordination of women even as they are invested, as political participants and combatants, with an agency that is unavailable to them in conventional society.

There are many antecedents for such containment in the heritage of the Indian subcontinent. A particular narrativisation of a mythological tale illustrates my point. The *Catakantarâvanan Katai* is an anonymous Tamil prose version of Sita's battle against the demon, Satakantharâvana, or Râvana of the hundred heads.[30] Sita, the epitome of the chaste, pure, dutiful and beautiful Hindu wife of King Rama takes on a martial role in this episode, and battles the devil on behalf of her husband. She has to seek permission to do so. She tells Rama:

We must seek a means of slaying Catakantaravanan. There is no need to be sad. With your grace I shall destroy the Raksasa Catakantan and his sea of armies. Give me the boon of achieving victory over him!

As she makes this request Sita "(falls) at the lotus-feet of Srîrâmâmurti and, bowing low with her hands raised above her head, asked this boon".[31]

Rama's reply is, not surprisingly, benevolent and paternalistic:

Listen, Lady Sita. Because you are a woman, you do not know the tricks of the Raksasas. Moreover, when Ravana kept you prisoner for ten months in Lanka, what did you do then? This is folly, or ignorance; how could you kill that Raksasa Catakantan? (p.109)

Sita does go to war however, for Rama, "by the eye of wisdom" knows that she can slay the enemy. (Note that foresight, wisdom and rationality are here invested solely in the male.) The tale continues with descriptions of Sita's feistiness and violent appetite for the utter destruction of the devil's kingdom, which mark what David Shulman sees as a significant dialectic informing the worldview of the folk-tale. For even as Sita unleashes her power, elsewhere the image of her locked in a box, house or shrine that recurs in many South Indian folk traditions, signifies that her "fiery power has to be somehow circumscribed and contained if it is not to bring about an unbearable destruction—hence the box motif". Shulman goes on to state that,

If we attempt. . . to extrapolate a conceptual scheme from such data, we find a vision of the world as dialectical and dangerous, a world in which powerful forces are constantly breaking through the barriers erected against them. But this state of continuing conflict reflects not only opposition but also a form of tense, productive symbiosis between container and contained, consuming energy and enveloping boundary. (p.119)

This antagonistic and complementary encounter of female power and sexuality, and male dominance which seeks to contain the former, is explicit throughout the *Catakantarâvanan Katai*. Sita's verbal and gestural supplications to her husband and master have already been noted. Although Rama remains outside the battleground, as Shulman points out,

he is still the ultimately powerful validating agency: he sees the outcome of the battle with his eye of wisdom. . . Sita conquers with *his* weapons and mantras, and in the name of his kingship. His presence is clearly necessary, even if others must do his fighting for him. (p.120)

After victory in battle the text concludes with Sita's return to Ayodhya where "Rama reigns virtuously", and therefore supremely. Hanuman the monkey, ally of Sita in war, asks for the title of a Brahman in return for his services, something which Rama promises to confer on him when the present Brahman reaches the age of one hundred. There is no mention of Sita. She is, then, the woman full of powerful potential, at times agent of terror and destruction but reined in when the need for such militancy is done, by a patriarchy that also demands of her the dutifulness and chaste loyalty of a wife, a secondary position to Rama, which she never questions.

The Enduring Past

> Time present and time past
> Are both perhaps present in time future,
> And time future contained in time past
> T. S. Eliot, "Burnt Norton"

These parallels are manifest in both the LTTE and JVP. The epithets of female containment within these militant groups have been, and remain, discipline and chastity. A militant guerrilla group, by its nature, is physically isolated from the larger community and strict disciplinary codes are applied to behaviour within it. Sexuality is seen as a threat to discipline, and strictures come into place that "police" both male and female sexual desire. Both the JVP and LTTE inculcate a notion of group kith and kin. Leaders are elder brothers—figures of authority in both Sinhala and Tamil cultures, and the comrades younger brothers and sisters. It is a hierarchy meant to deter sexual relations between combatants, even as it accords power to a leadership wishing to sexually exploit younger comrades. A former woman activist for the struggle for Eelam told me that women were seen as a "problem" within the LTTE.[32] Marriage was banned on the orders of both Prabhakaran and Rohana Wijeweera—until they themselves wanted to marry.[33] The move, then, is to "purify" the group and make it distinct from what happens outside it. Such control is all the more important in an environment in which the usual social boundaries that segregate male and female have dissolved. Within a guerrilla group the close proximity of men and women "requires" sexual containment. What we have here is an exact replication of the sexual taboos that exist in the outside world, despite the militants' denunciation of those very norms. The Stree Shakti Sanghatana observed of the Communist Party in the Telengana struggle:

The metaphor of the family constantly used to describe the Party reinforced aspects of a feudal culture that continued to assert itself within the organization, and perhaps served to keep women in their roles, which were extensions of their roles in the private sphere.[34]

This is borne out in Juliet's story. Hers was a symbolic role within the JVP as she functioned as a mnemonic of her dead brother, the district leader whose death the group mourned. "I had always to set an example," she said, "as my bother's sister. I understand now that I was nothing more than a symbol of my dead brother. I felt burdened by it, but I also accepted it."[35] When persuaded into a relationship with a man because, only then, would he agree to be recruited into the JVP, Juliet said the relationship indicated a certain "attachment"—they were seen as "belonging" to each other—but they had no physical contact, not even kissing. "In those days," she said, "we were very naive. The revolution was everything. Personal matters could come later."

We see here how Juliet's womanhood was de-sexualized. In the interregnum she had to subsume whatever sexual desires she may have had, in the service of her role within the movement. Operating here is a discourse that transforms the sacrifice paid on the personal terrain into a sense of *duty* towards the cause, and the woman militant accepts this as part and parcel of her struggle. She takes on, by choice, identities of abnegation and sacrifice rather than those of individual desire. This reflects, partly, her ideological commitment to the struggle, her understanding that life in existing society offers no real freedom for the individual; but it also signals an internalisation of existing social codes. Curbing sexual desire within the movement would be an extension of, and no different from, the norms of conduct expected from her within her home and until her marriage.

These norms included a collective silence about women's bodies, even when they had suffered transgression at the hands of the state. None of the JVP women who suffered sexual abuse while in police custody or prison. ever talked about those violations, and the JVP male leaders were at pains to deny the incidents. Their silence was in the service of preserving notions of women's sexual chastity and virginity;[36] yet, both the JVP and LTTE engaged in an instrumental use of sexuality when it suited them. Despite their silences over the sexual abuses suffered by living women cadres, both made icons out of raped, dead female colleagues. The fate of beauty queen Premawathie Manamperi, who was raped and killed by the army in 1971, continued to dominate JVP discourse in a highly sexualised manner for it was her violated body that was remembered and recovered in JVP songs, posters and articles that appeared in the JVP newspaper *Niyamuwā*.[37] Manamperi became a mnemonic by which to recall state terror. The JVP discourse on her rape and death also served to transfer the responsibility for acts of violence on to the state alone and to project the JVP as its victim, not perpetrator of violence in its own right. When Dhanu killed Rajiv Gandhi, the LTTE put out a message that she had been raped by the Indian Peace Keeping Force (IPKF) and that her act of violence was a fitting revenge for her shame and trauma. It is significant that in both instances, rape was publicised only after the women were dead. As for the living female cadre, the sexual abuses they suffered remain censored. This silence may have allowed the JVP women re-entry into the social mainstream, but it did nothing to redress the wrongs committed by the security forces or to inaugurate a public discussion on women's bodies as sites of war. The LTTE, on the other hand, does initiate such a public discourse by warning its women cadre that, if captured, they will be raped and tortured. To avoid this violence it insists that they commit suicide by biting on a cyanide pill following capture. In this case, the public discourse of women as booties of war may be articulated, but the woman whose chastity is defiled by enemy rape has to be eliminated altogether; the justification for the suicide is preservation of one's bodily integrity and of the collective good. When women members leave the LTTE due to ideological differences, it resorts to the rhetoric of sexual shaming to denigrate them. Both Rajani Thiranagama and her sister, Nirmala Nityanandan, were attacked as "loose women" after they distanced themselves from the LTTE's authoritarianism and violence. Their Christian family background, education in co-ed schools and freer interaction with men were misunderstood and misrepresented as grounds for sexual promiscuity.[38]

Vestiges of feudalism also remain in the highly centralised leadership of today's LTTE, as it did for the JVP of the past.[39] At the crux of the LTTE is a personality cult of Prabhakaran that produces a powerful, pervasive male discourse. Large cut-outs of the LTTE leader dominated Jaffna until Operation Rivirasa, when government forces gained control of the town in December 1995. A 47 foot cut-out of Prabhakaran, along with two huge maps displaying what he has achieved on the road to Eelam and what he hopes to achieve, dominate Mallavi in the Vanni.[40] In the volume of inspirational Tamil Eelam songs entitled "Songs from the Red-Blossomed Garden", released by the LTTE and repeatedly played in public places so that they have replaced the once-popular Hindi cinema music, Prabhakaran is invested with the aura of a deity.[41] In this, of course, Prabhakaran is not inventing history. Many guerrilla movements have been dependent on highly centralised organisational structures and leadership cults for their success. That women cadres have to negotiate this reality is implicit in the tension we confront in Adele Ann's *Women Fighters of the Liberation Tigers*. On the one hand, its avowed intent is to present the importance of women within the LTTE; but, on the other, there is an explicit (and politic) need to valorise Prabhakaran. Thus this book on women LTTE cadres begins with a full page photograph of Prabhakaran with the caption, "Mr. Velupillai Piribakaran, leader of the LTTE, who founded the Women's Military Unit of the Liberation Tigers." Homage is paid to him throughout in these terms:

He was confident that women had the potential for military training and combat. Unlike many of his fellow cadres caught up in male chauvinistic conceptions of women and their place in society, Mr. Piribakaran was determined that women should have equal opportunity for participation in all aspects of the armed struggle. Even he admits, however, that women have exceeded his expectations of them (p.7).

Here is the male who ushers in and creates a space for women within his organisation. He is thus the midwife of their agency. That this itself reinforces gender hierarchies which keep women in reliance on men, is never problematised in the book. Since Adele Ann's project is directed at revealing how Prabhakaran himself has broken out of the rigidity of patriarchal Tamil society, she endorses the construction of LTTE women as a site on which Prabhakaran's foresight is inscribed. The LTTE women refer to him as the "King of the Tigers".[42] Such is the acceptance of this that when members of the "Birds of Freedom," as the LTTE women's wing is known, were asked about feminist concerns, they confessed to much confusion within the movement regarding them, but "ultimately ended their argument with an expression of faith in their leader's ability to solve all problems".[43]

Such a reliance on the male leader, the elder brother (Prabhakaran is often referred to as "Anna") immediately begs the question as to whether the fourth clause of the LTTE Women's manifesto—"Ensure that Tamil women control their own lives"—can ever be fully realised. For even as the manifesto is anticipatory, with promises and aspirations for the future, in the interregnum patriarchy has already put into place strictures that will define/confine women in the future. Meanwhile, the woman militant internalises her containment, be it within the terrain of sexuality, rank, or division of labour. It is not surprising that accordingly, Juliet the JVP veteran, is now firmly within the ambit of traditional family values, married, a mother of three children;[44] nor is it surprising that the LTTE woman combatant has internalised her role as martyr in the struggle for Eelam.

The ideology of martyrdom is central to the LTTE's self-conceptualisation and recruitment drive. Peter Schalk argues that it has been effective in shifting the concept of martyrdom from the religious domain to secular space.[45] The LTTE does this by making a martyr synonymous with a great hero. The heroes of the Eelam struggle are commemorated through a series of mnemonics: from a Great Heroes Day which, once the deaths multiplied, was expanded to a Great Heroes Week, to paintings and posters, an office to administer the affairs of the heroes, and special cemeteries for them. The emphasis is on saluting the heroes, rather than on religious rites to mark their demise. However, these salutations take their vocabulary and cue from military rituals honouring brave soldiers—signifying, too, how crucial the legacy of militarism is as a foundational rubric of the anticipated Tamil state. And what of women within such a militarised state? In the current LTTE struggle for Eelam the leadership is careful to accord women combatants their due. They are officially acknowledged as martyrs/heroes as much as the males. The first woman LTTE combatant to commit suicide for the cause was Malati, who swallowed a cyanide capsule on 10 October, 1987, following clashes with the Indian Peace Keeping Forces. In 1989 on her second death anniversary, a large painting of her was made and placed symmetrically with that of the first male martyr, Cankar, in the Kokkuvil office of the Great Heroes in Jaffna district.[46] These early martyrs became role models for others to follow. A woman member of the LTTE propaganda wing declared:

I and my younger sister joined the movement. I am now not in a state to fight. The Leader of the Nation gave me a letter asking me to go home. But I have no mind to go home. I long to see the birth of Tamil Eelam while I am still a militant. After all, the militants who become Black Tigers turn themselves into torches and die the death of the brave. Following their example their brother or sister would come and join us to fight for the cause. Why do they do this? Is it not to win Tamil Eelam so that our generation can live in happiness and freedom? When they perform such sacrifices, can any sacrifice by you be too much?[47]

What is missing in this pledge to the movement, however, is an explanation of how and why the condition of Tamil women is part of the *explanation* for militarism itself. This lacunae encourages an understanding of women's role within militarism, not as a crucial contribution to the emergence and re-ordering of the anticipated state, but as a support service, an instrument (and one of many) in the leadership's armour. This woman's testimony also points to how circumscribed are the possible exits for those who wish to opt out of the movement. It is clear that Prabhakaran's sanction is needed to leave the LTTE. In the meantime, sacrifice for the collective good is valued above all others of self-preservation, family, profession. In the interregnum, during war, this is not hard to understand or demand, as alternatives to joining the movement are minimal, in terms of other jobs and occupations. The state sector has shrunk and the private sector has not expanded in the north and east because of the war. There is no strong women's movement in these areas outside the women's wing of the LTTE, and a few NGO groups working on women's issues. However, that recruitment is sometimes coercive says much about the LTTE's attitude to individual agency, even as it points to pockets of resistance to its ideology of militarism.

The University Teachers for Human Rights (Jaffna) report several instances of young girls forcibly picked up by LTTE recruiters, piled into a van against their will, and taken to LTTE camps for training and "lessons" in the LTTE way of life.[48] The heroic death, the martyrdom, remain important tropes in the rhetoric of recruitment. Students sitting for the G.C.E. "O" level examination were told, "One day you will have to die. If you die fighting, it will be a hero's death but if you die a natural death, it will be a coward's death. Your parents may today discourage you from joining. But later they would be ashamed of you."[49] What does this grammar of recruitment and ideology of martyrdom spell for the fe/male suicide bomber who, in being chosen for the task, is accorded the highest honour within the movement? Men and women vie for the privilege of being admitted to the Black Tiger squad, from which the suicide bomber awaits his/her call up. This can be viewed as an agentive moment in the militant's life, the pinnacle in a career of dedication. On the other hand, the cult of martyrdom is so ingrained and the concept of sacrifice already gendered, in that it is within the normative, pre-scribed roles for women, that at least the female suicide bomber's choice can be seen as culturally predetermined. Most recently, another development has taken place which points to an ever-tightening foreclosing of such agentive moments altogether. Fol-lowing the failure of some recent suicide bomb attacks, the LTTE suicide bomber's jacket is now wired up to detonate either by remote control or a time bomb.[50] The human being is no longer in control over his/her death.

It must be borne in mind, however, that if recruitment is at times coercive, there are women in Jaffna who resist its culture of violence even as the LTTE tightens its grip on the Tamil popu-lation. There have been LTTE women combatants who have left the movement with the blessings of the LTTE leadership, although it is difficult to ascertain how independent they really are of it. There are reports that some women LTTE members who have been allowed to leave the armed struggle, have had to continue to support the movement from outside by providing refuge to comrades, sharing intelligence information and/or securing funds for the LTTE. They have had the freedom to end their role as militants, but not their ideological and practical support for the LTTE cause.[51] At least their lives have been spared. Other women have not been as lucky. Two women poets who challenged the LTTE's authoritarianism and its cult of violence and so, can be heard in argument with the LTTE's Captain Vanathi, immedi-ately come to mind. They are Thiyagarajah Selvanity (known as Selvy) an internationally acclaimed poet, and Sivaramani, a young woman who was born and grew up in Jaffna. Selvy's condemna-tion of the lust for war and power is harsh:

In Search of Sun

My soul, full of despair
yearns for life
where ever I turn

                                    I see
                            primitive humans
                      yellow toothed, ugly mouthed
                        thirsting blood, slit flesh
                              saliva adribble
                    cruel nails and horrifying eyes
                         Bragging and jubilating
                         over victories are not new
                       legs lost from long walks for
                              miles and miles
                          in search of a throne
                   days wasted waiting for full moons
                          only boredom lingers. . .
                                                Jaffna, 1988

Sivaramani's tone is gentler, but she too shares the despair
and anger that pervade Selvy's verse. In an untitled poem
Sivaramani wrote:

                            I have no words
                            that give hope
                             and solutions
                             like a leaflet
                             in bold print.
                                 Dreams
                            their meaning
                             is lost to me
                             who is uncertain
                            that the sun will rise
                               tomorrow.
                             While a gun
                          aims at society's
                          umbilical cord,
                      the dreams of a butterfly
                          resting delicately
                             on the tip
                         of a fragile flower
                             are merely
                           an occurrence.

> In my attempts
> to be humane
> I would rather leave
> the flowers
> on the trees.
> Now,
> the beautiful night
> shaped by the day
> is only a dream.
>
> Jaffna, 1989

But what happened to these women? Selvy was taken into LTTE custody on 30 August, 1991 and is believed to have been killed.[52] Sivaramani, at the age of 24, burnt all the poems she could get hold of one night and, setting her room on fire, committed suicide.[53] As Sitralega Maunaguru commented, Sivaramani's tragedy went largely unnoticed; not dying by biting on a cyanide capsule in the honoured tradition of the LTTE, she was not praised as a martyr.[54] The ultimate tragedy is of a society trapped in its own epistemic ideology of militarism and violence. Rajani Thiranagama stated:

> If in a society like this, the dominant ideology under which the struggle is organised is itself an even more narrow, revivalistic and romantic one, well sprinkled with images of male heroes and male valour, and if nationalism is a type of aggressive patriotism, then a concept of women's liberation would be working against the inner core of such a struggle.[55]

The grip of a patriarchal LTTE leadership is such that in making this statement Rajani, too, signed her death warrant: she was shot dead on 21 September, 1989 as she cycled home in Jaffna town.

Notes

[1] Rajiv Gandhi was India's Prime Minister from 1984 to 1989, and brokered the Indo-Lanka Accord of 1987 which brought the Indian Peace Keeping Forces to Sri Lanka. The IPKF fought the LTTE from 1987–89 without success, before withdrawing and returning to India. The assassination of Gandhi by the LTTE in 1991 was widely seen as retaliation for these events.

228   WOMEN & THE NATION'S NARRATIVE

[2] In 1998, after 16 years, municipal council elections were held in Jaffna. Sarojini Yogeswaran of the Tamil United Liberation Front was elected mayor, but survived in office only a month. She was allegedly shot and killed by members of the LTTE, as was her successor, P. Sivapalan. Also killed was Pon Mathimugarajah, general secretary of the Jaffna TULF, who was tipped to succeed Sivapalan as mayor. Through such killings the LTTE has sent deadly signals that there can be no return to civilian rule which does not have their blessing.

[3] Michael Ignatieff, *Nationalism and Self-Determination: Is There an Alternative to Violence?*, ICES, Colombo, March 2000, pp. 9–10.

[4] The JVP and LTTE have mobilised women combatants in Sri Lanka; in India there are women members of the RSS (Rashtriya Swayamsevak Sangh) and Durga Vahini, militant wings of Hindutva, who participate in its violence against the Muslim minority and those deemed "anti-Hindu". In Kashmir the Dukhtaran-i-Millat is a women's wing affiliated to the All Party Hurriyat Conference fighting for a separate Kashmiri state.

[5] Peter Schalk, "Resistance and Martyrdom in the Process of State Formation of Tamililam," in Joyce Pettigrew (ed.), *Martyrdom and Political Resistance: Essays from Asia and Europe* in *Comparative Asian Studies* 18, 1997. p.71

[6] This has its parallel in the south. A team of journalists who reported on the women cadres of the Sri Lanka Air Force repeatedly stressed the "arduous" and "gruelling" training they undergo in Diyatalawa, which they accomplish with "dedication" and "stamina".*The Sunday Leader*, 5 March, 1995, pp.18–9.

[7] Rajan Hoole, Daya Somasundaram, K.Sritharan, Rajani Thiranagama, *The Broken Palmyrah: The Tamil Crisis in Sri Lanka—An Inside Account*. Claremont: The Sri Lanka Studies Institute, 1990, p.325.

[8] Captain Vanathi, quoted in Peter Schalk, "Birds of Independence: On the Participation of Tamil Women in Armed Struggle." *Studies in Lankan Culture* No.7, December 1992, pp.92–96.

[9] Adele Ann, *Women Fighters of Liberation Tigers*. Jaffna: LTTE, 1993, pp.8–9.

[10] Peter Schalk, "Woman Fighters of the Liberation Tigers in Tamililam: The Martial Feminism of Atel Palacinkam," *South Asia Research* No. 14, Autumn 1994, pp.163–83.

[11] Peter Schalk, "Resistance and Martyrdom," op. cit., p.69.

[12] For studies of the JVP movement in Sri Lanka see A.C.Alles, *Insurgency 1971.* Colombo: Apothecaries' Co.Ltd.; C.A.Chandraprema, *The Years of Terror: The JVP Insurrection 1987–89.* Colombo: Lake House,1991; Rohan Gunaratne, *Sri Lanka: A Lost Revolution? The Inside Story of the JVP.* Kandy: Institute of

Fundamental Studies, 1990. None of these studies however, show any interest in providing a gender-sensitive reading of the JVP. An exception is an article by Kelly Senanayake on "Women, Revolution and the JVP" in *Aya* No. 2, March–April 1996. Colombo: Women and Media Collective, pp.18–20, and work in progress by Manisha Gunasekera, "Gender in Counter-State Political Practice of the JVP 1978–1989," MA thesis, University of Colombo.

[13] C.A.Chandraprema draws attention to the divisions within the JVP itself over the issue of armed militancy. Op. cit., 1991, pp.31–2, 34–5. However, the second phase of JVP militancy had much in common with the LTTE and was indeed influenced by the latter. Like the LTTE, its rhetoric was nationalist, and class struggle was the duty of the patriot. The cult of martyrdom was adopted by the JVP in the 1987–90 period and the ideology of violence became one of its central tenets. See Jani de Silva, "Praxis, Language and Silences: The July 1987 Uprising of the JVP in Sri Lanka," in *Sri Lanka: Collective Identities Revisited* Vol. 2 op. cit., pp.174–5.

[14] This is mirrored in the relative lack of material on JVP women when compared to that—whether propagandist or not—on the LTTE women cadres. Moreover, there is a reluctance on the part of JVP women, who have now joined the socio-cultural mainstream and have families of their own, to talk about their agency in violence. Juliet for instance, insisted that her name not be divulged.

[15] Kelly Senanayake, op. cit., pp.18–19.

[16] Manisha Gunasekera, op. cit., chapter 4.

[17] Alles, op. cit., p.131.

[18] Juliet's testimony contradicts Alles's implication that when the JVP set off on its strike against Balapattuwa, the seven girls (sic) in the party went along merely to cook (Alles, p.124). As the Stree Shakti Sanghatana note, while recording the experiences of the women in the Telengana People's Struggle, this type of "contributory" historiography in which the participation of women in militant groups is "analysed and judged not according to their value or importance for women, but according to their 'use' for the movement in question" devalues the complex issues surrounding the woman militant. Stree Shakti Sanghatana, *"We Were Making History. . ." Life Stories of Women in the Telengana People's Struggle*. New Delhi: Kali for Women, 1989, p.263.

[19] Ibid., p.263.

[20] See C.S.Lakshmi, "Mother, Mother-Community and Mother Politics in Tamil Nadu," *Economic and Political Weekly* 20–9 October, 1990, pp.72–83; Sara S.Mitter, *Dharma's Daughters: Contemporary Indian Women and Hindu Culture*. New Delhi: Penguin, 1992, chapter 6.

[21] Susie Tharu and K.Lalitha, (eds.), *Women Writing in India*, op. cit., Introduction.

[22] Partha Chatterjee, "The Nationalist Resolution of the Women's Question," op. cit., pp.238–9.

[23] Such selflessness is carefully constructed in the propaganda put out by the government to buttress its war effort. *Rana gi*, or war songs, were produced, extolling the virtues of mothers whose sons fight for the motherland, and of lovers who demand of their men that they write home of their bravery on the battlefield rather than "tales of innocent love". Serena Tennekoon, '"Macho" Sons and "Man-Made" Mothers,' *The Lanka Guardian*, 15 June, 1986. It must be noted however that this is not only a woman's preserve. Male politicians, too, have constructed and exploited the notion of selflessness very successfully. See M.S.S.Pandian, *The Image Trap: M.G.Ramachandran in Film and Politics*. New Delhi: Sage, 1992.

[24] Cynthia Enloe, *Does Khaki Become You? The Militarization of Women's Lives*. Boston: South End Press, 1983, p.166.

[25] Sitralega Maunaguru, "Gendering Tamil Nationalism: The Construction of the 'Woman' in Projects of Protest and Control," in Pradeep Jeganathan and Ismail Qadri (eds.), *Unmaking the Nation*. Colombo: Social Scientists' Association, 1995, p.164.

[26] Cynthia Enloe, op. cit., p.166.

[27] Sitralega Maunaguru, op. cit., p.169.

[28] The Jaffna Mothers' Front was formed in July 1984, after an incident in which the Sri Lankan army rounded up between 700–800 males ranging from 12–30 years, and forcibly transported them to the Palaly and later, Boosa camps. In July 1984 the army began a new tactic of surrounding a village in force, with armoured tanks and guns, in order to comb it for LTTE militants. A plea was then issued by the army to the mothers of Jaffna to bring their children with their identity cards for voluntary checking. The mothers did so, and were at the end of the day rewarded with the detention and removal of their male children to army camps. Frustrated at the acquiescence of their husbands, male relatives and friends to the government, the women took it upon themselves to organize and form the Jaffna Mothers' Front. A very successful rally was held with 10–15,000 people attending, which ended in a march to the Government Agent's office, demanding the release of their sons. Sarvam Kailasapathy, personal communication. Colombo: 18 March, 1995.

[29] Sarvam Kailasapathy, personal communication.

[30] David D.Shulman, "Battle as Metaphor in Tamil Folk and Classical Traditions," in *Another Harmony*. Berkeley: University of California Press, 1986, pp.105–30. I am indebted to Shulman's reading of this text from which I draw my main points.

[31] Ibid., pp.108–9.

[32] Lakshmi, (pseudonym), personal communication. London, April 2000.

[33] The JVP leadership had in fact ordered that no JVPer should marry or have romantic links with anyone until the revolution was won. Kelly Senanayake, op. cit., pp.19–20.

[34] Stree Shakti Sanghatana, *We Were Making History*, op. cit., p.269.

[35] Juliet's second brother, Justin Wijesinghe, was also killed in JVP activity.

[36] Kelly Senanayake, op. cit., p.20.

[37] Manisha Gunasekera, op. cit., chapter 2.

[38] Lakshmi, personal communication. London, April 2000.

[39] This was so when Rohana Wijeweera was the leader of the JVP, although he was never able to control or decimate the many factions within the party as successfully as Prabakharan has done with the LTTE. Wijeweera was killed when captured by government forces in 1989.

[40] The University Teachers for Human Rights (UTHR) Jaffna. Sri Lanka —Information Bulletin no. 23, *The Island*, February 2, 2000, p.12.

[41] *Counterpoint*, Vol.1 No.8, November 1993, p.11.

[42] Peter Schalk, "Resistance and Martyrdom," op. cit., p.70.

[43] Hoole, et al., *Broken Palmyrah*, op. cit., p.328.

[44] Many of the women of the 1987–89 JVP too are now married, have children and are reluctant to talk about their JVP connections, partly because they wish to distance themselves from its violence, having entered the socio-cultural mainstream of Sri Lankan life. They may also fear possible future government reprisals. Manisha Gunasekera, personal communication.

[45] Peter Schalk, "Resistance and Martyrdom," op. cit., p.68. According to Schalk it was in 1989 that Heroes' Day was first institutionalised by the LTTE and the commemoration of heroes as it is manifest today, begun.

[46] Ibid., p.72.

[47] Quoted in University Teachers For Human Rights, Jaffna. Sri Lanka – *Information Bulletin* No. 23.

[48] Ibid.

[49] Ibid.

[50] These jackets, wired to detonate one hour into the operation, were used in the commando style attack mounted by the LTTE in Rajagiriya, a suburb of Colombo, and en route to Parliament in March 2000. Although the suicide bombers did have to press the switch that activated the timer, the fact that there was no possibility of retraction once the device was switched on, meant that the bomber could not change his mind. This was the first time such a device was used. *Tamil Times*, 15, March 2000.

[51] The difficulty at present in accessing information on the LTTE and analysing its role, particularly for scholars in the south, makes for a reliance on personal communications, which are often disparate accounts of the LTTE's politics and activities. Just as there are reports of ex–LTTE women being obliged to continue working for the struggle, there are other accounts that contest this, insisting that within the LTTE there is complete freedom of movement.

[52] Selvy was awarded the "Freedom to Write" award by International PEN in 1992. The award honours poets who suffer imprisonment or other infringement of their human rights on account of their beliefs and writing.

[53] About 23 of Sivaramani's poems were with friends at the time of her death, and so survive.

[54] Sitralega Maunaguru, Introduction to "Two Poems of Sivaramani," *South Asia Bulletin* No. 9, 1991, p.147.

[55] Hoole, et al., *Broken Palmyrah*, op. cit., p.327.

The Mothers' Front

5

MOTHER POLITICS AND WOMEN'S POLITICS

Notes on the Contemporary Sri Lankan Women's Movement

IN SEPTEMBER 1999, several events were held in Colombo to commemorate the 10th death anniversary of Rajani Thiranagama. Of these, a coalition of groups which included the Women and Media Collective, Mothers and Daughters of Lanka, University Teachers for Human Rights, the Movement for the Defence of Democratic Rights and the National Christian Council convened, variously and together, a commemorative meeting in Colombo at the Sri Lanka Foundation Institute on 13 September, and a picket at Lipton Circus on 21 September. While the organisers and several women activists attended both events, they were essentially supported by different constituencies. The presence of Kamla Bhasin from India at the earlier commemorative meeting, her keynote address in English,[1] the presence of Rajani's family and a Christian constituency who had known her, gave the SLFI event an urban, middle-class flavour, while the picket attracted a number of women from the south and east of the country, who took to the streets in a march from Lipton Circus to the Centre for Society and Religion, on Dean's Road. Some of the urban audience could lay claim to a larger sisterhood within South Asia, and Kamla Bhasin's reminiscences of Rajani's contribution to the South Asian women's movement was testimony to this. She recalled Rajani's presence at a workshop in Bangalore a few months before her murder; her contribution to the South Asian feminist declaration drafted at that workshop; and the participation of feminists from India and Pakistan who flew to Sri Lanka for a protest march in Jaffna denouncing her murder.[2] The activists who were on the streets on 21 September 1999, on the other hand, tapped into a different collective identity. That week, two atrocities had occurred. Government armed forces strafed the town of Pudukuduirippu in the Vavuniya district, killing 21 Tamil civilians. In retaliation the LTTE hacked 48 villagers to death in Gonagala, and murdered a further 12 villagers in Bandiressa and Boragala in the Amparai district. As they commemorated Rajani Thiranagama's life and death, these women appealed, with a renewed sense of urgency, to their fellow citizens *within* the nation to call for an end to the war and to a life free of both state and LTTE violence.

As with women's movements elsewhere, this signaled that the contemporary Sri Lankan women's movement comprised women of diverse origins and occupations, that it diverged as much as it converged on some issues, that its members spanned a cross-section of state and NGO personnel as well as professionals, academics and political party members, and that its methods of struggle were varied.[3] However, that Rajani Thiranagama's name and face had travelled from the north to enter the consciousness of those in the rest of the country indicated, as Sunila Abeysekera noted at the commemorative meeting, a singular achievement of the women's movement. This had in fact begun much earlier, in the 1993 campaign, "Freedom from Fear", organised by the Movement for Inter-Racial Justice and Equality (MIRJE). Rajani's smiling face, as well as that of journalist Richard de Zoysa, abducted and murdered by state security forces, also in 1989, had been on posters, T-shirts and placards as part of this campaign.[4] Together they symbolised the loss to life and challenge to democratic rights that violence had wrought both in the north and south. They became icons around which a renewed pledge could be made to free society from such fear and violence.

Amrita Basu has noted that, "Even women's movements that ultimately define themselves as autonomous from male-dominated parties and institutions are often closely intertwined with broader movements for social change."[5] These movements have had varied goals, and encompassed a range of activities from trade unionism to consumer protection, demand for civil liberties, employment and equal opportunities. In Sri Lanka in the 1980s, campaigns for equal pay for women in the plantations, elimination of night work for women in the Free Trade Zone,[6] and the campaign for enhanced maternity benefits were some of the prominent activities. They constituted what Maxine Molyneux termed "strategic" gender interests as opposed to practical ones.[7] By the late 1980s and early 1990s however, under severe state and non-state repression (in the militancy of the JVP and LTTE), women's groups in Sri Lanka linked their feminist demands to the language and principles of human rights. Sri Lankan society was in crisis. Thousands had "disappeared" in the south of the country in the brutal JVP violence and retaliatory crackdown by the UNP government of President Ranasinghe Premadasa. The Presidential Commission into Involuntary Removal in the south of the country found evidence of 7239 cases of "disappearances" since January 1988 from an alleged 8739 cases reported to it. Of these, 4858 cases were at the hands of state forces while 779 cases were JVP instigated.[8] Journalists and scholars who have written on the "reign of terror" however, have placed the numbers of deaths much higher, at around 40, 000.[9] The north and east were also theatres of civil war resulting in over 60,000 casualties, half of them civilian, with 55,000 maimed, over 750,000 people, mainly of Tamil origin, dispersed into a diaspora, and nearly a million Sri Lankans, mostly Tamil and Muslim, but Sinhalese too, internally displaced and in refugee camps.[10] The need of the hour was to campaign for a respect of and commitment to international standards of human rights and a political negotiation to end the ethnic war. It was a context in which it was difficult for women's groups to keep focusing on feminist/strategic issues as it had done up to the mid-1980s. Criminalising domestic violence, sexual harassment, equal opportunities, abortion, women's access to safe contraception and informed choice about contraceptive methods, women's reproductive health, the image of women in the media, etc., had to be kept on hold because of the socio-political crisis within the nation. When women's groups, such as the Women's Action Committee, themselves became targets of attack by the JVP for their support of the 1987 Indo-Lanka accord as a first step towards a political solution to the war, they could no longer ignore the need to campaign for human and democratic rights. This decision was not an easy one.

One of the reasons WAC ceased to exist by 1987 was because it could not agree on what its response should be to the complex and contradictory pulls of the IPKF presence in Sri Lanka, to Sinhala nationalist outrage and militant Tamil nationalism.[11] The context of state and JVP repression also jeopardised WAC's existence. The fact that three years later members of WAC regrouped with others to form Mothers and Daughters of Lanka, in 1990, indicates that women were willing to take up the challenges posed by militant nationalism and state authoritarianism. By the early 1990s, despite the multiplicity of NGOs focusing on a diverse range of women's issues, and the presence of women's organisations like the Kānthā Vibūshaṇa Peramuna which supported the war effort and continue to do so even today, a broad coalition of women's groups had formed around the issue of human rights.

This is not to say that feminist issues were altogether off the agenda. The 1995 Women's Conference in Beijing provided a forum for women's groups to put together a list of demands that directly addressed the state about women's concerns. In 1992 consultations began on the Women's Charter, spearheaded by the Ministry for Women's Affairs. The Charter, published in 1993, called on the state to ensure women's political and civil rights. It confronted the vexed question of nationality (currently a Sri Lankan woman married to a foreigner cannot pass on her citizenship to her children), and asked that women enjoy equal rights with men on issues of citizenship; it demanded that women be given the choice as to whether to marry under personal law or general law; that women enjoy the same rights as men in relation to the rights of marriage and custody of children; that the state secure women's right to education and training, economic activity and ownership of land, including land in settlement schemes; that the state redefine "heads of households" so as to ensure that women's contribution to the household is recognised and that they have access, as men do, to all state development programmes and distribution of benefits; that women receive maternity benefits and childcare and that they not be discriminated against on grounds of marriage and maternity. The issue of migrant women and the state's responsibility towards them was addressed in the

Charter, as well as women's right to reproductive health and nutrition, protection from social discrimination and gender-based violence. A National Committee on Women was formed to oversee the Charter although to date, it has not been ratified in parliament. Despite these efforts at working towards women's rights as strategic interests, the separatist war which began in 1983 and the overwhelming violence of 1989–1992 in the south of the country left most women's groups with little choice but to include the boundaries of women's issues in those of human rights and the question of minority self-determination.

The trajectory of the Women's Action Committee is a good example of this shift. WAC was the first significant women's group to be formed around some of these issues in 1982. As a coalition of women from a range of left political parties and trade unions, the members of WAC had a particular orientation towards the national question. For one, they were committed, in principle, to the right to self-determination of minorities. For another, many of them had been a part of active campaigning against the Prevention of Terrorism Act of 1979. Women from the Plantation Women's Group (Hatton) and the Women's Education Circle (Jaffna) were also original members of WAC. It was, therefore, one of the most broad-based groups of the time. It organised several workshops, campaigns and lobbying strategies linking women's rights to human rights, with the ultimate goal of establishing a far-reaching democratic culture within Sri Lanka.[12] It championed the right to self-determination of the Tamil people, raised consciousness about the consequences of the war, and called for its halt. WAC collaborated with a group of women academics and professionals comprising journalists, lawyers, doctors, administrators, writers and artists, to call for a negotiated settlement to the ethnic conflict and a cessation of hostilities. This effort resulted in a petition signed by over 100 women, published in 1984 in the name of a new collective called Women for Peace. As the war escalated during the 1980s and measures at counter-terrorism such as Emergency rule, the Prevention of Terrorism Act (under which arbitrary arrest and detention took place) and the Public Security Ordinance which permitted the disposal of bodies by the security forces came into

force, Women for Peace and WAC protested against these measures, held vigils and worked for humanitarian aid to those displaced by conflict.

The Indo-Lanka Accord of July 1987 proved a turning point
in Sri Lanka's recent history. The presence of the Indian Peace
Keeping Forces, although welcomed at first by women of WAC
drew immense hostility from a nationalistic Janathā Vimukthi
Peramuna comprising a Sinhala constituency in the south. Immediately after the IPKF arrival, it began a sustained campaign
of political assassination, arson and enforced work stoppages. It
protested at the "Indian occupation" of the country, and the "sell-
out" to India by the Sri Lankan UNP government under the leadership of President J.R. Jayawardena. The attacks were carried
out by the Deshapremī Janathā Vyaapāraya or Patriotic People's
Movement, which allowed the JVP to deny its involvement with
the assassinations. But it was widely known that the two groups
worked in tandem. Women who belonged to WAC and were
also involved in other community organisations which challenged
Sinhala nationalist positions, were threatened and harassed by
the JVP. Many of them had to leave their homes, particularly
from the provinces where they were known, to the anonymity of
the city. Under such an onslaught WAC could not survive, and
from 1987–1990 there was a period of hiatus, hiding and inac-
tion until the formation of Mothers and Daughters of Lanka
(MDL). The goal of MDL was a broader platform of unity within
Sri Lanka that all mothers and daughters—in the south as well as
north and east of the country—could join. It lobbied for a negotiated settlement to the ethnic conflict and the war. Its name was
not without controversy; there were women who protested against
the use of motherhood as a coalescing factor. However, the name
stuck and MDL launched an appeal addressed to the state, the
JVP and the LTTE to "stop all killing".[13]

"Mother politics" was to become an even greater force in the
wake of the formation of the Mothers' Front and its challenge to
the state during the years 1990–92. (Earlier, in 1984 a Mothers'
Front had been formed in Jaffna to protest against the arbitrary
detentions of youth taking place there, but as will be discussed
later, it soon disbanded under LTTE pressure.) The Mothers'

Front of the south has been, arguably, the most visible and potent women's protest movement in the history of post-colonial Sri Lanka. It brought together women from different regions in the south of the country and united across caste and class barriers. Several women from urban-based NGOs gave the movement support and leadership. Dr. Manorani Saravanamuttu, mother of murdered journalist Richard de Zoysa, became the president of the national committee of the Mothers' Front in 1991. A middle class medical doctor by profession, the daughter of a Tamil father and Scottish mother, bearing a Tamil name, she came to symbolise (for urban activists at any rate), the need for unifying across ethnic and class divides to focus on the issues at hand. The Mothers' Front radically challenged the government of the day, forcing it into a defensive position as never before provoked by a Sri Lankan women's protest movement. The Mothers' Front understood the weaknesses of its opponents well and planned its strategies accordingly, using both orthodox and unorthodox measures. In its highly visible public outing, in its achievements and weaknesses, lie several factors which characterise the legacy of the Sri Lankan women's movement, the context in which it operates today, and its engagement with Sri Lankan nationalisms.

The Reign of Terror

From 1987 to 1990 the south of the country lived through a time that has come to be known as the "reign of terror" (*bheeshana samaya*).[14] The JVP, in its bid to capture state power, began a violent campaign of threats, intimidation and assassination to assert its supremacy. It targeted the state—its military, police and bureaucracy—as well as politicians and activists classified as "traitors to the nation" because of their support for the Indo-Lanka peace accord. During this period the JVP engaged in violence on a scale as never before, in a departure from its earlier 1971 stance, perhaps because it was poorer then and less organised, and did not have the means to arms as the late-1980s JVP did. When the UNP came to power in 1977, President J.R.Jayawardena released the JVPers detained from the 1971 insurrection. It was free therefore to contest the 1981 presidential elections. Its abysmal failure in this election, as well as the 1982 referendum which extended the UNP's parliamentary life by another six years—causing frustration amongst the UNP's political opponents, including the JVP—and finally, the proscription of the JVP in 1983 following the July anti-Tamil riots, resulted in its resolve towards armed militancy. By 1987 it had systematically collected weapons and raised funds for its efforts through armed robberies. It had created the Deshapremī Janathā Vyapāraya (DJV), signaling its nationalist bent in the word "patriotic". This nationalist fervour found its target in the Tamil separatist cause and India's involvement in Sri Lanka's ethnic conflict. In line with the JVP's long mistrust of Indian expansionism, it launched a campaign of unrest following the Indo-Lanka accord of July 1987. Its first salvo against the accord was in Leading Seaman Wijayamunige Vijitha Rohana's attempt on the life of Indian Prime Minister, Rajiv Gandhi. Vijitha Rohana attempted to hit the Indian Prime Minister on the head with his rifle butt as Gandhi walked past a naval guard of honour minutes before his departure to India, having signed the accord with the Sri Lankan authorities. Gandhi narrowly missed the attack. It took place simultaneously with the DJV setting fire to buses and public buildings in Fort, an important government and commercial district in Colombo. In January 1988 the DJV issued a leaflet named "The National Movement to Punish the Enemies of the Motherland", warning left-wing political parties, women's groups, the Independent Students' Union of the universities and other NGOs that "All Those Killed were Traitors who Deserved Punishment."[15]

The Provincial Council elections held under the 13th amendment to Parliament, adopted in 1987 as a provision of the Indo-Lanka accord, was again seen by the JVP as a prelude to Tamil separatism and a legitimate target for attack. Through leaflets and posters it demanded a boycott of these elections and warned that anyone who disobeyed would be shot. The JVP kept its word. A number of electoral candidates, as well as ordinary citizens who turned up at polling booths to exercise their right to vote, were killed. Given this climate of intimidation and assassination, the voter turnout was very low. In the districts of Matara and Hambantota in the south of the country where the JVP was active, the turnouts were, respectively, a mere 20.34 per cent and a staggeringly low 7.97 per cent.[16] The JVP then went on to campaign against the presidential elections of December 1988 which brought Ranasinghe Premadasa to power. Once again it succeeded in keeping the voters away. This election saw only 55.32 per cent of registered voters casting their ballot, in the lowest voter turnout for a presidential election for the time. Premadasa was elected president with only 27.40 per cent of the vote.[18] The general elections of February 1989 became the next target of JVP attack. On 1 January 1989, it called for people to boycott this election and stepped up its violence, with a record 600 assassinations which took place between the presidential elections of December 1988 and the beginning of the February 1989 general elections.[17]

These anti-election campaigns achieved their goal of intimidating the voter through the tactics of terror, bolstered the JVP's sense of power and furthered its desire for it—1989 saw the worst of JVP terror. Marking the anniversary of the April 5, 1971 JVP uprising, it called for a general *hartāl* or stoppage of work from 5–15 April, 1989. Schools, transport and health services came to a halt. Traders and government officers who did/could not comply with its orders were, in many cases, killed. The country was paralysed for six days and the government was on the brink of collapse. The JVP killing spree continued. The incumbent vice chancellor of the University of Colombo was shot dead in his office. The JVP cracked down on UNP politicians and security service personnel close to the government, in particular, wiping out entire families as in the case of DIG of Police, Premadasa Udagampola, whose whole family, including his aged mother, was killed in a JVP attack.

The UNP launched an equally brutal counter-offensive. That the police force had been particularly targeted by the JVP meant that the police and other security personnel had a vested interest in revenge, and were motivated to wipe out the JVP. Those targeted, however, were not only JVPers (many youth were killed on mere suspicion of JVP sympathies), but also men who worked for the opposition SLFP party in its various organisational committees. Words associated with terror like *bheeshanaya* (terror), *athurudahanwoowo* (the disappeared), *wadhākagāraya* (torture chamber) entered the popular vocabulary.[19] The women of the south faced the trauma of seeing their sons, husbands and brothers either taken away or brutally killed in front of their own eyes. Security personnel and para-military groups like the Black Cats and Kola Koti (Green Tigers) specially formed to eliminate the JVP, conducted what is analogous to a scorched-earth policy. This is the story of one woman we interviewed. She is Mangalika and lives in the Matara district:[20]

> I was living at my brother's house when he was attacked and killed. I was in an utter state of shock, but I went to the police station to lodge an entry. Before going I asked my 10 year old daughter to wait in the house with her younger brother and sister until I returned. But she wanted to go with me as she was frightened. At the police station they even refused to take down my entry. Then I heard a big sound and people shouting. I ran back to find that they had set fire to our house. My other two young children, nine and seven years old, died in that fire. I had to be hospitalised that day. My eldest daughter lives with the guilt of being a survivor of that attack in which her two younger siblings died. When I returned from hospital, the children had already been buried. The authorities refused to give me death certificates, saying that it was not possible as inquiries had not been held into the circumstances of their deaths.

Others either witnessed their men being shot and/or burnt alive, and lived in fear of the sound of revving engines and knocks on their doors, that foretold their menfolk being arrested and dragged away. Very soon, women began to search for their men in the camps where detainees were housed. It was the women who went and confronted the authorities because they were afraid that if the remaining men went, they too would be detained. For many of them the search was in vain. Their men were not produced before them, the authorities were indifferent to their appeals and disingenuous with the truth.

The UNP government was able to act with such impunity because violence had been a systematic tool of socio-political control in both colonial and post-colonial Sri Lanka which, as marked in the introduction to this book, had resulted in several states of Emergency. But from 1977 onwards, under the leadership of President J.R. Jayawardena, the systemic use of violence for political

gains became heightened. The landslide electoral victory of
J.R.Jayawardena and the UNP in 1977, as well as the new Constitution of 1978 which ushered in a presidential system to Sri
Lanka with wide executive powers to the president, gave the party
a sense of untrammelled power. It institutionalised violence as a
defining aspect of the state apparatus as never before. The trade
union of the UNP, the Jāthika Sevaka Sangamaya (JSS) was used
to stoke industrial strife, and act as a well-organised band of
thugs when required. Gananath Obeyesekera notes how, during
the seventeen years the UNP was in power, working class jobs
were given to people who joined the JSS. Its leadership, in turn,
owed personal allegiance to party politicians; before long it became an organised force acting in concert with other local thugs
and lumpens, with the ability to even control government offices
and corporations and harass officials unpopular with it.[21] The
JSS, with the blessings of the UNP leadership, was instrumental
in the violence unleashed in July 1983 against the Tamils. Moreover, as the movement for Tamil separatism took hold, the UNP
and the state security forces resorted to para-military and extra-
judicial action to curb the Tamil rebels. The legislature was used
to protect those engaged in such acts from prosecution. A wide-
ranging Prevention of Terrorism Act came into force, and an
Indemnity Act No. 20 of 1982 restricted legal action against persons who had resorted to violence during the period 1 to 31 August, 1977, the month the UNP came to power. Police officers
who had used violence to intimidate citizens engaged in rightful
protest (eg., when Vivienne Gunawardena went to deliver a petition to the U.S. embassy and was beaten up) were promoted.
Not surprisingly, the increasingly politicised police force looked
the other way when thuggery and violence were applied to the
UNP's political opponents. Through the cynical use of the legislature, the experience gained by its clandestine use of para-military groups to fight the Tamil separatists in the north and east,
and repeated immunity afforded the police and armed forces
engaged in violence in its service, the UNP was well equipped, in
policy and practice, to meet the JVP challenge with a high level
of force and violence, backed by all the state and non-state muscle
at its disposal.[22]

In this climate of terror and militancy, the Mothers' Front was inaugurated on 15 July, 1990 in the southern town of Matara, as a response to the UNP government's human rights abuses. Two members of parliament, Mahinda Rajapakse of the SLFP and Vasudeva Nanayakkara of the NSSP, first broached the idea of a Mothers' Front.[23] They had attended the sessions of the UN Commission on Human Rights and other international meetings to raise the issue of the "disappeared". SLFP MP, Mangala Samaraweera, joined the movement later. These MPs had heard of the Latin American Mothers' Fronts, particularly the Mothers of the Plaza del Mayo of Argentina. Following that example and recognising the potential of politicising motherhood in a situation of anarchy, they held their first meetings with the mothers and families of the disappeared. Their immediate goals were to try and find the disappeared and obtain the release of those detained without charges. They demanded death certificates and compensation for those missing for over a year.[24] They pledged to try and alleviate the misery of the women who had suffered personal trauma, and were now in tremendous economic difficulties with the loss of their breadwinners. Even from an orthodox point of view, the meetings were an enormous success.[25] Within six months of its inauguration, branches of the Mothers' Front had been formed in ten other districts. In Matara alone, 1500 women elected officers to co-ordinate the group's activities in the district. By 1992 there were 25,000 members of the Mothers' Front. The UNP government was disturbed enough by these series of events for President Premadasa himself to openly declare sympathy for the mothers whose children had been led astray by undesirable elements. He told the mothers that many of their children were being rehabilitated in the camps in which they were held, implying, as Malathi de Alwis points out, that the state had taken over the responsibility of undoing the deficiencies of their bad mothering. Defence Minister Ranjan Wijeratne was more blunt. He openly blamed the mothers for having failed their duty by their children and the nation, chastised them for taking part in demonstrations, and stepped up police surveillance on the group.[26]

On 19 February, 1991 the Mothers' Front held its first convention at the Town Hall in Colombo. The following ten resolutions were passed unanimously at this meeting:

1. That the President and the government release information on the whereabouts of the disappeared and what has happened to them, and that local and foreign human rights organisations like the Red Cross insist on such information from the government.
2. That the government appoint a fully powered independent Commission, free from state interference and including Supreme Court judges, to verify the facts around arbitrary arrests and detention.
3. That the government pay compensation to the dependents of the disappeared as well as for damage of house and property.
4. That the government harness state-funded social service institutions to guide the orphaned children who had lost their parents who were disappeared.
5. That the government issue death certificates to the dependents of the disappeared and alleviate their trauma.
6. That the government give priority to the families of the disappeared in giving state jobs, houses and compensation.
7. That the government release information on those who have been held under the Emergency Regulations and the Prevention of Terrorism Act; that the government preserve their lives and act in a manner respectful of basic human rights; allow parents to visit detainees at proper intervals to see to their well-being; appoint an independent investigation commission consisting of representatives of all political parties, which has the power to inspect camps at any time if proper prior notice is given.
8. That people in custody who have not been charged be released immediately; that the government confirm security of their lives and present them in front of the judiciary.
9. That the government confirm the security of life of those rehabilitated and released, and provide them means of employment.
10. That the government nullify all controlling acts and disarm all armed groups.[27]

This meeting was followed by a rally in Nugegoda, a suburb of Colombo, on the same day. A large number of women from the south and a few from the north and east attended this rally, despite rumours spread by the government of LTTE attacks on them, other acts of intimidation and withdrawal of adequate transport facilities.[28] The rally was addressed by Dr. Manorani Saravanamuttu, now appointed co-ordinator of the Mothers'

Front, Sirimavo Bandaranaike and Chandrika Kumaratunga, amongst others. A woman representing the Tamil community also addressed the gathering. While Dr. Saravanamuttu appealed for a non-partisan approach within the Mothers' Front and insisted that the Front gain strength from the goodwill and support of mothers world wide, Mrs. Bandaranaike pointed out that the UNP government should be held responsible for the violence that had rocked the country, that not only Sinhala but Tamil and Muslim youth had been affected by the violence, and dismissed as baseless, reports that the LTTE would attack the Mothers' Front. She informed the crowd that, on the contrary, the LTTE had issued a statement from its London office in support of the Front.[29] President Premadasa responded by "shaming" the SLFP and human rights activists. He stated that the very same people shedding tears for the mothers had asked that his government crush the JVP with brutal force, and pointed out that at the height of the JVP violence, there had been no marches or protests against *its* brutal slayings of innocent people, including a number of Buddhist priests.[30] The SLFP and the human rights community were thus singled out for ridicule of their hypocrisy.

From then on the Mothers' Front and the UNP government were locked in antagonistic combat, with each responding to the others' tactics, claims and counter-claims. The second rally of the Mothers' Front was held in Colombo a month after its initial one, on 8 March, 1991, to coincide with International Women's Day. The government tried to ban the rally on grounds of security threats from the LTTE. Hema Premadasa, the President's wife, then held a separate rally on the same day, in which women mourned the deaths of those killed by the JVP and the LTTE. Much publicity was given to this rally in the government media. One year later, in July 1992,[31] the government responded to the challenge of the Mothers' Front by inaugurating its own Mothers' Front, comprising UNP women of the Gampaha district. Thus the agitations of the earlier Mothers' Front marked a singular achievement in bringing the agenda of human rights before the public. The UNP Mothers' Front may have focused on its own dead, but it was forced, nevertheless, to follow the terms of reference set by the original southern Mothers' Front.

What this also indicates is that, despite the strenuous efforts of Dr. Manorani Saravanamuttu and its leadership to maintain the independence of the Mothers' Front, and despite Mrs. Sirimavo Bandaranaike's claim at the Nugegoda rally that the Mothers' Front was not a political movement, that the SLFP's involvement was only to support and fortify the Front, [32] both Mothers' Fronts had begun to acquire distinct political tones by the end of 1992. The first "SLFP Mothers' Front", however, had the support of a large umbrella of human rights and women's organisations, that the UNP Mothers' Front totally lacked. The first was thus seen as the legitimate Mothers' Front, more neutral and with a greater moral force, given the UNP's use of state power to curb opposition and obliterate international standards on and respect for human rights. (The Mothers' Front was quick to capitalise on this by inviting international agencies like the Red Cross to look into the UNP's human rights record—as per its 19 February 1991 resolution—thereby internationalising the issue.)

However, that there *were* women who felt that the UNP Mothers' Front provided them refuge at a time of need, shows that the first Mothers' Front did not do enough to cut across political party lines and recruit mothers of all those who were killed and had disappeared, irrespective of their political affiliations to its cause. In all the resolutions unanimously passed at its first convention on 19 February, 1991, it was President Premadasa and the UNP government who were named as adversaries. Neither the JVP nor the LTTE were called upon, as non-state militant groups engaged in terrorist activity, to halt violence. Rather, the demand was once again to the government to disarm all armed groups. In this, there was a failure to keep to its goal of being an independent watchdog. Its actions fell short of forging a "lateral cosmopolitanness" with interlocking political and cultural links that would have brought together all mothers—not just in the south, but also the north and east where Tamil youth were disappearing by the day at the hands of the state armed forces. While there had been a Jaffna Mothers' Front active in the mid-1980s, engaged in earlier moves to get their sons out of detention camps and the clutches of the security forces, and some women from the north and east took part in the Mothers' Front rallies in Colombo, there was no effective networking between these groups thereafter, under a broad umbrella of a united Mothers' Front. Its resolutions at its first convention, demanding information on those held under Emergency Regulations and the Prevention of Terrorism Act, and its call for the lifting of these instruments of social and political control, were lobbied by independent human rights groups based largely in Colombo, rather than by the Mothers' Front as a whole. When pressed to comment on this lacuna and the absence of Tamil women in the Front, all the women we spoke to said that they had not met any Tamil women at their Mothers' Front activities. Many of them however said that it would have been good if Tamil women, too, had joined because these mothers shared a common concern and common grief. None of them drew attention to the fact that Dr. Manorani Saravanamuttu was herself of Tamil ethnicity. For them, it was not so much her ethnic, but class and urban identities, that were significant. She was a woman who, despite her location in the professional middle class of Colombo, had suffered the same fate as them. We can speculate from this, that if the Mothers' Front had been able to achieve a broader coalition that united Sinhala and Tamil women from all regions, including the north and east, it would have survived to be a powerful protest movement today working for peace and a negotiated settlement to the ethnic conflict. It would have admitted the "impure" and the "non-citizen" into its ranks, in a cosmopolitanness that would have challenged both dominant Sinhala and Tamil nationalisms, while at the same time drawing from nationalism's sense of solidarity to forge a strong feminist, coalition politics.[33] As it happened, its focus on the single issue of disappearances in the south became so intimately connected with ousting President Premadasa and the UNP from power, that when the President was killed by an LTTE suicide bomber on 1 May, 1993, and Chandrika Kumaratunga became President as head of a People's Alliance in November 1994, the Mothers' Front all but fizzled out. It still maintains a presence today and joined other organisations in a 100,000 signature "Petition for Peace" presented to the President on 8 March, 2000, which called on the government to bring about a speedy solution to the ethnic conflict, [34] but it no longer holds centre stage. On the other hand, it can be argued that the Mothers' Front achieved what it had to in its day and, as with shifting coalitions, the movement fragmented into different organisations with diverse foci. Instead of calling themselves the Mothers' Front, many of these groups now work around the issues of widows and women as heads of household. Manorani Saravanamuttu herself started the organisation called the Family Rehabilitation Centre.

As already noted, the numbers of women who joined the Mothers' Front were impressive. These included not just mothers, but also the widows and sisters of the disappeared. Numbers and rallies aside however, it was the unorthodox nature of the Mothers' Front protests that radically challenged the UNP government. Many of the bereft women had supplicated the gods and goddesses at temples (*devāles*) in their local districts, seeking answers to and solace for the disappearance of their loved ones. In the Matara district, many women had made vows at the Seenigama and Devinuwara *devāles* for their return. What the Mothers' Front was able to do as an organisation was to convert these essentially private quests and pilgrimages into highly public and politicised religious rituals. It held two successful *pāda yatrās* or marches in March and April 1992, which led to the Devinuwara and Kataragama *devāles* where women heaped curses on President Premadasa in revenge for the loss of their loved ones. It is reported that a superstitious President Premadasa attempted to counter their curses by consulting a Malayali priest who recommended that he be bathed by seven virgins. Recognising a weak link in the government's armour, the Mothers' Front increasingly began to target President Premadasa's superstitiousness in its by now highly visible and politicised activities. Another *Deva Kannalaawa* or beseeching of the gods was held to coincide with Premadasa's birthday on 23 June, 1992. This took place at the Kaliamma Kovil in Modera. The police were out in full force and the mothers who approached the temple found its gates locked. When they decided to break their coconuts and heap curses in front of the gates anyway, a senior police officer had the gates opened, although the inner sanctum of the temple remained out of reach. Again curses were heaped on the President—a woman we spoke to said she had beseeched Kaliamma and broken a coconut with the wish that the President's head be split into seven.[35] Many women like her saw President Premadasa's violent death at the hands of an LTTE suicide bomber as a direct answer to their supplications. In contrast was the response of Dr. Manorani Saravanamuttu. Senior DIG, Ronnie Goonetilleke, widely suspected in Richard de Zoysa's abduction and killing, had also been blown up with President Premadasa. When a three-wheeler driver expressed his jubilation at the deaths and told Dr. Saravanamuttu that justice had been done at last, she replied—"I too want justice for my son, but not this way. I want a democratic process to convict the guilty."[36] While both responses sought justice, the different routes these women took—one rooted in folk justice, the other in the judicial and secular processes of a modern state—did surface after all, even when their common endeavour took its most dramatic turn.

Mother Culture

In her work on the women's movements in India, Raka Ray observed that protest movements are influenced as much by local cultures, histories and institutions of politics, as by other social movements.[37] The complex cultural field of motherhood in Sri Lanka played a central role in the formation of the Mothers' Front, its success and, at the same time, its vulnerability to attack and appropriation. In a culture where motherhood is valorised, the appeal to mothers to come together as protectors of their sons, searching for the truth of their whereabouts, proved most compelling, as the numbers of the movement proved. The value of motherhood also gave the women moral and emotive power as victimised mothers in a culture supposedly deferential and respectful to them. Their marches on the streets and beseeching of gods and goddesses pointed to the transgressions of the state in this regard. They were successful shaming mechanisms, bringing ignominy on the UNP government which had denied them their rights of motherhood in the most brutal fashion. The public looked on in awe and sympathy as aged mothers marched together with younger women, weeping and wailing, proclaiming their loss in a highly public display of private grief.

Motherhood was also valorised within the JVP ideology that some of these mothers had lost their sons to. Hemasiri Gamalath, an ideologue of the JVP, noted in an interview with Manisha Gunasekera in 1996, that Lenin had bestowed the title of "Great Mother" (*Uthum Māthā*) upon a woman who had produced a great number of children, thereby doing a great service to the nation's revolutionary cause.[38] Gamalath quoted Lenin with approval, "unproblematically and simplistically" as Gunasekera points out, at a time when Sri Lankan women were aspiring to a different identity for themselves in professional careers and planned motherhood, if at all. The JVP men, at best caught in the ambivalence towards the family within socialist orthodoxy itself, which both criticised and valorised it, nevertheless by and large remained stuck in traditional patriarchal prescriptions for women. The JVP poetry of the 1980s is another case in point. Many of the "mother-son" poems had the poet-subject appropriating the role/ voice of a mother, who pledges to protect her rebel son even if she eventually loses him. She understands her sacrificial loss in terms of a larger gain:

Son—possess not I
Palaces nor robes hewn in gold
Nor gourmet dishes,
Son—possess I
A son who will
Some day mount red flags of victory
Fighting for a world
Where all live and die as equals.[39]

In this way motherhood, and the mothers' espousal of the JVP cause, were used to legitimise the JVP, and the photograph of old mothers taking part in the JVP May Day rally in 1981, published in the JVP newspaper *Niyamuwpa*, reinforced this message.[40] When these mothers demanded justice for their disappeared sons they were seen as legitimate supplicants, with the full weight of moral authority behind them.

Mother-value and the successful politicisation of motherhood by the Mothers' Front has been repeatedly appropriated by women politicians, too. It is Chandrika Kumaratunga, who has benefited the most from identifying with the Mothers' Front. In the run-up to the 1994 presidential election, Kumaratunga, herself the daughter of an assassinated father and widow of an assassinated political leader/actor "cleverly articulated the mothers' suffering as both a personal and national experience".[41] An advertisement for her candidacy foregrounded this. She was presented as the daughter who lost her father to an assassin, the wife who lost her husband to an assassin, and therefore the daughter, widow and mother best placed to understand the suffering of the families of the disappeared. There was a vote bank of mothers and families of the disappeared in the south of the country which was important to capture, and it is still Kumaratunga's stronghold today. A Presidential Commission on Disappearances was established in 1995[42]—this was one of the demands of the Front—and the Kumaratunge government continues to claim it as one of its achievements. Another Commission, popularly known as the Batalanda Commission (named after the notorious Batalanda camp at which alleged acts of torture and killing took place) was simultaneously set up. The Batalanda camp is in the electorate of Ranil Wickremasinghe, the leader of the UNP opposition, and this Commission was used by the People's Alliance to politically embarrass and corner him. While nothing has come of the Commission and no prosecutions have taken place to date, it is revived in the memory of the electorate each time an electoral campaign is in swing.

In the run-up to the Wayamba provincial council election in January 1999, the UNP's reign of terror, Batalanda, the Mothers' Front and its cause were resurrected by Chandrika Kumaratunga who pledged compensation to the families which had suffered under the UNP terror of the late 1980s, once the war with the LTTE was over (*The Island*, 23 January 1999).

The use of the Mothers' Front for government propaganda on 8 March 2000, was again significant for demonstrating its usefulness to the President. With the UNP in opposition, the front page headline of the *Daily News* (9 March 2000) proclaimed, "Mothers appeal to President to punish perpetrators of 88–89 reign of terror." The lead article went on to say that members of the Mothers' Front expressed gratitude to the President for "ending the fear psychosis and restoring democracy and human rights", thanked the government and the President for compensation received, and asked that the perpetrators of violence be brought to justice. The really newsworthy event that day, however, was the petition signed by 100,000 women asking the government and the UNP to enter into dialogue with each other in the pursuit of a peaceful settlement of the ethnic conflict and the war. It is noteworthy that, with the exception of the Sinhala language newspaper *Dinamina* , none of the other government-controlled Lake House newspapers, nor those of the opposition media, thought this feat worthy of publicity. The handing over of the Petition for Peace to President Kumaratunga only merited a front page photograph in the *Daily News,* covering Women's Day events. Its content was not divulged. Instead, the publicity given to the Mothers' Front's alleged congratulatory remarks to the President and demand that the (UNP) perpetrators of violence be punished, suited the government's divisive political strategy which went totally against the spirit of the Petition for Peace, which asked the PA and UNP to evolve a bipartisan approach at this time of national crisis.

That the *Daily News* chose to publicise the Mothers' Front's call for justice and reported its gratitude to the President for her attentiveness to its cause, indicates the enormous political potential of motherhood for those politicians who want to claim it. Conversely, even when, as already noted, (bad) motherhood was the focus of the UNP's retaliation against the Mothers' Front, motherhood remained the yardstick by which to judge these women. The UNP's was a counter-shaming strategy, of accusing the mothers of wantonly abandoning their duties as good mothers and not teaching their children civil obedience. The UNP's record on human rights was so tarnished by this time, however, that this counter-rhetoric failed to cut any ice with the public.

That motherhood was placed at the very centre of both the protest discourse and counter-discourse, caused concern among some urban sections of the Sri Lankan women's movement. The militancy of the mothers' protests was another factor that created unease.[43] Whether mothers should appropriate hysterical weeping and revengeful curses as public political strategy became a topic of debate. The unease expressed was on the grounds that these images reinforced a stereotype of women as hysterical and crazy.[44] Weeping and wailing in public is also a class issue. While middle-class women are taught to suppress grief in public, working class women have license to publicly display grief. The debates around the "tears and curses" of the Mothers' Front were, then, as much about class as about feminist strategy. The counter argument to this was that sorcery, charms and supplication of gods and goddesses were always within Buddhist practice, and that the mothers were drawing on indigenous cultural forms for their protests. These had proved highly effective, particularly against a superstitious President and his regime. At a time when the UNP government was carrying on a brutal onslaught against opposition youth, was itself corrupt and militaristic in waging wars both in the north and south of the country, militancy was very much part of the political culture. The state was in crisis and the Mothers' Front was born of that crisis. Its militant protests were therefore of a piece, albeit with a different goal of human rights in view.

Chandrika Bandaranaike Kumaratunga, who addressed the Mothers' Front rally in 1993 as "one of them", became President in November 1994. The Presidential Commission on Disappearances was appointed by her in 1995, and the two MPs who had spearheaded the Mothers' Front were appointed cabinet ministers. Following these events, a number of questions come to mind. What has happened to the women of the Mothers' Front ten years on? How have they re-shaped their lives after the traumas suffered? How have they adapted to being heads of household? Has their world-view changed and how have they been able to influence and shape new directions in thought within their communities and families? What is their reaction to the ethnic war? What is their engagement with national politics today? What has the Mothers' Front bequeathed its leadership? And how has it strengthened the Sri Lankan women's movement today?

Recorded here are interviews with women from various parts of the south who took part in the Mothers' Front and its ancillary organisations. These women are foregrounded as individuals who responded to their crises, but participated nevertheless in the collectivity the Mothers' Front and other organisations offered in their time of need. The sense of community fostered by these organisations by bringing the bereft women together was important, for many of them did not receive the expected support from their village communities and extended families. As a study of women who became heads of household in the context of political violence and terror in the Moneragala and Hambantota districts shows, the very fabric of a community itself ruptures at a time of generalised violence.[45] People were reluctant to come forward to help the bereaved. Poverty was another reason for withholding support, but patriarchy was at play too. Given that men are the link in kinship networks, their disappearance/death meant that their relatives became estranged or even hostile to the surviving wives and children. In the Hambantota district, of 50 women interviewed, only 10 maintained cordial links with their husband's families.[46] Quite often, the dead husband's brothers or parents took over the land his wife and children lived on. As the legal titles of these lands were not in the wives' names, they had no alternative but to return to their parents. Thus, even their marital material entitlements were lost to them. Moreover, existing cleavages of caste, class and differences in political affiliations within a village became sharpened in this context of violence. Competition among families and traders, and intra-caste conflict manifested itself in betrayals of the other to the security forces or the police, so that much of the violence at this time originated from *within* the village and its intimate community.[47] The women who came together under the umbrella of the Mothers' Front therefore found a welcome provision of collective support they sorely lacked in their immediate neighbourhoods. While some women like Nalini from Buttala said that it was primarily to seek economic support that they first went to a meeting of the Mothers' Front, they nevertheless received comfort from the collective spirit of the women and discussions of their common problems.[48]

These women are therefore positioned as if in dialogue with each other, as much as they are in dialogue with us. They come

from Matara, the large southern town and current seat of People's
Alliance MP, Mangala Samaraweera, founder member of the
Mothers' Front; from Buttala, also in the south, which holds a
traditional farming community, where the women spoken to derived their livelihoods from cultivation of home gardens; from
Kuliyapitiya, close to Colombo and so, a more urbanised setting.
In placing these women's voices in dialogue with each other we
see their commonalities, but also their differences, in focus, their
priorities, approach and strategies rooted in the diversity of class,
region and language. We note their relationship to leadership
and the Colombo-based women's organisations. We note their
(in)dependence from politicians as well as their deep
(dis)engagement with national politics. Their responses are, of
course, conditioned by our questions, in turn located in authority and the privilege of the researcher. They are also determined
by the environment in which the dialogue takes place. The women
from Matara were interviewed in the office of Minister Mangala
Samaraweera, while attending a planning meeting for a religious
bōdhi pooja to invoke blessings on President Chandrika
Kumaratunga for the presidential election of 21 December, 1999.
These women are therefore the most overtly linked to a political
party and its politicians, and their responses bear this out. Others were interviewed in the privacy of their homes, and still others, who were members of NGOs in leadership roles, at their
offices. Taken together they represent an alternative account to
that of the UNP's official narrative of what happened during the
reign of terror. They can be read as counter-narratives to the
UNP's which hounded and delegitimised JVP and SLFP supporters, and denied their disappearances.

That the interviews with the women were recorded ten years
after these events occurred has enabled several possibilities that
could not have opened up earlier. For some, the searing pain of
the trauma is muted, although their loss continues to be felt on a
daily basis. It is noteworthy that many of the women from Matara
began their narrative by weeping at the loss of their loved ones.
This was not evident among the other women. What does the
weeping, an integral part of the Matara women's narrative, signify? Can we read into this the dependence these women continue

to have on their politicians for support, that they are still economically disadvantaged and personally unempowered, so that their public weeping signifies their loss at many levels? The absence of weeping, but a fatalistic acceptance or anger or disappointment that we encountered among the other women could, then, be read as a sign that their roles in life have changed, that they have been altered in the process. Again, that the JVP is now a recognised political party which has sought democratic election and done fairly well at the local government and national level, has opened up a space for those women whose menfolk were involved with the JVP to claim them as such—a claim they could not have made easily and with confidence before January 1999 when the JVP joined the electoral process, campaigned for local government elections in the Wayamba province and obtained 3.92 per cent of the vote and ten seats in Parliament in the General Elections of October 2000. Moreover, the setting up of NGOs in the 1980s and 1990s working around the issues of women in conflict, women and development and violence against women, has provided some alternative employment and political participation for the women. They have offered the possibility of leadership roles and alternative affiliations, however tentative, for the women, and altered their sense of identity, of who they are and their role in society, ten years after their fateful tragedies.

1. Piyaseeli, Secretary, Akuressa Mothers' Front [49]

On July 16, 1990, my only son disappeared. I have been talking about losing my son for the past ten years and I do not want to dwell on it. Yet, it is important to point out that during a time when we were discarded by society as mothers of murderers, Minister Mangala Samaraweera set up this organisation and it was later that other women's organisations and youth organisations came to be. I can also say that our President came to power because of the support she gave to the Mothers' Front.

We are against the UNP as a political party but we are willing to take in any mother in our situation having lost a child even if she supports the UNP. But there are no such mothers in our movement, but in the future there may be women of different political loyalties who will join the Front expecting various benefits.

The slogans and placards carried in our walk were designed and created by us. They were spontaneous efforts and we wrote them based on our emotions. No one instructed us or influenced us. They were our own thoughts. In our demonstrations and placards we often talked about taking revenge and rejected the then government vehemently. Even today the thought of taking revenge is strong in our minds especially when we think of our children. We will never forget. The way we will take revenge is by ensuring that the UNP never comes to power again as long as we live.

I participated in village activities, organisations and programmes before joining the Mothers' Front and worked voluntarily. People in the village support me. The education I have received gives me the ability to take on leadership and even here, I have come in grief looking for relief and consolation. I still come forward to take on leadership roles. My husband always supports and encourages me, even with money to spend on various activities.

The Front as a whole decides on activities—walks and marches—and the cost is borne by us. However poor we are, any mother in the movement will join any activity and we help each other. Other than *pāda yatrā*, *pol gaheema* (breaking coconuts) and satyagraha, we used to go to *devāles* and visit soothsayers in order to find our children. But now we know that our children will never come back and not even the President and Ministers can give us what is gone forever. At first we thought the government was not making an effort to find our children but now we know they are dead. I attended the Presidential Commission recently but nothing came out of it. But what can the present government or any commission do? They cannot give back our children. If my son were alive he would have been 29 years old, who can give me a 29 year old son now? Our only aim now is to keep the UNP from coming to power.

As such, the Mothers' Front cannot be called an independent organisation. It is a very political organisation in the sense that it is against the UNP. We would like all Mothers' Front organisations to get together and this effort has to come from the mothers themselves in the different branches.

Before we joined the Mothers' Front, we were outcasts, known as mothers of murderers. Today the situation is different. Today as members of a group we are strong and no one, not even the President, can influence the Mothers' Front.

We will come forward in the future to support the PA. No one in our movement has thought of coming forward to contest elections but we support the government and our Minister. Our issue will never be solved by contesting and winning elections. We can never get our children back; we only want people to never forget what happened.

2. Sweneetha, 34 years old
My husband worked at a saw mill, stripping coconut timber, and during the JVP period he was at home for a day as he had hurt his leg. Villagers

informed the army that he was involved in the JVP and that he had been shot at. The army took him away that night. When my mother-in-law, four children and I went to the camp the next day, I was told that he was never brought to the camp. Later we found out that he had been killed. I was 24 and he was 29 and we have four children. Due to hardships now my two older children do not go to school. I appealed to the Minister and we have got a grant with which we are building our house.

I have never participated in a society or organisation before this but I found consolation only after I joined this movement. We got a place to talk and assurance from the present government and compensation. I cannot take part in a lot of activities because of my children. I have three daughters and a son and I have to provide security for them, so I cannot take part in activities that happen away from home, only in Matara. I also find difficulty in finding the money to come for them. I am unemployed. I can sew well but I do not own a sewing machine.

Before my husband was taken away I used to be very backward, never stepped out of the house at night. But now, after he was taken away and killed, I have the strength to face anything, even step out at night and fight someone. I am not scared of anyone.

The President knows what we are going through because she herself has gone through it. I have a brother in the war, but I don't feel sad about the war or if I lose someone in the war. I cannot accept the unnecessary killing of my husband and because the army did it, I do not feel sad about soldiers dying.

3. Leela, Kamburupitiya

I am from Kamburupitiya and lost my fourteen year old son, abducted on his way to school. To date I have no news of him. I joined the Mothers' Front in November 1989. At the inception there were 300 mothers and now the number has grown to 3000. There are still about 500 mothers in the Matara district who have not joined the movement.

I have served on the Executive Committee of the Front and we have made visits to virtually every kovil in the area and organised meetings. The Minister, Mangala Samaraweera is very supportive. It was he who provided food for our visit to the Modara Kovil (the Kaliamma temple). We went in four buses.

We are a very united movement. We attend all meetings we are called for and participate in discussions with visitors.

We request assistance from the government although we feel the government has done whatever possible. But we would like employment for our children. We received assurance of this when we met the President at Temple Trees (then the President's office-cum-residence.) We have also been promised support to start income generating activities and also Samurdhi (Poverty Alleviation) benefits.

All mothers in Sri Lanka are aware of this movement which is very important to us. We believe that we won our fight for justice when President Premadasa was killed. Our belief in the gods and the Buddha helped us through.

We have discussed the disappearances in the north and we attended the rally at Nugegoda where mothers from Batticoloa and Jaffna participated. We also attended the rally at Town Hall. We would like mothers from the north to join us but there is no opportunity to do so. This is so even with mothers from other districts. We talk when we meet but there is no further collaboration.

Before I joined the movement I was not involved in any organisation and was confined to my home. There was no necessity for me to take part in community activities. But with the disappearance of my son and my joining the movement, I have become self-confident and now I can go alone to police stations, courts, and move with people. This is the strength I have gained through my pain and sorrow. We have sold our land to fulfil vows and meet soothsayers to find our children. We have walked miles for long periods of time and suffered illness. But now we are able to speak freely and we have faith in our Minister.

Several mothers who received letters attended the Presidential Commission but nothing has resulted from the meeting.

4. Nalini, Buttala.

I lost both my husband and brother. I was a mother of four and the youngest was only one month and ten days old when this happened.

I got to know about the Mothers' Front through Seela of the Uva-Wellassa Govi Kantha Sanvidanaya (Uva-Wellassa Farm Women's Organisation). I got to know it as a programme of Dr. Manorani Saravanamuttu. As far as I know this was formed to work for the welfare of women who lost their husbands and sons. Our Samithiya was formed not during the *beeshanaya* (terror) but later. During the *beeshanaya* we were members of the UWGKS. Even before we joined the Mothers' Front there were some awareness programmes conducted to give us confidence.

I did not have to search for my husband as he was murdered in front of me.

When we started the Samithiya we all had hopes of forming a successful organisation. At the beginning the Samithiya enrolled single women whose husbands had been killed. But one woman got remarried and at that stage there was disagreement amongst the members as to whether she should be allowed to stay in the group. If the Samithiya was for widows and married women were allowed, then what would be our identity? was a question asked. This issue was not taken up openly and this led to conflict amongst the officials of the Samithiya and its members. In 1995 there were about 40 women in the Samithiya and at present all these women have dispersed.

While we were in the Samithiya we went to Colombo to take part in the exhibition held at the Mahaveli Kendraya (Mahaveli Centre) but I did not take part in any political rallies.

Before joining the Samithiya we were depressed and isolated, always thinking of the killings. We took part in the Family Rehabilitation programmes at Hambantota. But after some time the Samithiya collapsed. At the moment I do not have time to get involved in the activities of the UGKS. I have an ailing mother and four children to look after. My economic activity is farming but I also have sewing skills. Because I do not own a sewing machine I am unable to derive an income.[50] My only ambition is to bring up my children to be useful citizens to this country. I live because of my children but I am not really very happy.

I am now 38 years old and when my husband was killed I was 27. It is true that my husband was involved with the JVP and I still believe that he was correct. They were not robbing people. They had a goal to achieve. They had principles and I am proud of him because he sacrificed his life for a cause.

We were looked down upon by the community after my husband's killing. We were cornered as if we had committed a great crime. But today things have changed and my children can go about freely. Maybe we had this notion that the people around us were thinking badly of us but in reality they may not have.

Economically I have difficulties but I am happy to say that I don't depend on others. At the beginning I did not have the courage even to go to the boutique, but today I have the confidence to go anywhere in the world and attend to my work. It took time for me to change from the dependent person I was when my husband was living. Now I realise my responsibilities.

5. Udula, Kuliyapitiya

When I lost my husband during the JVP insurgency I was only 26 years old with two small children who were three and a half years and 7 years. I was a dependent housewife throughout my married life. The unexpected loss of my husband left me with many responsibilities. I had very little experience of how to handle them. My family and relations helped enormously during these difficult times. Gradually I learnt how to cope on my own.

When the Delwagura Post Office was burnt down my husband was taken in for questioning alongwith another person named Nimal. The UNP supporters had presented a petition with 20 names alongwith my husband's name to the police. Nimal's brother who held a higher office in the navy managed to get him out. But my husband remained. This was the last time I ever saw him.

My husband was taken in on Monday and they were beaten that evening. According to the information I received my husband had died by Tuesday night and his body was brought to the Pilipanna beach. After seven days a *billa* (a disguised informant) informed my husband's relations that there is no point in searching for him. I was not aware of this. Though they came with me in search of my husband, sometimes they were not happy on the amount of money I was spending on my search. I searched for him for almost a year.

I followed every clue in the search for my husband. He was the Village Secretary to the SLFP office. I was never involved in politics but assisted my husband by arranging our house for meetings, etc.

It was when I went to Mr. Samarasuriya's office (the SLFP area organiser) that I learnt of the inaugural rally of the Mothers' Front. Madam Sirimavo Bandaranaike had informed all the Gampaha District MPs and organisers to call this meeting at the Nittambuwa Sangabodhi Vidyalaya in Attanagalla. Mr. Samarasuriya provided transportation for us to attend this rally.

The rally was a turning point in my life. There were more than 300 people there. I was amazed by this number. Although I knew many women had met the same fate as mine I did not expect to see such a large crowd. At the meeting an Executive Committee was elected and I was elected Vice President. We visited S.W.R.D Bandaranaike's memorial monument and prayed for his guidance.

I felt a strong organisation was needed for these women and spoke to Mr. Samarasuriya in this regard. He was willing to give assistance provided I take on the initial responsibilities.

Two or three months later another meeting of the Mothers' Front was held in Nugegoda. More than 25 people from here went to this rally in a bus organised by Mr. Samarasuriya. At this rally Dr. Manorani Saravanamuttu, who was the President of the Sri Lanka organisation, spoke. This speech inspired me. There were more than 2000 women, island-wide there. Until this moment I had no contacts outside the Gampaha District. I made an effort to meet Dr. Saravanamuttu. Through my son's acquaintance with Ms. Karuna Perera, editor of *Surathala*, I was directed to see Sita Ranajani.[51] I told Sita my life story—how I had lost my parents when I was four years old; that my married life had lasted only eight years, and that they were the only happy years of my life. Sita Ranjani didn't promise me anything but she had spoken to someone and I got a telegram asking me to come and meet Dr. Saravanamuttu.

This was the first time I came to Colombo without anyone's assistance, except my son's. I was feeling very uncomfortable and scared. Then Sita walked in with Mahinda Rajapakse (a member of parliament). Seeing him calmed me down because he was someone I knew—we had spoken with each other over the phone. Dr. Manorani spoke to me and I said how much I think the Mothers' Front is useful for us. I meet Dr. Manorani only occasionally now. She thinks I don't have patience, and complains that I want everything very fast! I love her very much though we hardly meet now.[52]

During this time the SLFP organised the Parents and Childrens' Society of the Disappeared (Aturudahanvunage Māpiya Dūdaru Samāgamaya) in the Divulapitiya electorate to assist women who had lost their menfolk, to get compensation. I chaired this organisation and made a great effort to ensure that everyone received their compensation. I realised the lack of awareness of these women and conducted a seminar to impart information to them with the assistance of the regional secretary.

I was a field officer in the empowerment programmes organised by the Family Rehabilitation Centre and learned to work together with Tamil women from the north. The activities of the Mothers' Front caused confusion amongst people. "JVP women getting together" was the popular accusation of the time. These rumours made us think of changing the name of our organisation from the Mothers' Front to the Widows' Society.

Our contacts with the Mothers' Front gradually declined. I worked closely with the other women and began to work as a separate organisation. On 6 December, 1991 I came with eleven others to Colombo and formed our organisation for widows under the name Janashakthi Kāntha Sanwardana Samithiya (Janashakthi Women's Development Organisation). I became its secretary.

We wrote some proposals to receive aid from CIDA. This aid was spent on self-employment projects for those who most needed economic stability. At the beginning we received Rs. 91,200/- in aid. CIDA was very pleased with the achievements we have made. Women and Media Collective helped us all the way in getting this aid.

I then formed another Widows' Front in Minuwangoda. I had plans to make 13 such organisations within the Gampaha district. We assist the projects of the NGOs and our main link is with Women and Media Collective. Rather than the Mothers' Front we believe that our organisation helps us develop ourselves and assist in our problems.

6. Rajini, Kurunegala

All of us who lost our husbands got together to search for them. In our efforts we became a small community. When Indrani came to organise the women, the villagers opposed this saying they were trying to convert us to Christianity. Even the priest in the temple took this line and when the women requested the temple hall (Prajā Sālāva) to conduct their meetings, they were kicked out of the temple and onto the street by force, by more than 50 villagers. The women were ridiculed and isolated in the village.

But now they are accepted, and the people of the village who opposed them even assist them in their work.

7. Nanda, Kurunegala

I don't know anything of the Mothers' Front. I was introduced to this society through Indu. The society has given us great encouragement and created social awareness. The villagers looked at us then in the most degrading manner, specially because we were living alone without husbands. Until Indu came there was no one to assist us. Now many have forgotten the past and those who did not help us then ask our assistance now.

When I lost my husband I had two very small children. I started a chicken farm at the beginning, but couldn't manage it on my own, so I decided to leave the country and get work abroad. I went abroad for two years and returned just two months ago. I now live with my parents. My mother-in-law who had four sons, lost all of them during the insurrection.

8. Gunawathie, Kurunegala

My husband was taken away when he was working with his brother in the paddy fields. I was informed that he had been taken to the camp. When I visited the camp they informed me very harshly that he had been taken away and burnt. I collapsed. The guards insisted that my mother who was with me take me away.

I lost all my property when my mother-in-law's house was burnt down in 1989, with one of her sons and his wife inside.

The organisation provided Rs. 2000/- initially. We were harassed. My children suffered greatly and many dropped out of school because of the harassment. Our children were ridiculed by other children and the teachers. When Indu organised a Children's Society (Lama Samajaya) the villagers opposed it. They believed it was organised by Christians. "Pallikarayo" (church goers/people) was the term they used. But many people who were against us then are now with us. Some have even joined the organisation.

9. Sumika Perera, Women's Development Foundation, Kurunegala

I have no personal experience of losing a family member during that time. But I assisted women who had to form their organisations and to face up to their problems. I was involved in political activities during this period which was against the terrorism of the JVP.

When my group started working again in 1991, we met Dr. Manorani Saravanamuttu through our programmes. We had a meeting in Kurunegala at the Ibbagamuva Women's Development Foundation. Dr. Manorani asked us to assist them find female volunteers to help their work in Kurunegala. On their next visit we informed Dr. Manorani that we were willing to work with her, as many of our women had lost their husbands.

When I asked for training I was introduced to Indrani who trained us to handle this work.

We first worked in Galgamuwa but realised the greater need was in Kattiyawa and so decided to settle and work there. We made continuous visits to the residents there and informed them of the organisation. We managed to get 27 women participants. Many obstacles were placed in the way of these women and they were deliberately isolated. They were not allowed to hold meetings and were kicked out of the local Buddhist temple. Many of the meetings had to be conducted on the road!

These women were helpless and had no direction nor aim for the future of their lives. The organisation gave them a feeling of unity and shared responsibility. This brought psychological satisfaction in that they shared their problems together, not alone. Their children were often humiliated and ridiculed in schools so programmes were created to enhance their talents, improve their education, give mental guidance to control their fears and temper, and psychotherapy provided for the children in shock.

My group and I assisted these women. A committee called Sahana Kamituva was organised to improve their economic position. The aid programmes have created a more stable economic position for them.

My group and I also organised a programme for 18 families from different districts which was a success. Many of them were from the Samastha Lankā Govi Sammelanaya (All Island Farmers' Association) in Thammanna.

The women in this programme were not involved in the Mothers' Front. Many were even ignorant about it. All they wanted was to have a better life and create a better future for their children. Our organisation is non-partisan and we stand for no ideology in political activities. But what we do is another kind of politics.

We have not been involved in any political party. It was our men who were involved. We have unpleasant memories of what happened to these men when they got involved in politics. These fears and their painful histories may prevent women from taking part in the future in political activities. But the women are much stronger individuals now and in a much more secure position. They can face up to their problems better. All they need is good leadership and a little backing to do work. There is no need to nurse them as it was done ten years ago.

Several common factors surface in the testimonies of these women. Their initial trauma, now conveyed more in terms of economic despair due to unemployment or, at best, a meagre income, is coupled with the responsibility of single parenthood. A depressed economy in which unemployment was 10.2 per cent (in 1999) does not help.[53] It is significant however that none of the women mentioned the separatist war as a factor influencing their economic status. The absence of their men meant that theirs were not households from which males were recruited into the army, except for Sweneetha who has a brother in the forces. Thus the war has not offered them employment prospects or direct income. They did not speak either of the spiraling cost of living as a direct consequence of the war. This points to a conspicuous silence on the part of politicians, the media as well as certain NGO and community development organisations that work in these areas, but have failed to encourage a significant peace movement among the Sinhala people in the south with awareness of the exact economic, social and developmental costs of the war.[54]

Pro-war nationalist sentiment is the other reason a peace movement has not taken hold. Interestingly, none of the women we spoke to overtly subscribed to a Sinhala ethno- nationalism which insists that the LTTE/Tamils must be militarily defeated. In fact all of them acknowledged that Tamil women had undergone similar suffering, and wished the Mothers' Front had accommodated more of them within its ranks. But while there was silence on all other aspects of the conflict, Sweneetha's comment that she would not feel sad if she lost someone in the war and that she has no sympathy for the army because the army killed her husband in the first place, is significant for voicing a different sentiment. What made her say this? It clearly goes against the grain of whatever nationalist sentiment there is in the south that supports the war effort and regards the Sinhala soldiers as war heroes. It was clear when speaking to Sweneetha, however, that she was not an *insider* in the group gathered at Mangala Samaraweera's office in Matara. She is poorer than the others and has to travel from farther afield. While we were in the office, Matulata, the organiser of the Mothers' Front for the Matara district, asked her why she did not attend more of their events. Sweneetha replied that she could not afford to and then shrugged indifference. She was told thereafter that if she did attend, "something could be done for her". Clearly, Sweneetha refuses to be co-opted totally into the politics of the Mothers' Front in Matara She is a marginalised subaltern voice and from that location can dare to critique the armed forces at a time when they have reached their apogée in the nation's consciousness.[55]

The dependence on the political patronage afforded by Mangala Samaraweera was clear from the Matara women's statements. They looked to him for jobs, housing and future prospects. They had no aspiration to join other organisations in leadership roles. The link between the Mothers' Front and the PA, its oppositional stance to the UNP and its intrinsically political character were made clear and supported. The strong link Mangala Samaraweera maintains with the Matara Mothers' Front and his continued use of it as a political tool is the main reason for the patron-client relationship evident in Matara, but not in Kurunegala. Urbanisation has also played its part. While many of the Matara women we spoke to came from the interior of the district, the Kurunegala women live in closer proximity to urban areas and are, by now, familiar with organisations and events in the capital, Colombo. They tap into a more cosmopolitan sensibility and are able therefore to venture farther, independent enough to work in villages other than their immediate ones. The decision of Sumika and her fellow workers to organise among the women of Katiyawa is such an example. Having occupied positions of leadership, participated in socio-political movements—Udula with the SLFP and Sumika with Deva Sarana (a community organisation based in Kurunegala, which had 1971 JVP affiliates and worked on issues of women in agriculture)— and now affiliated to NGOs, both Udula and Sumika enjoy a mobility that neither the Matara women nor Nalini from Buttala have. Both these women come from middle-class families within their respective villages (Udula mentioned that she had some private property of her own) and have achieved a higher level of education than most other women in their communities (Sumika told us of her mother's insistence that her daughters receive a good education); this plays an important part in their ability to assume leadership and obtain acceptance by other women.

While the collective spirit of the Mothers' Front and/or its ancillary organisations provided the women comfort and solidarity, and brought ordinary wives and mothers who had not been politically vocal before into the public/political sphere, it is clear from their testimonies that this vocalising also made them targets of attack from within their own communities. They were noted with suspicion and for some, the stigma of being single women was keenly felt. Their children were ostracised at school, marking a climate of mistrust and the suspension of normative socio-cultural codes at a time of crisis, which did not spare even the children from a hostile gaze. The women's association with NGOs made them vulnerable to accusations in Kattiyawa that they were western agents working towards Christian conversions. We see in this reaction a nationalist response, current at the time, to NGO presence and work in the country. (The UNP government had begun a witch-hunt against NGOs and had set up a NGO Commission to monitor NGO activity.) NGOs were constantly accused of being the spokespeople of interested western lobby groups, working towards the disintegration of Sri Lanka as a unitary state and so, working against the nation's Buddhist culture and its primacy. The hostility of the Kattiyawa Buddhist priest to Sumika and her colleagues is part and parcel of this response to the bogey of western imperialism in the Third World. It is a response which fails to be a really radical critique of globalisation that has ushered the Third World into an unequal global trading system, and falls short of a nuanced critique of the structures of class, caste, ethnicity and gender within the nation itself.

The Mothers' Front was born of the crisis of the state, and in its strategies and focus was frankly anti-state. Where there is a conjuncture between the state (as it stands for forms of governance) and the nation (as it represents a socio-cultural category describing forms of community), where the state has subsumed the nation in an attempt "to eliminate the hyphen",[56] any anti-state activity gets read as anti-national. The women of the Mothers' Front were quite often confronted with this accusation. While they may have been silent on the separatist war or unable to forge links with women from all regions in the country, their efforts nevertheless were aimed at reinstating the distinction between the state and the nation by insisting on a form of governance that was internationally accountable on the issue of human rights.

However, that the Mother's Front is largely written about in the past tense, except when politicians appropriate it for their own ends, indicates its structural inability to cross over from issues of human rights to women's rights, and vice versa. It was a movement that came together and fulfilled the need of the hour at a time of crisis in Sri Lanka's post-coloniality. Beyond that it was unable to transform itself into a movement with significant links to other areas of activism that were the preoccupation throughout the 1990s—the protection of labour within a globalised economy, the preservation of the environment, demilitarization, devolution and peace. That the women of the southern Mothers' Front could not be retained within any form of women's activism also points to the failure of feminist politics within the Sri Lankan women's movement.

Notes Towards the Future

The trajectory and work of two other women's groups, however, points to the potential within the contemporary Sri Lankan women's movement for bridging issues and building a platform for intra-regional coalitions that could also foster a sense of lateral cosmopolitanism *within* the nation. This notion of cosmopolitanism is particularly apt when we also take into account the rapid globalisation of the economy and the mass media, that make the borders between village and town, province and metropolis increasingly porous and blurred. The two organizations are the Women's Development Foundation, based in Kurunegala, and the Uwa Welassa Govi Kantha Sanvidanaya (Uva Welassa Women Farmers' Organisation) based in Buttala. They show that there were women's organizations that existed before "the reign of terror" which were able to cross over from strategic and practical women's issues to human rights and back. Their interest and activities in forging links with Tamil plantation workers, Tamil women of the north and east, as well as southern women from other provinces pursue a lateral cosmopolitanism that seeks to pare down the fixed boundaries within nationalist ideology and ethnic divides, towards an alternative view of society and how it should be constructed. These are moves that have made them distinct from other political or single-issue centred groups and have ensured their long-term survival within Sri Lankan civil society.

The Women's Development Foundation traces its origins to the Progressive Women's Front (PWF) which began in 1982. The PWF in turn grew out of the All Lanka Peasant Congress and Deva Sarana, a community-based group in Kurunegala which worked on issues concerning agricultural labour, had its own farm and provided medical and library facilities to the local community. Among members of the group were those associated with the 1971 JVP who had distanced themselves from the JVP politics of the 1980s. (Deva Sarana was in fact attacked by the latter JVP in 1987.) As discussed in the introduction to this book, the failure of left-wing parties to answer to the needs of Sri Lankan youth and provide a progressive structure to youth politics, free of feudal and patriarchal hierarchies, created a context in which many young women of the left were, by the 1980s, in search of progressive alternatives to existing party politics. The JVP, with its male-dominated bureaucracy and politics of violence, was unattractive to many of these women as were the mainstream political parties with their family dynasties, cynical politics and corruption. By 1984, the PWF had begun working in agricultural communities. In the Moneragala district, in Polgahagama and Dematabedda, the PWF organised women into Women Farmers' Societies to protest against the imposition of the water tax on farmers which would affect their costs of production; the privatization of state enterprises such as the Pelwatte sugar plantation; its monopoly over the supply and demand of sugarcane and its restructuring of farm labour. It ran pre-schools for the children of women working on the sugar plantations. The organising of these women and their participation in public demonstrations and strikes attracted the hostility of the community's men at first, but the women stood their ground; as Sumika Perera, a founder member of the PWF noted, their strategy was not to be confrontational with them, since the men were important members of the community, but to seek a consensus on their common issues and methods of protest.[57]

From its inception it is clear that the PWF engaged in both strategic and pragmatic women's interests. Its work-plan in 1984 attests to a range of activities, from lectures on the history of women's oppression and a seminar on the "reasons for raping

women", to organizing women farmers, visiting the
Anuradhapura prison to check on the conditions of its women
prisoners, campaigning for the abolition of night work for women
(this was carried out in conjunction with the WAC campaign),
holding Montessori Teacher Training programmes and sewing
classes for women, so that they could gain employment in the
garment factories opening up. Throughout these activities the
PWF's main interest in organising female agricultural workers
was paramount. In September–October 1984 branches of the
Women Farmers' Societies were established in Dombagahawela,
Kivulayaya, Mahakalnagolla, Madugama and Siyamabalanduwa
in the Moneragala district. Protests were staged in
Siyambalanduwa against the proposed takeover of the sugar plantations in the area by Meta International. Discussions on the
progress of these Women Farmers' Societies were held in
Ibbagamuwa (where the PWF had its headquarters), Madahapola
and Doraveruwa in the Kurunegala district. In 1985 a rally was
organized in Thambuwa, in the Kurunegala district, against the
imposition of the water tax on farmers.

With the outbreak of the ethnic war, the 1987 Indo-Lanka
Peace Accord and its aftermath of civil unrest the PWF, as an
affiliated member of WAC, committed itself to a pro-Accord
position as a first step towards a peaceful resolution to the ethnic
conflict. It worked in various district councils towards the acceptance of the need for the Indian Peace Keeping Forces.[58] For this
the PWF was attacked by the JVP, as was WAC. That the PWF
was supportive of the Accord signals perhaps a failure on the
part of women's groups in the south to fully understand the ground
situation in Jaffna where the IPKF was present and where, sty-
mied by its lack of success against the LTTE, its troops took out
their frustration on the civilian population in Jaffna. Jaffna Tamil
women became the victims of rape and molestation during this
onslaught.[59]

That the PWF was able to take on the political issues related
to the war, such as the need for devolution and negotiations
with the LTTE, was helped by its proximity to Kurunegala, a
cosmopolitan city, 58 miles from Colombo, in a district which
sees a constant mix with the dry zone and has a tradition of

migrant farm workers who move east during the farming season into the Polonnaruwa and eastern provinces. This
(re)crossing of provincial borders has meant an extended contact with Tamil as well as Muslim communities. Soon after the
1983 anti-Tamil riots, the PWF worked towards Sinhala-Tamil
ethnic reconciliation. This was a time when, under Emergency
regulations, the distribution of leaflets and posters was banned.
Yet the PWF was active in a poster and leaflet campaign that it
carried out surreptitiously, without attracting official attention.
Given that post-1983, the PWF had already moved into minority
rights work in this way, it was not difficult for it to support the
campaign of the Mothers' Front in the late 1980s. What is extraordinary however is that it did so, despite being a target of
attack by the JVP for its support to the Indo-Lanka Accord.
Many of the disappeared during the reign of terror were
JVPers—it was their mothers who were out marching on the
streets, seeking justice and redress from the UNP government.
The decision of the PWF and other women's groups like it (for
example, members of WAC who had joined to form Mothers
and Daughters of Lanka) to support these mothers was not without controversy. There were members of the PWF, as well as
village neighbours, who questioned why the organisation should
struggle on behalf of the JVP which had vilified and attacked it
in the first place.[60] However, those supporting the PWF's coalition with the Mothers' Front won the debate. The commitment to human rights was paramount. This was a stance
fostered by the cosmopolitan links that organisations like the
PWF had established with leaders of the women's movement
in Colombo, and by their exposure to debate and discussion on
international standards of human rights and the growing internationalism of a global women's movement that took up these
causes.

After the difficult years of 1987–90, members of the PWF re-
organized to form the Women's Development Foundation (WDF)
in 1991. The organization shifted from Ibbagamuwa to
Kurunegala town itself. It is through the WDF that women like
Sumika lent their support to the post-1991 activities of the Mothers' Front, by helping in the work of the Family Rehabilitation

Centre set up by Dr. Manorani Saravanamuttu. The WDF formed its own widows' societies, and its activities became more focused on the issue of minority rights and women's rights as human rights. Its monthly journal, *Athwela* (Chain of Hands) repeatedly published articles by women throughout the 1990s, arguing for an end to the war and a political negotiation to the ethnic conflict. The articles highlighted the suffering of women living in the border areas and conflict zones, and went hand in hand with the WDF's lobbying among the mainstream political parties like the People's Alliance and United National Party, for a negotiated settlement to the war. *Athwela* also highlighted the need for strengthening democratic practise, and severely criticised the election violence that overshadowed the Wayamba provincial council election in January 1999.

Dialogue through cultural exchange was a strategy the PWF had adopted in the 1980s. Street theatre was an attractive means for communicating a message. Its use of mime, sound and visuals surmounted the barriers of language. It was cheap to produce, mobile, and was an entertaining and creative medium that could be both insightful and didactic in getting its message across to the audience. The PWF's location in Kurunegala also offered it the opportunity to avail itself of the expertise of Gamini Haththotuwegama, the foremost street theatre practitioner in Sri Lanka, who teaches English in Kurunegala. With Haththotuwegama's help, as well as others interested in drama, the PWF formed a street theatre group in 1984-85. In particular, it facilitated a significant exchange which brought Sinhala and Tamil people, peasants, plantation workers and urban activists together. The estate of Delhena in Raddegoda was a site of unrest in 1984-5 following the assault on a Tamil estate worker by the superintendent. A strike, which demanded the transfer of the superintendent, was in full swing. It subsequently succeeded. During the strike the PWF organised a theatre workshop on the estate dramatising the issues facing estate plantation workers. The Sinhala-speaking street theatre group which facilitated the workshop worked with Tamil plantation workers of Delhena estate who took part in the performance. The spoken medium was bilingual, Sinhala and Tamil.

What is noteworthy is that one of the street theatre troupes involved in this event was from Thambuwa in the Kurunegala district and had as its name, Weera Puran Appu Kalā Kavaya. Puran Appu became a Sinhala nationalist hero for fighting against the British in the 1848 rebellion. Although from Moratuwa, a coastal area near Colombo, he was one of the claimants to the throne of the Kandyan kingdom. He acquired the honorific "weera" or courageous, for challenging the British. Despite the reference to such a nationalist moment and sentiment in the naming of their group, the actors of the Weera Puran Appu Kalā Kavaya had learnt, through their profession, to interact creatively with people of Tamil ethnicity. When asked about the cross-fertilisation that took place over the events on Delhena estate, Sumika noted that it was only when activists from the Sinhala-speaking areas went to the estate that the conditions under which the Tamil plantation workers lived and worked, became tangible and apparent to them. For the street theatre group from Thambuwa, too, the workshop and performance on Delhena estate had been a curtain-raiser to its growing awareness of the conditions under which Tamil plantation workers laboured. The links formed in the 1980s between the plantation workers and PWF activists continue today through the members of the WDF. These continuities, both at the level of cultural interaction and solidarity around issues of labour and minority rights, have the potential to create the necessary groundwork for fostering a lateral cosmopolitanism. This can ultimately challenge dominant ethnic nationalisms which have long classified Tamil plantation workers as non-citizens with few rights of their own.

The Uwa Welassa Govi Kantha Sanvidanaya (UWGKS) was formed in 1978. Its work, like that of the Women's Development Foundation, is primarily with women farmers but more intensive, given its location in Buttala, in the south-east Moneragala district, which is almost wholly agricultural. Like the PWF, the Buttala women also agitated in the 1980s against the imposition of the water tax on farmers, and the privatisation of the Pelwatte sugar plantation. Pelwatte is in close proximity to Buttala and the effect of its privatisation was felt most acutely by the farmers in the area. The privatisation agreement allowed the British company which took over the management of the sugar plantation, to decree that *a*) the management company had control over the plots of sugarcane, *b*) farmers in the area could sell their sugarcane only to the Pelwatte factory, *c*) the factory decided the quantity of sugarcane purchased, and *d*) farmers could not grow other crops during the off-season. These conditions were clearly unfavourable to local farmers and the privatisation saw wide-scale protest.

The UWGKS formed women farmers' committees in surrounding villages, and facilitated self-employment and health care programmes. It campaigned against the use of chemical fertilizers and environmental degradation, and facilitated programmes on childcare.[61] Some of its women had been trained in Montessori teaching methods by the Community Education Centre, an organisation in Colombo to which it is closely affiliated. This interest in children's welfare and education is evident in other activities of the UWGKS—in 1999 it undertook to encourage children's savings societies and held programmes for children on the need to protect the environment.

The Moneragala district was the heartland of the 1818 Uva rebellion against the British, and nationalist sentiment still holds fast. But the district is one of the most underdeveloped in the country, and so its nationalism is tempered by poverty and lack of employment opportunities. Recruitment to the army is high among male youth in Buttala, but it is the lack of alternative avenues of employment that send them to the warfront. While the women of the area survive by farming, working in the garment factories or leaving for the Middle East as migrant labour, the young men have no such alternatives. The ethnic conflict, the attendant economies of war and their effect on women, are therefore particularly pertinent to the women of the Uva Welassa Govi Kantha Sanvidanaya. Their location in Buttala, in the Moneragala district which borders the eastern province and which has seen LTTE raids into its territory, has also given them an added incentive to grappling with issues around the war. Their sensibilities are quite different to those of the women we spoke to in Matara, with the exception of Sweneetha. Matara is the focal point of the Ruhuna district in the south of the country, and a strong base for Sinhala nationalism. The district is also the base for indigenous mercantile capitalism which feels most threatened by Tamil and Muslim traders. The Buttala women, occupying a border area, were far more open to dialogue and exchange with their Tamil counterparts, and therefore far less nationalistic. Their interventions and programmes on the ethnic question have taken their cue from the leadership of Anita Fernando of the Community Education Centre, which funds the organisation.[62] At the same time, the UWGKS' location in the border area of Buttala/ Moneragala makes it a valuable partner for Colombo-based groups wishing to work in the border areas and conflict zones. Many of the UWGKS programmes on raising awareness around the issue of war have been held with organisations like Movement for Inter-Racial Justice and Equality and the Community Education Centre. At the periphery, the UWGKS has been an ideal coalition partner for Colombo-based NGOs.

The women of the Uva Welassa Govi Kantha Sanvidanaya participated in a study tour of Batticoloa town, in the conflict zone of the eastern province, in July 1999. They interviewed women from Athugala and Muthugala in Welikanda, a border village area in the Uva Welassa region, for a documentary film entitled *Donkaraya* (The Echo) produced by the Social Economic Development Centre (SEDEC). The documentary highlighted these women's displacement, insecurities and personal losses, and stressed the need for an end to armed conflict. The women of the UWGKS also joined in a peace march held in Vavuniya in the northern province. They stated that their study tour of Batticoloa had been greatly beneficial in understanding and gathering information on the problems confronting Tamils living in conflict zones, and Tamil women in particular. They saw for themselves a town under strict military rule, with army checkpoints and constant surveillance. They noted that people seemed to move about freely in what appeared to be LTTE controlled areas, where the army was absent. They also commented on the sense of solidarity they felt with the Tamil women who staged a demonstration in Batticoloa town, while they were there, demanding the right to live without fear. They thought that the Tamil women who were with them at the demonstration were heartened by their support, and also felt that the participation of Tamil women in their local campaigns would strengthen their own struggle. However, the prevailing security situation which made it easier for Sinhala women from Buttala to visit Batticoloa, prevented such coalition-building on a regular basis. Even though the security checkpoints and arrangements for the trip to Batticoloa were a hassle, the women from Buttala were aware that they were privileged in their inter-regional mobility in a way that was denied, or at best made difficult, for Tamil women in the adjoining region.[63]

While the need for strategic alliances and coalition-building around different issues between Sinhala, Tamil and Muslim women (on their study tour to Batticoloa the Buttala women also visited Kathankudy, a Muslim village in the district) was acknowledged by the women of the UWGKS, a cultural exchange among the communities, commensurate with these strategic alliances over political issues, has not taken place. Even though the inter-ethnic contact they experienced when they participated in the Vavuniya peace march, the trip to Batticoloa, and the documentary produced for SEDEC, was recalled by them with pride and offered as a basis for future work, there was little enthusiasm for fostering cultural contact between the communities through the mediums of art, song, dance, oral folk performance and drama. Why is this the case? The barrier of language was offered as a reason. Apart from Indra, none of the Buttala women knew Tamil. When asked whether forms of art cannot overcome linguistic barriers, the women expressed reservations. They pointed to some events in Tamil that they had attended but not been able to understand fully. Seela, who leads the organisation in Buttala, noted however that they have planned a cultural event for the following year which would bring Sinhala and Tamil women together. Whether it would be held in Buttala or not has still to be decided.

Why does cultural exchange lag behind strategic alliances to prevent cultural cosmopolitanism, that can complement political, lateral cosmopolitanism from coming about? One reason is that unless the culture one wishes to acculturate is associated with power, there is little incentive to learn from it. The colonial elite adopted European culture because it was strategic and useful to do so. It provided access to social mobility and political power. The Sinhala women of Buttala see little reason, at this present moment in Sri Lanka's story of nationalism, to understand Tamil cultural paradigms. Despite their expressions of solidarity the wide gap, that they felt existed between them and the Tamil women of Batticoloa, in terms of cultural praxis, also points to the fact that the legacy of nationalism on both sides prevents the two communities from exchanging a deep cultural understanding which would preserve and cherish their differences, but on an equal basis. Such a compolitanism would not universalize on the basis of an elite metropolitan one. The fact that the women of both the Women's Development Foundation in Kurunegala and the Uva Welassa Govi Kantha Sanvidanaya in Buttala have been able to show solidarity and support for each other's struggles, as well as work for women's rights as human rights, indicates an enabling mobility across varied issues. Their work with the Mothers' Front (even as they were the target of the JVP), and with Tamil plantation labour and Tamil women farmers living in the border areas of the south-east shows that the basis for a radical challenge to the constraining paradigms of nationalism is there to be built on. To foster this politics, its intrinsic commitment to a variety of goals which could alter how society is viewed and constructed, as well as its intra-regional, class and inter-ethnic potential will be the challenge for the Sri Lankan women's movement of today.

Notes

[1] Kamla Bhasin, keynote address, published in *Options* No. 19, 3rd Quarter 1999. Colombo: Women and Media Collective.

[2] This march in Jaffna was one of the few events at which, post-1983, women from the south travelled to the north to participate in a common front with the women there. The presence of Govind Kelkar from India and Nighat Said Khan from Pakistan marked the new sense of solidarity between South Asian feminists.

[3] See introductions in Amrita Basu (ed.), *The Challenge of Local Feminisms: Women's Movements in Global Perspective*. Boulder, Colorado: Westview Press Inc, 1995; and Haleh Afshar (ed.), *Women*

and Politics in the Third World. London and New York: Routledge, 1996.

4 Kumuduni Samuel of Women and Media Collective noted that the use of Rajani as such a symbol was perhaps mooted by the women's groups present at the planning stage of this campaign. Personal communication, May 2000.

5 Amrita Basu, op. cit., p.9.

6 Following the ILO convention, the Sri Lankan government accepted the prohibition of night work for women, but in 1980 sought to re-introduce it. Women's groups actively lobbied against this reneging.

7 Maxine Molyneux, quoted in Raka Ray, *Fields of Protest: Women's Movements in India.* New Delhi: Kali for Women, 1999, p.5.

8 *Final Report of the Commission of Inquiry into Involuntary Removal or Disappearance of Persons in the Western, Southern and Sabaragamuwa Provinces.* Colombo: Department of Government Printing, September 1997, pp. 13, 29 and 159.

9 Rohan Gunaratne, *Sri Lanka A Lost Revolution? The Inside Story of the JVP.* Kandy: Institute of Fundamental Studies, 2001, p.269 and C.A. Chandraprema, *Sri Lanka: The Year of Terror—The JVP Insurrection 1987–1989.* Colombo: Lake House Bookshop, 1991, p.312.

10 D.B.S.Jeyaraj, "Lions and Tigers," *Himal,* April 1999, Kathmandu, p.25.

11 Sunila Abeysekera, Director, INFORM, and founder member of WAC personal communication.

12 Kumuduni Samuel, "Gender Difference in Conflict Resolution: The Case of Sri Lanka," *Options* No. 14, 2nd Quarter 1998. Colombo: Women and Media Collective, p. 9.

13 Ibid.,p.10

14 For a detailed account of JVP and UNP violence during this period see Sasanka Perera, *Stories of Survivors: Socio-Political Contexts of Female-Headed Households in Post-Terror Southern Sri Lanka,* Vol. 1. Colombo: Women's Education & Research Centre, 1999, chapter 2.

15 Ibid., pp. 29–30.

16 Ibid., p.29.

17 Ibid., p.33.

18 Ibid.

19 Ibid., p.19.

20 All the names of the women victims of JVP or state terror are pseudonyms.

21 Gananath Obeysekera, quoted in Sasanka Perera, *Stories of Survivors,* op. cit., p.22.

[22] Sasanka Perera, *Stories of Survivors*, op. cit., pp.20–25.

[23] Sunila Abeysekera, personal communication. SLFP MP, Mangala Samaraweera is also associated with the formative stages of the Mothers' Front, but he appeared on the scene later, following a split between Mahinda Rajapakse and Vasudeva Nanayakkara, and the formation of two groups—the Mothers' Front on the one hand and also in 1990 the Organisation of Parents and Families of the Disappeared on the other.

[24] *The Island*, 9 February, 1991.

[25] Malathi de Alwis, "Motherhood as a Space of Protest: Women's Political Participation in Contemporary Sri Lanka," in Patricia Jeffery and Amrita Basu (eds.), *Appropriating Gender: Women's Activism and Politicized Religion in South Asia*. New York & London: Routledge, 1998, pp.187–92.

[26] Ibid., p.188.

[27] *Divaina* newspaper, 21 February, 1991.

[28] *The Island*, 19 and 20 February, 1991.

[29] Ibid.

[30] *The Island*, 26 June, 1992.

[31] Malathi de Alwis, op. cit., p.189.

[32] Sirmavo Bandaranaike, excerpts from a speech at Mothers' Front rally in Nugegoda. *The Island*, 19 and 20 February, 1991.

[33] See Bruce Robbins, *Feeling Global: Internationalism in Distress*. New York & London: New York University Press, 1999, pp. 6–7.

[34] *Ceylon Daily News*. 9 March, 2000, p.1

[35] Chandralatha Samarasinghe, Matara, 10 December, 1999.

[36] Dr. Manorani Saravanamuttu, personal communication, 1994.

[37] Raka Ray, *Fields of Protest*, op. cit., p.8.

[38] Manisha Gunasekera, "Gender in Counter-State Political Practice of the JVP 1978–89." MA thesis, University of Colombo, work in progress.

[39] Quoted in Manisha Gunasekera, no pagination.

[40] Ibid.

[41] Malathi de Alwis, op. cit., pp.198–9.

[42] The first Presidential Commission on Disappearances was appointed by President Premadasa in 1991 following agitation by civil rights groups.

[43] Discussion at the course on "Identity Politics, Ethnicity and Gender in South Asia" conducted by the International Centre for Ethnic Studies, Colombo, August 1992.

[44] See also Jayadeva Uyangoda, "Tears and Curses" in Jayadev Uyangoda, and Janaka Biyanwila (eds) *Matters of Violence*. Colombo: Social Scientists' Association, 1997, pp.153–55.

[45] Sasanka Perera, *Stories of Survivors*, op. cit., p.53.

[46] Ibid., p.68.

[47] Ibid., p.54.

[48] Nalini, personal communication, Buttala, 5 January 2000.

[49] The names of the women have been altered except those in leadership capacities who are public figures.

[50] Subsequent to the interview, Nalini has been given a sewing machine by the Uwa Welassa Govi Kantha Sanvidanaya's welfare programme. When I met her in Buttala in July 2000, she was very happy at this turn of events.

[51] Sita Ranjani, poet and human rights activist worked at this time for the newspaper *Yukthiya*, published by Movement for Inter-Racial Justice and Equality, Colombo.

[52] Dr. Manorani Saravanamuttu subsequently died in March 2001.

[53] Central Bank of Ceylon Annual Report, 1999, p.113.

[54] An exception is a small booklet published by the National Peace Council entitled "The Cost of War." Ratmalana: Sarvodaya, 1996.

[55] The most recent public manifestation of this adulation was when Valentine Day 2001 became the occasion for many advertisements and full-page newspaper supplements declaring the nation's love for its soldiers, in a bizarre co-mingling too, of globalisation and nationalism.

[56] See Radhika Vyas Mongia, "Race, Nationality, Mobility: A History of the Passport," in *Public Culture* 29, 1999, p.529.

[57] Sumika Perera, interview with Neloufer de Mel, July 2000.

[58] Ibid.

[59] Rajan Hoole, et al., *The Broken Palmyrah: The Tamil Crisis in Sri Lanka*, op. cit. For alleged rapes of Jaffna Tamil women by the IPKF or complicity in such rapes, see particularly pp. 309–320.

[60] Sumika Perera, interview, Colombo, August 2000.

[61] Work plan of the Uva Welassa Govi Kantha Sanvidanaya.

[62] Interview with U.D.M.S. Seelawathie who heads the UWGKS, Buttala, July 2000.

[63] Interview with members of the UWGKS, Buttala, July 2000.

BIBLIOGRAPHY

Abhayavardhana, Hector (1997) "Selina Perera-The Forgotten Socialist-Militant." *Pravada* 4, Nos.10 & 11. Colombo: Social Scientists' Association.

Adele, Anne (1993) *Women Fighters of Liberation Tigers*. Jaffna: LTTE.

Afshar, Haleh (1996) *Women and Politics in the Third World*. London & New York: Routledge.

Ahmed, Syed Jamil (1994) "Female Performers in the Indigenous Theatre of Bengal," in Firdous Azim and Niaz Zaman (eds.), *Infinite Variety: Women in Society and Literature*. Dhaka: Ahmed University Press.

Al-Ali, Nadje, (2000) *Secularism, Gender and the State in the Middle East: The Egyptian Women's Movement*. Cambridge: Cambridge University Press.

Alles, A C *Insurgency 1971*. Colombo: Apothecaries' Co. Ltd.

Amerasinghe, Y Ranjith (1998) *Revolutionary Idealism and Parliamentary Politics: A Study of Trotskyism in Sri Lanka*. Colombo: Social Scientists' Association.

Amunugama, Sarath (1997) "Ideology and Class Interest in One of Piyadasa Sirisena's Novels. The New Image of the "Sinhala Buddhist" Nationalist," in Michael Roberts (ed.), *Sri Lanka. Collective Identities Revisited* Vol.1. Colombo: Marga.

_____ (1978) "John de Silva and the Nationalist Theatre," in *The Ceylon Historical Journal* Vol. xxv Nos.1–4. Dehiwela: Tisara Prakasakayo.

Anderson, Benedict (1989) *Imagined Communities: Reflections on the Origins and Spread of Nationalism*. London: Verso.

Arasanayagam, Jean (1993) *Shooting the Floricans*. Kandy: Samjna Books.

_____ (1973) *Kindura*. Kandy: Godaumunne & Sons.

_____ (1987) *Out of Our Prisons We Emerge*. Kandy: Arya Printers.

_____ (1987) *Trial by Terror*. Hamilton: Rimu.

_____ (1991) *Reddened Water Flows Clear*. London & Boston: Forest Books.

_____ (1995) *All is Burning*. New Delhi: Penguin.

_____ (1996) *Peacock and Dreams*. New Delhi: Navrang.

_____ *A Nice Burgher Girl* (unpublished manuscript).

Aretxaga, Begona (1998) "What the Border Hides: Partition and Gender Politics of Irish Nationalism," in *Social Analysis,* 42 No.1.

Ashcroft, Bill, Gareth Griffiths, Helen Tiffin, (1989) *The Empire Writes Back.* London & New York: Routledge.

Bagchi, Jasodhara (ed.) (1995) *Indian Women: Myth and Reality.* Hyderabad: Sangam Books.

Basu, Amrita (1998) "Appropriating Gender," in Patricia Jeffery and Amrita Basu (eds.), *Appropriating Gender: Women's Activism and Politicised Religion in South Asia.* New York & London: Routledge.

———— (1995) "Introduction," in Amrita Basu (ed.), *The Challenge of Local Feminism: Women's Movements in Global Perspective.* Boulder, Colorado: Westview Press Inc.

———— (1992) *Two Faces of Protest: Contrasting Modes of Women's Activism in India.* Berkeley: University of California Press.

Bastian, Sunil (1987) "Plantation Labour in a Changing Context," in Charles Abeysekera and Newton Gunasinghe (eds.), *Facets of Ethnicity in Sri Lanka.* Colombo: Social Scientists' Association.

Bhabha, Homi (1994) *The Location of Culture.* London: Routledge.

———— (ed.) (1990) *Nation and Narration.* London: Routledge.

———— (1986) "Remembering Fanon," Introduction to Frantz Fanon's *Black Skin White Masks.* London & Sydney: Pluto Press.

Bhattacharya, Rimli (1998) *Binodini Dasi: My Story* and *My Life As an Actress.* New Delhi: Kali for Women.

Boehmer, Elleke (1992) "Motherlands, Mothers and Nationalist Sons: Representations of Nationalism and Women in African Literature," in Anna Rutherford (ed.), *From Commonwealth to Post-Colonial.* Sydney: Dangaroo Press.

Bonner, Frances, Lizbeth Goodman, Richard Allen, Linda Janes, Catherine King, (1992) *Imagining Women: Cultural Representations and Gender.* Cambridge: Polity Press.

Brennan, Tim (1989) "Cosmopolitans and Celebrities," *Race and Class,* July–Sept.

Brohier, Deloraine (1994) *Dr. Alice de Boer and Some Pioneer Burgher Women Doctors.* Colombo: Social Scientists' Association.

Brubaker, Rogers (1996) *Nationalism Reframed: Nationhood and the National Question in the New Europe.* Cambridge: Cambridge University Press.

Brydon, Diana and Helen Tiffin (1993) *Decolonising Fictions.* Sydney: Dangaroo Press.

Chandrapreman, C A (1991) *The Years of Terror: The JVP Insurrection 1987–89.* Colombo: Lake House.

Chatterjee, Partha (1993) *The Nation and Its Fragments: Colonial and Postcolonial Histories.* New Delhi: Oxford University Press.

Chatterjee, Partha (1989) "The Nationalist Resolution of the Women's Question," in Kumkum Sangari and Sudesh Vaid (eds.), *Recasting Women: Essays in Colonial History.* New Delhi: Kali for Women.

Chatterjee, Sudipto (1995) "Mise-En-(Colonial) Scene: The Theatre of the Bengal Renaissance," in Ellen Gainor (ed.), *Imperialism and Theatre: Essays on World Theatre, Drama and Performance.* London & New York: Routledge.

_____ (1999) "The Nation Staged: Nationalist Discourse in Late Nineteenth Century Bengali Theatre," in Helen Gilbert (ed.), *(Post) Colonial Stages: Critical and Creative Views on Drama, Theatre and Performance.* Hebden Bridge: Dangaroo.

Coomaraswamy, Radhika "Women of the LTTE," *Frontline*, 10 January 1997.

Coombs, Orde (ed.) (1974) " Timehri," *Is Massa Daly Dead?* New York: Anchor & Doubleday.

Cooray, Christy (ed.) *Tower Hall: Theatre and Culture Centre.* Colombo: Tower Hall Theatre Foundation.

Davies, Carole Boyce & Elaine Savory Fido, (1990) "Women and Literature in the Caribbean: An Overview," in Carole Boyce Davies & Elaine Savory Fido (eds.), *Out of the Kumbla.* Trenton: Africa World Press Inc.

Davy, Kate (1992) "Fe/male Impersonation: The Discourse of Camp," in Janelle G Reinelt and Joseph R Roach (eds.), *Critical Theory and Performance.* Ann Arbor: University of Michigan Press.

Dalmia, Yashodhara (1995) "From Jamshetjee Jeejeebhoy to the Progressive Painters," in Sujata Patel and Alice Thorner (eds.), *Bombay: Mosaic of Cultures.* Bombay: Oxford University Press.

de Alwis, Malathi (1998) "Motherhood as a Space of Protest: Women's Political Participation in Contemporary Sri Lanka," in Patricia Jeffery and Amrita Basu (eds.), *Appropriating Gender: Women's Activism and Politicised Religion in South Asia.* New York & London: Routledge.

_____ (1997) "The Production and Embodiment of Respectability: Gendered Demeanours in Colonial Ceylon" in Michael Roberts (ed.), *Sri Lanka Collective Identities Revisited* Vol.1. Colombo: Marga.

de Mel, Neloufer (1990) "Responses to History: The Re-articulation of Postcolonial Identity in the Plays of Wole Soyinka & Derek Walcott 1950–76". Ph.D dissertation, University of Kent at Canterbury, U.K.

de Mel, Neloufer & Ramani Muttettuwegama, (1997) "Sisters in Arms: The Eksath Kantha Peramuna." *Pravada*, Vol.4, Nos.10 & 11.

Dept. of Census and Statistics, Colombo (nd.) *Women and Men in Sri Lanka.*

_____ (1998) *Statistical Profile of Sri Lanka.*

_____ (1997) *Changing Role of Women in Sri Lanka.*

de Silva, Anil (1955) *The Life of the Buddha*. London: The Phaidon Press.

de Silva-Vigier, Anil (1964) *Chinese Landscape Painting in the Caves of Tun-huang*. London: Methuen.

_____ (1992) *This Moste Highe Prince . . . John of Gaunt 1340–1399*. Durham: The Pentland Press.

de Silva, Jani (1998) "Praxis, Language and Silences: The July 1987 Uprising of the JVP in Sri Lanka" in Michael Roberts (ed.), *Sri Lanka Collective Identities Revisited Vol. 2*. Colombo: Marga.

de Silva, John (1992) *Collected Plays Vol. 1*, (ed.) Sunil Ariyaratne. Colombo: S Godage & Sons.

_____ (1992) "Sri Vickrama Rajasinghe: Our Last King," in *Collected Plays Vol. 2*, (ed.) Sunil Ariyaratne. Colombo: S Godage & Sons.

de Silva, Minette (1998) *The Life and Work of an Asian Woman Architect*, Vol. 1. Kandy: George E de Silva and Agnes Nell de Silva Trust.

Dissanayake, Wimal (1974) *John de Silva and Sinhala Theatre*. Colombo: Cultural Affairs Department.

Enloe, Cynthia (1983) *Does Khaki Become You?: The Militarization of Women's Lives*. Boston: South End Press.

Erdman, Joan L & Segal, Zohra (1997) *Stages: The Life and Adventures of Zohra Segal*. New Delhi: Kali for Women.

Fisher, James David (1988) *Romain Rolland and the Politics of Intellectual Engagement*. Berkeley: University of California Press.

Garber, Marjorie (1992) *Vested Interests: Cross-Dressing and Cultural Anxiety*. New York: Routledge.

Gluck, Sherna Berger (1997) "Shifting Sands: The Feminist-Nationalist Connection in the Palestinian Movement," in Lois A West (ed.), *Feminist Nationalism*. New York & London: Routledge.

Gombrich, Richard & Gananath Obeysekere (1988) *Buddhism Transformed: Religious Change in Sri Lanka*. New Jersey: Princeton University Press.

Gooneratne, Yasmine (1968) *English Literature in Ceylon 1815–1878*. *The Ceylon Historical Journal*, Vol. 14, Dehiwala: Tisara Prakasakayo.

_____ (1986) *Relative Merits: A Personal Memoir of the Bandaranaike Family of Sri Lanka*. London: C. Hurst.

Gunaratne, Rohan (1990) *Sri Lanka: A Lost Revolution? The Inside Story of the JVP*. Kandy: Institute of Fundamental Studies.

Gunatilleke, Godfrey (1998) "The Ideologies and Realities of the Ethnic Conflict—A Postface," in Michael Roberts (ed.), *Sri Lanka. Collective Identities Revisited*, Vol. 2. Colombo: Marga.

Hansen, Kathryn "Making Women Visible: Female Impersonators and Actresses on the Parsi Stage and in Silent Cinema," *Economic and Political Weekly*, 29 August 1998.

Hansen, Kathryn, Review of Binodini Dasi, *My Story* and *My Life as an Actress, Theatre Journal* Vol. 5 No.4, Dec. 1998.

Hapuarachchi, D. V. (1981) *The History of Sinhala Drama 1860–1911.* Colombo: Lake House.

Harlow, Barbara (1987) *Resistance Literature.* New York: Methuen.

Hassan, Dahabo Farah, Amina H Adan, & Amina Mohamoud Warsame, (1997) "Somalia: Poetry as Resistance Against Colonialism and Patriarchy," in Saskia Wieringa (ed.), *Subversive Women: Women's Movements in Africa, Asia, Latin America and the Caribbean.* New Delhi: Kali for Women.

Hensman, Rohini (1996) "The Role of Women in the Resistance to Political Authoritarianism in Latin America and South Asia," in Haleh Afshar (ed.), *Women and Politics in the Third World.* London & New York: Routledge.

Hill, Errol (1972) *The Trinidad Carnival.* Austin & London: University of Texas Press.

Hobsbawm, Eric & Terence Ranger (eds.) (1983) *The Invention of Tradition.* Cambridge: Cambridge University Press.

Hoole, Rajan Daya Somasundaram, K. Sritharan, Rajani Thiranagama, (1990) *The Broken Palmyrah: The Tamil Crisis in Sri Lanka—An Inside Account.* Claremont: The Sri Lanka Studies Institute.

Hulme, Peter (1986) *Colonial Encounters: Europe and the Native Caribbean 1492–1797.* London: Methuen.

Ignatieff, Michael, (2000) *Nationalism and Self-Determination: Is There an Alternative to Violence?* Colombo: International Centre for Ethnic Studies.

Jahan, Roushan (1995) "Men in Seclusion, Women in Public: Rokeya's Dream and Women's Struggles in Bangladesh," in Amrita Basu (ed.), *The Challenge of Local Feminism.*

Jayasuriya, Wilfred (1994) "Roots," in *Sri Lanka's Modern English Literature.* Delhi: Navrang.

Jayawardena, Kumari & Mala de Alwis (eds.) (1996) *Embodied Violence: Communalising Women's Sexuality in South Asia.* New Delhi: Kali for Women.

Jayawardena, Kumari (1995) *The White Woman's Other Burden: Western Women and South Asia During British Rule.* London: Routledge.

———— (1972) *The Rise of the Labour Movement in Ceylon.* Colombo: Sanjiva Prakashana.

———— (1986) *Feminism and Nationalism in the Third World.* London: Zed Books.

———— (1990) *Ethnic and Class Conflict in Sri Lanka.* Colombo: Sanjiva.

———— (1993) *Dr. Mary Rutnam: A Canadian Pioneer for Women's Rights in Sri Lanka.* Colombo: Social Scientists' Association.

Jayawardena, Kumari (1993) "Aspects of Religious Cultural Identity and the Construction of Sinhala Buddhist Womanhood" in Douglas Allen (ed.), *Religion and Political Conflict in South Asia*. New Delhi: Oxford University Press.

_____ (1997) "Vivienne Goonewardena: 'La Pasionaria' of Sri Lanka," *Pravada* 4, Nos.10 & 11. Colombo: Social Scientists' Association.

_____ (2000) *From Nobodies to Somebodies*. Colombo: Social Scientists' Association.

Jeganathan, Pradeep and Ismail Qadri (eds.) (1995) *Unmaking the Nation*. Colombo: Social Scientists' Association.

Jeyifo, Biodun (1985) "Tragedy, History and Ideology: Soyinka's Death and the King's Horseman and Ebrahim Hussein's 'Kinjeketile'," in George Gugelberger (ed), *Marxism and African Literature*. London: James Currey.

Juneja, Monica (1996) "Imaging the Revolution: Gender and Iconography in French Political Prints," in *Studies in History*, Vol.12, No. 1. New Delhi: Sage.

Kandiah, Tiru (1988) "This Language and These Women," in Rajiva Wijesinha (ed), *An Anthology of Contemporary Sri Lankan Poetry in English*. Colombo: British Council & (EASL).

Kandiyoti, Deniz (1997) "Identity and Its Discontents: Women and the Nation" in *Dossier 20* Grables: Women Living Under Muslim Laws.

Kapur, Anuradha (1993) "The Representation of Gods and Heroes: Parsi Mythological Drama of the Early Twentieth Century," in *The Journal of Arts and Ideas*, Delhi.

Kapur, Geeta (1997) "Body as Gesture: Indian Women Artists at Work" in Vidya Dehejia (ed.), *Representing the Body: Gender Issues in Indian Art*. New Delhi: Kali for Women.

Kariyawasam, Tissa (1997) Introduction to W C Perera, in *Eugene Nadagama*. Colombo: Cultural Affairs Department.

Kodikara, S U (1965) *Indo-Ceylon Relations Since Independence*. Colombo: Ceylon Institute of World Affairs.

Kosambi, Meera (1995) "British Bombay and Marathi Mumbai: Some Nineteenth Century Perceptions" in Sujata Patel and Alice Thorner (eds.), *Bombay: Mosaic of Modern Culture*. Bombay: Oxford University Press.

Lakshmi, C S (1990) "Mother, Mother-Community and Mother Politics in Tamil Nadu," *Economic and Political Weekly*, 20–29 October.

Lamming, George (1984) *Pleasures of Exile*. London: Allison & Busby.

Liyanage, Pulsara (1998) *Vivi: A Biography of Vivienne Goonewardena*. Colombo: Women's Education & Research Centre.

Ludowyk, E F C (1962) *The Story of Ceylon*. London: Faber & Faber.

Manchanda, Rita (1999) "Kashmir's Worse-off Half," in *Himal*, 12. No. 5, Kathmandu.

Manor, James (1989) *The Expedient Utopian: Bandaranaike and Ceylon.* Cambridge: Cambridge University Press.

Markovits, Claude (1995) "Bombay as a Business Centre in the Colonial Period: A Comparison with Calcutta," in Sujata Patel and Alice Thorner (ed.), *Bombay: Metaphor for Modern India.* Bombay: Oxford University Press.

Manyoni, Joseph (1973) "Emergence of Black Power" in Robert Moss (ed.), *The Stability of the Caribbean.* London: Institute for the Study of Conflict & Centre for Strategic and International Studies.

Menon, Nivedita (1998) "Women and Citizenship," in Partha Chatterjee (ed.), *Wages of Freedom: Fifty Years of the Indian Nation State.* New Delhi: Oxford University Press.

Menon, Ritu and Kamla Bhasin, (1998) *Borders & Boundaries: Women in India's Partition.* Delhi: Kali for Women.

Mills, Sara (1991) *Discourses of Difference: An Analysis of Women's Travel Writing and Colonialism.* London: Routledge.

Mitter, Sara S (1992) *Dharma's Daughters: Contemporary Indian Women and Hindu Culture.* New Delhi: Penguin.

Mitchell, Juliet (1973) *Women's Estate.* New York: Vintage Books.

Mongia, Radhika Vyas (1999) "Race, Nationality, Mobility: A History of the Passport, *Public Culture*, No.29.

Mosse, George L (1985) *Nationalism and Sexuality: Middle Class Morality and Sexual Norms in Modern Europe.* Madison: University of Wisconsin Press

Muller, Carl (1993) *Jam Fruit Tree.* Delhi: Penguin.

———— (1994) *Yakada Yaka.* Delhi: Penguin.

Murphy, Richard (1989) *The Mirror Wall.* Newcastle upon Tyne: Bloodaxe Books.

Nadkarni, Dnyaneshwar (1988) *Bal Gandharva and the Marathi Theatre.* Bombay: Roopak Books.

Nadkarni, Mohan (1988) *Bal Gandharva.* New Delhi: National Book Trust.

Naik, J.V. (1995) "The Seed Period of Bombay's Intellectual Life 1822–1857," in Sujata Patel and Alice Thorner (eds.), *Bombay: Mosaic of Modern Culture.* Bombay: Oxford University Press.

Nixon, Rob (1987) "Caribbean and African Appropriations of the Tempest," *Critical Inquiry*, No.13.

Obeysekera, Gananath (1997) "The Vicissitudes of the Sinhala-Buddhist Identity through Time and Change," in Michael Roberts (ed.) *Sri Lanka, Collective Identities Revisited Vol 1.* Colombo: Marga.

Obeysekere Rajani (1999) *Sri Lankan Theatre in a Time of Terror: Political Satire in a Permitted Space.* Colombo: Charles Subasinghe & Sons.

Ondaatje, Michael (1984) *Running in the Family.* London: Picador.

Osofisan, Femi (1986) "The Alternative Tradition: A Survey of Nigerian Literature in English Since the Civil War," *Presence Africane*, 139, 3rd Quarter.

Pandian, M.S.S (1992) *The Image Trap: M G Ramachandran in Film and Politics*. New Delhi: Sage.

Paranavitana, S (1959) *The History of Ceylon*, Vol. 1 Part 1. Colombo: Ceylon University Press.

Patel, Geeta (2001) *Lyrical Movements, Historical Hauntings: On Gender, Colonialism, and Desire in Miraji's Urdu Poetry*. Berkeley: University of California Press.

Patel, Sujata and Alice Thorner (eds.) (1995) *Bombay: Mosaic of Modern Culture*. Bombay: Oxford University Press.

———— (eds.) (1995) *Bombay: Metaphor for Modern India*. Bombay: Oxford University Press.

Pateman, Carole (1989) *The Disorder of Women: Democracy, Feminism and Political Theory*. Stanford: Stanford University Press.

Perera, Sasanka (1999) *Stories of Survivors: Socio-Political Contexts of Female-Headed Households in Post-Terror Southern Sri Lanka*, Vol. 1. Colombo: Women's Education & Research Centre.

Prakash, Gyan (ed.) (1995) *After Colonialism: Imperial Histories and Postcolonial Displacements*. New Jersey: Princeton University Press.

Pradhan, Sudhi (ed.) (1979 & 1985) *Marxist Cultural Movement in India: Chronicles and Documents (1936–1947)* Vol.1. Calcutta: Santi Pradhan.

Presidential Commission on Youth (1990) Report. Colombo: Sri Lanka Government Publications Bureau.

Raha, Kironmoy (1978 & 1993) *Bengali Theatre*. Delhi: National Book Trust.

Ratemar, Roberto Fernando (1974) "Caliban: Notes Towards a Discussion of Culture in Our America". *Massachusetts Review*, No.15.

Ratnayake, L D A (1963 & 1965) *The History of Proctor John de Silva's Plays*. Colombo: Private Publications.

Ray, Raka (1999) *Fields of Protest: Women's Movements in India*. New Delhi: Kali for Women.

Robbins, Bruce (1999) *Feeling Global: Internationalism in Distress*. New York & London: New York University Press.

Roberts, Michael (1999) "Sinhala-ness and Sinhala Nationalism," Colombo, Marga.

———— (1994) *Exploring Confrontation. Sri Lanka: Politics, Culture and History*. Chur: Harwood Academic Publishers.

———— (1997) "For Humanity. For the Sinhalese. Dharmapala as Crusading Bosat," in *Journal of Asian Studies*, Vol.56.

———— (ed.) (1997) *Sri Lanka. Collective Identities Revisited* Vol.1. Colombo: Marga.

Roberts, Michael (ed.) (1998) *Sri Lanka. Collective Identities Revisited* Vol. 2. Colombo: Marga.

Roberts, Michael, Ismeth Raheem, Percy Colin-Thome, (1989) *People Inbetween: The Burghers and the Middle Class in the Transformations Within Sri Lanka 1790s–1960s.* Colombo: Sarvodaya.

Russell, Jane (1981) *Our George: A Biography of George E de Silva.* Colombo: Times of Ceylon.

Rushdie, Salman (1997) "Notes on Writing and the Nation", *Index on Censorship,* No.3.

———— (1991) "In Good Faith", *Imaginary Homelands.* New Delhi: Penguin.

Rutherford, Anna (1994) *Unbecoming Daughters,* Sydney: Dangaroo Press.

Ryan, Bryce (1993) *Caste in Modern Sinhalese Tradition.* New Delhi: Navrang.

Saeed, Fouzia & Adam Nayyar (1991) *Women in Folk Theatre.* Islamabad: Lok Virsa.

Said, Edward (1993) *Culture and Imperialism.* London: Chatto & Windus.

———— (1978) *Orientalism.* London: Routledge & Kegan Paul.

Samarasinghe, Gameela (1999) "Stories of Coping," in *Stories of Survivors: Socio-Political Contexts of Female-Headed Households in Post-Terror Southern Sri Lanka,* Vol. 1. Colombo: Women's Education & Research Centre.

Sangari, Kumkum & Sudesh Vaid (eds.) (1989) *Recasting Women: Essays in Colonial History.* New Delhi: Kali for Women.

Sanghatana, Sthree Shakti (1989) *"We Were Making History. . ." Life Stories of Women in the Telangana People's Struggle.* New Delhi: Kali for Women.

Sarachchandra, E R (1952 & 1966) *The Folk Drama of Ceylon.* Colombo: Cultural Affairs Department.

———— (1951) "Sinhalese Drama," in *The Ceylon Observer Pictorial.* Colombo: Lake House.

Sarvan, Charles (1998) "Appointment with Rajiv Gandhi", in Michael Roberts (ed.) *Sri Lanka Collective Identities Revisited* Vol.2. Colombo: Marga.

Sawker, Indrani (1983)"The Living Legend Narayanrao Rajhans alias Bal Gandharva," *The Economic Times,* Bombay, 7 August.

Schalk, Peter (1997) "Resistance and Martyrdom in the Process of State Formation of Tamililam," in Joyce Pettigrew (ed.), *Martyrdom and Political Resistance.* Comparative Asian Studies 18, Amsterdam: VU University Press for Centre for Asian Studies.

———— (1994) "Women Fighters of the Liberation Tigers in Tamililam: The Martial Feminism of Atel Palacinkam, *South Asia Research* No. 14.

Sen Gupta, Bhabani (1972) *Communism in Indian Politics*. New York & London: Columbia University Press.

Sivanandan, S (1997) *When Memory Dies*. London: Arcadia Books.

Shiveshwarkar, Shyamala (1976) "The Rise and Decline of the Parsi Theatre," in *The Hindustan Times*, 21 March 1976.

Shahani, Roshan G. (1995) "Polyphonous Voices in the City: Bombay's Indian-English Fiction", in Sujata Patel and Alice Thorner (eds.), *Bombay: Mosaic of Culture*. Bombay: Oxford University Press.

Shastri, Amita (1999) "Estate Tamils, The Ceylon Citizenship Act of 1948 and Sri Lankan Politics," in *Contemporary South Asia*, No.8.

Shulman, David (1986) "Battle as Metaphor in Tamil Folk and Classical Traditions," in *Another Harmony*. Berkeley: University of California Press.

Southard, Barbara (1995) *The Women's Movement and Colonial Politics in Bengal 1921–1936*. New Delhi: Manohar.

Soyinka, Wole (1976) *Myth, Literature and the African World*. London: Cambridge University Press.

Spivak, Gayatri (1991) "Feminism in Decolonization" in *Differences: A Journal of Feminist Cultural Studies*, Vol.3, No.3.

_____ (1990) in Sarah Harasym (ed.), *The Post-Colonial Critic: Interviews, Strategies, Dialogues*. London: Routledge.

_____ (1988) "Can the Subaltern Speak?" in C.Nelson and L. Grossberg (eds.), *Marxism and the Interpretation of Culture*. Basingstoke: Macmillan.

_____ (1987) *In Other Worlds: Essays in Cultural Politics*. New York: Methuen.

Stoler, Ann (1992) "Sexual Affronts and Racial Frontiers: European Identities and the Cultural Politics of Exclusion in Colonial Southeast Asia," in *Comparative Studies in Society and History*, Vol.34, No. 3.

Sullivan, Michael (1969) *The Cave Temples of Maichisan: An Account of the 1958 Expedition to Maichisan by Anil de Silva*. London: Faber.

Sullivan, Zohreh T (1998) "Eluding the Feminist, Overthrowing the Modern? Transformation in Twentieth Century Iran," in Lila Abu-Lughod (ed.), *Remaking Women: Feminism and Modernity in the Middle East*. New Jersey: Princeton University Press.

Sunder Rajan, Rajeswari (1993) *Real and Imagined Women: Gender, Culture and Post-colonialism*. London: Routledge.

Sunder Rajan, Rajeswari (ed.) (1999) *Signposts: Gender Issues in Post-Independence India*. New Delhi: Kali for Women.

Tagore, Rabindranath (1996) "The Union of Cultures" in Sisir Kumar Das (ed.), *The English Writing of Rabindranath Tagore*, Vol.3. Delhi: Sahitya Akademi.

_____ (1996) "East and West" in *The English Writing of Rabindranath Tagore* Vol.3. Delhi: Sahitya Akademi.

Tampoe, Manel (1997) *The Story of Selestina Dias: Buddhist Female Philanthropy and Education.* Colombo: Social Scientists' Association.

Tambiah S J (1986) *Sri Lanka : Ethnic Fratricide and the Dismantling of Democracy.* London: I B Tauris & Co. Ltd.

Thapar, Romila (1997) *Traditions Versus Misconceptions.* Colombo: Social Scientists' Association.

————— (1992) *Interpreting Early India.* Delhi: Oxford University Press.

Tharu, Susie & K. Lalitha (eds.) (1993) Introduction to *Women Writing in India,* Vol. 2. London: Pandora.

Thorner, Alice (1995) "Bombay: Diversity and Exchange," in *Bombay: Mosaic of Modern Culture.* Bombay: Oxford University Press.

Traub, Valerie (1992) *Desire and Anxiety: Circulations of Sexuality in Shakespearean Drama.* London: Routledge,

Uyangoda, Jayadeva (Forthcoming) "A State of Desire? Some Reflections on the Unreformability of Sri Lanka's Post-colonial Polity," University of Colombo.

Vindhya, U I (1998) "Comrades-in-Arms: Sexuality and Identity in the Contemporary Revolutionary Movement in Andhra Pradesh and the Legacy of Chalam," in Mary E John and Janaki Nair (eds.), *A Question of Silence?: The Sexual Economies of Modern India.* Delhi: Kali for Women.

Vittachi, Tarzie (1958) *Emergency '58: The Story of the Ceylon Race Riots.* London: Andre Deutsch.

Vogel, Lise (1983) *Marxism and the Oppression of Women: Towards a Unitary Theory.* New Jersey: Rutgers University Press.

Walcott, Derek (1970) "What the Twilight Says: An Overture," in *Dream on Monkey Mountain and Other Plays.* New York: Farrar, Straus & Giroux.

————— (1986) "Crusoe's Journal," *Collected Poems: 1948–1984.* New York: Farrar, Straus & Giroux.

Weeraratne, Neville (1993) *43 Group: A Chronicle of Fifty Years in the Art of Sri Lanka.* Melbourne: Lantana.

West, Lois A (1997) Introduction to *Feminist Nationalism.* New York & London: Routledge.

Wickremasinghe, Nira (1992) "Some Comments on Dress in Sri Lanka", *Thatched Patio.* 5 No. 1, Colombo: International Centre for Ethinic Studies.

Wijekoon, Nancy (1918) "Our Motherland," *Young Lanka,* Vol. 1, No. 1.

Wilson, A J (1974 & 1979) *Politics in Sri Lanka 1947–1979.* London: Macmillan.

Woodward, F L (1906) "Girls, Wives and Mothers," *The Ceylon National Review.* Colombo: Ceylon Social Reform Society.

Wood, Elizabeth (1997) *The Baba and the Comrade: Gender and Politics in Revolutionary Russia.* Bloomington: Indian University Press.

Wriggins, Howard (1960) *Ceylon: Dilemmas of a New Nation.* New Jersey: Princeton University Press.

Yuval-Davis, Nira (1997) *Gender and Nation.* London & New Delhi: Sage.

Yuval-Davis, Nira & Floya Anthias (eds.) (1989) *Woman-Nation-State.* London: Macmillan.

Zackariya, Faizum and Zulfika Ismail (1998) "Early Marriage and Perpetuation of the Cycle of Violence in a Displaced Situation," in *Confronting Complexities: Gender Perceptions and Values.* Colombo: CENWOR.